JANE ADDAMS

ALSO BY LOUISE W. KNIGHT

Citizen: Jane Addams and the Struggle for Democracy

JANE ADDAMS, CIRCA 1910

JANE ADDAMS

Spirit in Action

LOUISE W. KNIGHT

W. W. NORTON & COMPANY

New York London

For information about permission to reproduce
selections from this book, write to Permissions,
W. W. Norton & Company, Inc.,
500 Fifth Avenue, New York, NY 10110

For information about special discounts for bulk
purchases, please contact W. W. Norton Special Sales
at specialsales@wwnorton.com or 800-233-4830

Manufacturing by Courier Westford
Book design by Joanne Metsch
Production manager: Julia Druskin

Library of Congress Cataloging-in-Publication Data

Knight, Louise W.
  Jane Addams : spirit in action / Louise W. Knight.
    p. cm.
  Includes bibliographical references and index.
  ISBN 978-0-393-07165-8 (hardcover)
 I. Addams, Jane, 1860–1935. 2. Women social reformers—United States—Biography.
 3. Social reformers—United States—Biography. 4. Women social workers—United
States—Biography. 5. Social workers—United States—Biography. I. Title.
  HV28.A35K65 2010
  361.92—dc22
[B]
                                                              2010020648

W. W. Norton & Company, Inc.
500 Fifth Avenue, New York, N.Y. 10110
www.wwnorton.com

W. W. Norton & Company Ltd.
Castle House, 75/76 Wells Street, London WIT 3QT

1 2 3 4 5 6 7 8 9 0

We are at the beginning of a prolonged effort to incorporate a progressive developing life, founded upon a response to the needs of all the people, into the requisite legal enactments and civic institutions. . . .

JANE ADDAMS, *Newer Ideals of Peace* (1907)

CONTENTS

LIST OF ILLUSTRATIONS

PREFACE

In JULY 1933 the United States was in the midst of the Great Depression, Adolf Hitler had recently been appointed chancellor of Germany, and the possibility of war hung over Europe. People on both sides of the Atlantic were worried about rampant nationalism, unemployment, and starvation and wondering why they found themselves in such a troubling and dangerous situation. Jane Addams, who had become the second woman and the first American woman to be awarded the Nobel Peace Prize a few years before, gave a speech in which she addressed these issues, but also took up what she thought was an underlying problem—mental conformity.

At seventy-two Addams was willing to be blunt. She told her audience, hundreds of women attending an international congress of women in Chicago, that it was dangerous when people clung to old ideas, whether they did so out of loyalty to tradition or fear of appearing radical. What people needed to do now, she said, was imagine new possibilities while also seeing life as it was. Such "free and vigorous thinking," she promised, would "liberate new sources of human energy" and make it possible to build "a bridge between those things which we desire and those things which are possible."[1] It was the advice of a rare kind of person—a pragmatic visionary. Addams was integrating both sides of her worldview into one profound message: If you think for yourself in choosing your hopes and then are realistic about what it will take to achieve them, you will release your own spirit into action with wonderfully useful results.

This book is the story of how Jane Addams (1860–1935) did just that—how she increasingly thought for herself, released her own spirit, and, working with others, accomplished remarkable things. She cofounded Hull House, the nation's first settlement house (and one of the earliest community-based nonprofits) in Chicago, and in time became one of the nation's most effective reform leaders, as influential in her day on both the national and the world stages as Eleanor Roosevelt was in hers. She worked to end child labor, support unions and workers' rights, protect free speech and civil rights, respect all cultures, achieve women's suffrage and women's freedom, and promote conditions that nurtured human potential and therefore, she believed, the spread of peace. She served on the founding boards of the National Association for the Advancement of Colored People and the American Civil Liberties Union, advised every president from William McKinley to Franklin Delano Roosevelt, wrote ten books, gave hundreds of speeches, and was one of the greatest American women this nation has yet produced. Indeed, in 1912—eight years before the federal amendment giving women the vote became law—there were wistful discussions of her running for president. For the last third of her life, as founding president of the Women's International League for Peace and Freedom, she was known worldwide as an advocate for peace and women, and in 1931 she was awarded the Nobel Peace Prize.

But a biography is about more than a person's accomplishments—or failures. It is most of all a story about what she learned, or not; about how and when a person stretched herself, or was stretched, and what wisdom was gained, or refused, and why. It is about the quests of the human spirit. We seek these stories everywhere, wanting to know more about how others tackle the burden and bliss of being human. Sometimes we find the stories in conversation, other times in movies, television, or radio, and still other times in theater, blogs, or books. Biographers want to know these stories, as well as to share them. I have written this book, first to know Jane Addams's story, and then to share it.

JANE ADDAMS

||||||||||||||||||||||||||||||||||||||||||||||||||||||||||||||||||||||||||||||||||||||||||||||||||||||||||||||||||||||||||||||||||||||||||||

DREAMER

JANE, TWO AND a half years old, stands at the door. Her mother is inside, but no one will let her in, and she is desperate. She pounds on the door with her fist. Then she hears her mother say, "Let her in, she is only a baby herself," and the door opens.[1] She runs to her mother, who is in bed, and receives tender words; a gentle hand reaches out to comfort her.

The mother, Sarah Weber Addams, had had a serious accident the night before. Seven months pregnant, she had gone out on a cold January night to help a neighbor give birth to a child and had fallen on her way up an icy hill. Though she attended the birth, she collapsed soon after from internal bleeding. The next day she began premature labor, and the day after that she gave birth to a stillborn daughter. Then she slipped into unconsciousness.

Throughout the two days the family had gathered at her bedside. Sarah's five children, including Jane, were there. Sarah's husband, John, had been out of town the night she fell, serving as a state senator at the Illinois State Capitol, but a telegram had summoned him home to Cedarville, and now he was there too. While most of the family talked

Sarah Weber Addams, Jane Addams's mother

and moved about, Jane stood still, never taking her eyes off her mother's strangely quiet face. Suddenly Sarah sat bolt upright, her eyes filled with terror. Jane, the first to notice, shrieked. Abruptly Sarah lay back down and was soon unconscious again. In the days that followed, she was able briefly to recognize John and say the Lord's Prayer, but five days after her fall she was dead.

Sarah's death devastated the family; it was also a blow to the close-knit town of Cedarville. She was loved, especially among the large number of German immigrant families who lived nearby, for her generous neighborliness. Her obituary in the local German-language newspaper praised her for her "constant willingness to . . . help . . . the suffering" and remarked how she was "always present when sympathy was needed or required."[2] (Both she and John, despite his Anglo last name, were of mostly German descent.)

Many people came to Sarah Addams's funeral, but Jane was not allowed to go. Perhaps the family regretted having let her into her mother's bedroom. Her initial exclusion from her mother's presence and later from the ritual of shared grieving, and the family's subsequent refusal to speak of their great sorrow, left scars. For the rest of her life Jane remembered her desperate effort to be admitted to her mother's bedroom. She told her nephew the story when she was seventy-three. In 1910 she railed at parents who did not let their children see the difficult realities of death and suffering. "Perhaps I may record here," she wrote in her memoir *Twenty Years at Hull House*, "my protest against the efforts, so often made, to shield children and young people from all that has to do with death and sorrow. . . . Young people themselves often resent this attitude . . . they feel set aside and belittled as if they were denied the common human experiences."[3]

The loss of her mother left the biggest scar. What sadness can compare with that of a motherless child? There was also fear. Suddenly, with Sarah gone, the world felt horribly unsafe and full of large, unseen forces, the most terrifying of which was death.

And there were more deaths to come. When she was six, Jane lost her sixteen-year-old sister Martha, away at a distant boarding school, to typhoid fever. Again the family shielded her from death. While her father and siblings went to the funeral, she was left behind with a servant, Polly. Terrified, she kept a lonely vigil sitting on the stairs to the second floor, where the blank wall beside her seemed to "afford protection . . . against the formless peril."[4] When she was sixteen herself, Jane finally saw death's face. She was present, alone, when Polly, who had helped raise Jane's mother back in Pennsylvania, died. The experience, she later remembered, left her feeling "unsheltered in a wide world of relentless and elemental forces."[5] When she was twenty, she was to see her father die.

For all these reasons, death became a haunting presence in Jane Addams's life. Beyond her fear of losing another loved one, she feared death's power to make life purposeless. But if a biographer realizes this, should she conclude that these deaths "made" Jane Addams the person she became? The idea is obviously too simplistic to be trusted. Some people suffer early bereavements but do not do as Jane Addams did and redeem life's meaning by devoting their lives to good causes. The forces that shape our lives are more complicated than that. A life is like a poem: Its content is inspired partly by unconscious feelings but also by mindful judgment. Jane Addams's life was shaped by choices as well as by fate, by opportunities seized or created as well as by the after effects of unavoidable tragedies. Her life may have started with a terrible loss, but that life and her strengthening ability to shape it—an ability evident when she knocked so fiercely on the bedroom door—had just begun.

||||||||||||

After Sarah's death, Jane's oldest sister, Mary, took up the task of mothering. It was a burden that, at nearly eighteen, she was scarcely equipped to bear. Besides Jane, there was an eleven-year-old boy, John Weber, called Weber (pronounced "Wee-ber"), and two girls, Alice, ten, and Martha, thirteen. (Four others of Sarah and John's children, including the baby whose death brought Sarah's own, had died in infancy or soon after.) At only two, Jane was the most bereft, and Mary took her into her heart. Jane always felt a special devotion to Mary for being her substitute mother.

Still a child knows who her real parents are. Jane was soon completely absorbed by her devotion to her father, John Huy Addams. She remembered later her "doglike affection" for him.[6] He was a successful man. Originally from Pennsylvania and trained in milling, he and Sarah had come west to northern Illinois in 1844 as newlyweds, settling in the small town of Cedarville. Using capital from John's innkeeper father, they purchased a flour mill and a sawmill on a small creek, along with 675 acres of timber, grazing, and farmland. In time, as he bought an additional 1,200 acres and acquired other businesses—including a bank he founded in 1864, a woolen factory, and an insurance company, a good deal of railroad stock, and commercial real estate—they became the wealthiest family in town and one of the wealthiest in the township. Notably, although his location was rural, his wealth was industrial.

The house Jane grew up in was a stone's throw from the flour mill, where her father had once spent much of his time. Adoring him, she wanted to have as flat a thumb as he did—millers tested the consistency of ground flour with their thumbs and index fingers, and a flat thumb was proof of their profession—and she tried hard to acquire one by pressing flour between the two fingers of her small hand for as much time as she could manage before becoming bored.

She held him in awe, of course. She later recalled how she worried terribly that because she had a crooked back, her elegantly dressed and proud father would be embarrassed to have her walk with him to Sun-

John Huy Addams,
Jane Addams's father

day school. (Her back was crooked but not *that* crooked; she was self-conscious about the effects of spinal tuberculosis, an illness she had suffered when she was four.) She walked with her uncle instead. Soon after, her father accidentally dispelled her fears by doffing his tall black silk hat and bowing formally to her as she joined him on a sidewalk in the nearby larger city of Freeport. This public display convinced her that he was not ashamed of her after all. In these stories, which she tells in her memoir *Twenty Years at Hull House*, she mocks her childish self but also captures the child's longing to be like her parent and her hunger to have his respect.

As a child she was eager to learn about her parent's ways of engaging with the world, and as she grew older, she wanted to know more about his political career. John Addams served as a state senator in the Illinois legislature from 1854 to 1870, retiring from office when Jane was nine. As she grew older, she could rarely persuade her busy father to take the time to talk to her about his days in the legislature, but, eager to catch glimpses of this side of him, she used to eavesdrop when his old political friends dropped by to chat. And she pestered him to show her his letter from Abraham Lincoln, stuffed into a cubbyhole in his desk, in which the future president asked Addams for whom he would be voting. The state senate was soon to elect a U.S. senator, and Lincoln was a candidate. Would John Addams have been more encouraging of her interest if Jane had been a boy? Perhaps. In any case, Jane inadvertently revealed in her memoir that he did not encourage her, although her political ambition and accomplishments would turn out to be much greater than his own.

||||||||||||

Jane was raised in an evangelical Christian household. Her father refused to formally join any of the Protestant churches in town because he could not, as required, agree completely with all the doctrinal tenets of any of the denominations.[7] Still, the family went to church every Sunday, generally to the Presbyterian church. But for Jane's religious instruction, he sent her to the "union" (nondenominational) Sunday school in town that he had helped found and in which he taught.

When Jane was young, her image of God, she remembered, came from "a most outrageous picture which adorned a song-book used in Sunday school, portraying the Lord upon His throne surrounded by tiers and tiers of saints and angels all in a blur of yellow."[8] She struggled with the Presbyterian Church's teaching of predestination—the idea that God had already decided whether or not a person would go to heaven when he died, regardless of how he might live his life. The idea made no sense to her, since her father and Mary taught her that her actions, good or bad, had moral consequences. She asked her father to explain and was relieved when he told her that neither of them had the kind of mind that could grasp the teaching and that she should not worry about it. The most important thing, he told her, was "not to pretend to understand what you didn't understand and that you must always be honest with yourself inside, whatever happened." She called it a "valuable lesson."[9]

The religious revivals that came through town posed an opposite dilemma. These preachers, not believing in predestination, warned with bellicose authority that those who did not repent of their sins before they died would burn in hell. Five-year-old Jane heard the talk in town and was worried, terrified really, that her neighbors would suffer this fate. She decided that the magic word with the power to save them was somewhere in the Bible and that she should read that book out loud to find it. But the task was too much for her, and she had to give it up. Her childish struggle, the memory of which came back to her when she was in her fifties, captured not only her unusually fierce desire to protect others from suffering after death but also the realities of her world—that sinfulness was a given and that repentance, achieved when a person accepted Jesus Christ as her savior, was essential.[10] Jane, like her siblings, had not been baptized as a baby because her parents expected her to convert and be baptized when she was older. The expectation hung over her head, ever present.

She also observed her father's faith. John was not just nondenominational and evangelical; he was also a perfectionist Christian. Believers in this wing of the evangelical movement, which spread with alacrity in the 1840s, held that once a person had been saved, or reborn, his new soul was without sin and all his deeds were for the benefit of others or, in the favorite word of the day, benevolent. In simplest terms, the perfectionist could do no wrong. John's early library held many books by believers in this sect, including the journal of Elias Hicks, an evangelical perfectionist Quaker and the founder of the Hicksite movement. John's good friend Luther Guiteau, who managed John's bank, was a follower of John Noyes, the founder of the perfectionist utopian Oneida Community in western New York State.

Equally telling, John Addams had a reputation for moral probity. One friend remembered, after he died, how he "was sure to be right on all moral questions, he was given to the right with his whole soul." Jane too recalled her father as being "the uncompromising enemy of wrong and wrong doing."[11] As a child and youth Jane Addams drew strength from and admired her father's unshakable moral surety and his emphasis on "mental integrity," as he called it.[12] Jane was raised to believe that self-righteousness was a good thing. It was many years before she understood its arrogant, blind, and selfish sides.

John may have come to his interest in perfectionism through his Quaker background. Most Quakers were not perfectionist, but some, like Hicks, were. John's mother was a Quaker, and he often used "thee" and "thou" in letters to his Pennsylvania family and sometimes avoided the first and second person when he spoke to his children, addressing them in the third person instead. Jane Addams noted that because of his "Quaker tendencies," he left the front door unlocked. Still, he was no pacifist, having funded local troops to fight in the Civil War. His Quakerism consisted of the lesson he taught Jane to be "honest with yourself inside"—in other words, as Elias Hicks taught, to trust one's inner light, rather than what others thought.[13] In matters of personal morality, John was an independent thinker. His determination to listen to his inner truth was a legacy he bequeathed his daughter.

Growing up in a small town, Jane Addams was fascinated by the "wider world," hints of which drifted her way from the overheard talk of men and women who returned from journeys and the overheard stories about politics, and from what she read in her father's newspaper, the *New York Tribune*, which came in the mail from faraway New York City.

It was the *Tribune* that first bore the tragic news to her father that President Lincoln had been assassinated and later that Giuseppe Mazzini, a leader of the Italian campaign to overthrow the Hapsburg monarchy, had died. Both times Jane watched her father weep. His tears taught her that he had a profound sense of connection to the distant realm of national struggles. She was four and a half years old when Lincoln died. She recalled the sight of her father's tears then as the moment of "my baptism . . . into the thrilling world lying quite outside the two white gateposts" of their home. When Mazzini died seven years later, Jane, now an opinionated eleven-year-old, told her father she did not understand why he wept for a man he did not know and who was not American. His gentle rebuke to her chauvinism opened her eyes. It gave her "a sense of the genuine relationship which may exist between men who share large hopes and like desires, even though they differ in nationality, language, and creed."[14]

||||||||||||

Is it the child who loves books who becomes a dreamer? Or is it the born dreamer who, inevitably, loves books? Whether cause or effect, books were Jane's passion throughout her life. The day she died, she had a pile by her bedside she was reading. Throughout her life books fed her curiosity, her intellect, her imagination, and especially her soul, which was hungry for beauty and meaning. They filled her hours when she was bored, depressed, or sad, but most of all, they connected her to the great minds of men (and a few women) who challenged her to become someone she did not feel herself to be. Books, particularly those she chose to read as she grew older, were her lifetime mentors and friends.

The first public library in Cedarville, population four hundred, was John Addams's private collection, which he made available to his neighbors and which contained books about history as well as about Christianity. Living in a bookish house was one of the great blessings of Jane's childhood. For a time, ever eager to imitate her father, she rose at 4:00 A.M. every day, a miller's rising time her father habitually kept, in order to read her way chronologically through his library, just as he had once read his way through the library of the town where he was a miller's apprentice.[15] She succeeded no better at this than at acquiring a miller's flat thumb.

However, she did read many books. To encourage her to read his favorite biographies of heroic men, John paid her (ever the capitalist, he believed in money as a motivator) to read Plutarch's *Lives*, about the great Roman and Greek leaders of the classical world, and the five volumes of Washington Irving's *Life of George Washington*. Later she read his copy of Thomas Carlyle's *Heroes and Hero Worship*, which swept her away. All these books, and many more, relentlessly pressed upon the reader a key message of nineteenth-century American secular culture: the urgent need to cultivate self-reliance, courage, and moral ambition. When this message was combined with the powerful influences of evangelical Christianity, including its emphasis on personal accountability for the soul's redemption, it is no wonder the century produced many morally earnest men and women. In her ethical ambitiousness, Jane was like her father and her mother, whose ethic of Christian self-sacrifice had led to her death, but also of her times.

The message did not take with everyone. A case in point was John's second wife. Raised in Pennsylvania, Anna Hostetter had come west to join her brothers; married a modestly successful miller, William Haldeman, a competitor of John's; and eventually settled with her husband and two sons in Freeport, the city south of Cedarville. Anna's seriousness was channeled not into morality but culture. Always drawn to the fine arts, she loved music (she could play the piano and the guitar); read widely in fiction; and adored the great British poets, most particularly the eighteenth-century Scots bard Robert Burns. A woman of refined tastes and elegant manners whose husband's death left her and her sons on the brink of poverty, she saw in John a man whose wealth could solve her financial problems and allow her to live in a style she had long aspired to. Having lost her own mother when she was a small child, she also felt some sympathy for his motherless children, especially Jane. Anna became Jane's third mother, after Sarah and Mary, and would change Jane's life.

Anna and her younger son, seven-year-old George, moved into the Addams homestead when Jane was eight. Jane gained a companion in George and new stimulations in Anna's enthusiasms for reading, conversation, good manners, lovely clothes, and travel. Anna subscribed to the *Atlantic Monthly*, with its rich array of articles and etchings, and nudged and prodded John Addams to take his family on sightseeing trips. Soon after their marriage, the family visited the State Capitol in Madison, Wisconsin, where Jane saw for the first time a large, architecturally beautiful space and found it thrilling. When Jane was fifteen, Anna prevailed on John to take them East to attend the nation's first world's fair, the Centennial Exhibition in Philadelphia, where the latest inventions, including the telephone, and the latest ideas about social reform, including the German educational innovation called the kindergarten, were on display.

But Jane also found it difficult to adjust to Anna as her stepmother. Having been used to Mary's gentle touch, she rebelled against Anna's sterner discipline. A friend of Mary's saw what was going on when she visited and later reminisced in a letter to Jane how Mary's "service of love ... [was] more acceptable to you ... than the word of authority from your stepmother." Temperamentally Jane and Anna mixed like oil and water. It was not only that Jane was used to Mary's kinder ways but that Jane was also a cooler personality. One family member, comparing Jane with Anna, thought Jane was "reserved," "never dramatic,"

Jane Addams at twelve

"quieter . . . and more equitable." Anna *was* dramatic; she also had a fierce temper. Jane's sister Alice later remembered Anna's "explosions."[16] She had a reputation in town too, for having, as one Cedarville resident put it, "a quick temper." A family letter refers to a heated argument between Anna and John over whether Alice, who had fallen in love with Anna's older son, Harry, should marry him. John, knowing that Harry had a serious drinking problem, was opposed.[17]

Hints of the tensions between Jane and Anna survive in fourteen-year-old Jane's briefly kept diary. She complained, for example, when Anna found the pies Jane had baked unsatisfactory (Anna, having a servant, refused to cook, but insisted Jane learn). Another time Anna compelled Jane to cancel a visit to see Mary, who had married and moved to a neighboring town, because the servant was unexpectedly away, and someone needed to cook breakfast for John Addams (again, Anna refused to cook). The scenes can only be imagined, as Jane did not describe them in her diary. Perhaps, when Jane did something of which

Anna did not approve, Anna would erupt in a rage, and Jane, whose greatest passions in later life were for accuracy and fairness, would argue back, for she had her own fierce temper when sufficiently aroused, and plenty of self-righteous conviction that she was right. Anna would become more furious, and Jane, more angry, hurt, and frustrated. Such pointless fights were likely a daily part of Jane's life as she grew up.

The depth of her frustration can be measured in her adult conclusions. She grew up to have a passionate dislike—"hatred" might be a better word if its use here were not ironic—for what she called antagonism. Anger, conflict, and opposition: Jane believed these should be avoided at all costs. Her argument was both pragmatic—that antagonism achieved nothing—and moral—that antagonism was never aroused for a "good" reason but only for personal reasons, perhaps because a person enjoyed opposing others or felt hurt or insulted.[18] But one senses that antagonism's pointlessness and pettiness were not the only issues. Anna's repeated fury seared into Jane's soul the pain that hostility causes; she aroused in her stepdaughter a profound longing to avoid such pain and to avoid inflicting such pain if she possibly could.

Unable to risk wholehearted love for Anna, Jane safely invested that love in her calm father. He was not a man to lose his temper. When the teenaged Alice, home from boarding school, irritated him by being late for breakfast every day, he waited to express his disapproval of her undisciplined ways in a letter she received from him after her visit ended. He told her that her lateness "annoyed me although I did not say much. Hope you will break [this habit]." The reasons he gave were practical: "I am a businessman and know how annoying tardiness is—it is no small thing." Although John tended to be a bit serious and taciturn, he was also ready to hear what a child had to say. A grandson later recalled how he was always "wondering what his thoughts must be—and yet I was so absolutely certain always of his love[.] . . . [I]f I did dare to speak to him, a certain look would come into his eyes and I felt he was never putting me off or only having to listen."[19]

In keeping with the customs of the age, John had certain expectations for his daughters that he did not have for his son. Not only were they to learn the skills of good housekeeping—it was particularly crucial, Jane Addams remembered, that she be able to bake a perfect loaf of bread for her miller father—but they were also to think of ways to make him more comfortable or happy. Every night Mary brought him his slippers. Jane later remembered how women of her generation were taught from "babyhood" to be "self-forgetting and self-sacrificing." Anna's *Atlantic Monthly* was one of the instructors. It reminded its readers in 1878: "The woman who does not please is a false note in the harmony of nature."[20] The person being pleased, it went without saying, was the man of the house. When Jane was a child, the sacrifices, perhaps a missed chance to visit a sister, were small. But when she was older the sacrifices became larger. John Huy Addams enjoyed without guilt exercising the familial tyranny of the nineteenth-century patriarch. Though, like most Americans, he hated the political tyranny embodied in Great Britain's royal government, he could not see that the benevolent despotism with which he ruled over the women in his family (or in Anna's case, attempted to rule) was anything except good.

John Addams was a businessman first, but he also had politics in his blood. He came from a family of Pennsylvania Whigs who enjoyed legislating. His grandfather had served in the state assembly, and he had two political uncles. One had run unsuccessfully for the U.S. Congress, and the other had served as a state assemblyman and a two-term congressman. Jane Addams never mentioned this family history—it is possible she never knew it—but her father's political service was part of a family tradition.

Beyond that, he seems to have been a good party man. His disapproving attitude toward immigrants (except for those from Germany, the country from which the bulk of his ancestors had come) was a case in point. By the 1840s the Whig Party, which attracted businessmen and other men of wealth, was opposed to the recent trend, pushed hard by the Democratic Party, to give the vote to men without property, including immigrants. The effort had been successful in Illinois. When John Addams arrived, he discovered that any man residing in the state for six months had the right to vote. As a resident for only four months on election day he could not cast a ballot in the presidential election of 1844. He stood around the polling place, watching men he considered his inferiors exercise the franchise. Disgusted, he wrote his brother-in-law back home: "An ignorant Norwegian . . . who knows nothing but says he has been here six months and 1 day" can vote, while "the Pennsylvanian who paid [property] tax in his native state and has been here five months and 29 days stands back at the polls. This is shameful."[21] He was not speaking of himself but of the hypothetical new resident who could miss qualifying to vote by one day.

One newer party practice, however, he did not accept—that of legislators taking bribes. He dealt with the situation himself after he had been elected state senator in 1854. Remarkably, he became famous during his sixteen years in the Illinois senate, no doubt somewhat apocryphally, as the only man who was not offered a bribe because, as his daughter later explained—she was relying on what a friend of her father's told her—"bad men were instinctively afraid of him." It wasn't simply that he considered bribes immoral. His critique went deeper. He refused to be influenced by the views of regular citizens too. He believed that a man should vote according to what he thought would be best for the people, not what they thought best. A grandson wrote: "John Addams did not so much care to know what the people wanted. . . . He took advice only from his own conscience."[22]

John Addams's practice of American democracy was constrained by his religion, his ethnicity, and his class. His sense of superiority was deeply ingrained, and he did not hesitate to judge his fellow citizens as inadequate, ignorant, and ill informed. Still, neighbors remembered him as always greeting rich and poor alike with equal courtesy, as behooved a small-town politician. Those on the lower economic rungs, however,

did not suppose he thought they were truly his equals. Instead they
gave him a moniker that summed up neatly just who he was, "the king
gentleman of the district."[23]

|||||||||||||

John Addams was a reformer of sorts. A Whig when he moved to Illinois, he joined the new Republican Party as soon as it organized in
Illinois in 1854 and was immediately elected a Republican state senator. He believed, like most Whigs and Republicans, that the government should be used for positive good—to protect the vulnerable and
strengthen the economic infrastructure—and he favored Congress's
preventing the spread of slavery. Perhaps his boldest action, during the
Civil War, was to risk a fine and imprisonment by serving as a conductor
on the Underground Railroad. When Jane was not yet four, she entered
a room of their house to find him talking with an African American
who had been enslaved and was escaping north.[24] Her father told her to
keep secret what she had seen. There is no record, however, that he ever
took a controversial political stand or aroused public ire for anything
he said or did. Except for his opposition to slavery, his beliefs did not
lead him into dangerous waters.

For her part, Jane Addams had an early urge to fix the world. Anna
recalled how Jane wanted to have a "career" while still in high school.[25]
The career she chose was social reform. At the time Ralph Waldo Emerson was her favorite author, and his essay "Man the Reformer" no doubt
deserves some credit for awakening that ambition. Emerson described
the reformer as "a brave and upright man" who called "the institutions
of society to account," a "restorer of truth," and a person who removed
"impediments" in order that mankind might flourish.[26] It seemed to
Jane a highly worthwhile kind of person to become.

She was also inspired by magazine stories about particular reformers. When she was twelve, she read a three-part series in the *Atlantic
Monthly* about the utopian Robert Owen and his short-lived 1830s community, New Harmony, in Indiana, and found his belief that man's

Jane Addams, age fifteen, on the right; her stepmother,
Anna Haldeman Addams, in the center; and
her stepbrother, George Haldeman, on the left, 1876

character was formed by his environment compelling and his vision for a classless, cooperative society "thrilling." The radical abolitionist John Brown was featured in another long series published when she was fifteen. Decades later she told a friend, "I have always had a secret sympathy with [Brown's] impatience and his determination that something should . . . happen." In later years she named Lucy Stone, the abolitionist, suffragist, and advocate for women's rights, whose accomplishments in the 1870s were reported in the *New York Tribune*, as the woman she most admired.[27]

And her interest in politics continued. As she grew older, it expanded to include presidential elections. When the election of 1876 was so close it had to be resolved in the U.S. House of Representatives, Jane followed the news with fascination. After it was settled, she wrote a cousin: "I enjoy politics very much and was especially interested last fall and winter. It seems rather tame now when the excitement has stopped."[28]

Sometime in her teens Jane's ambitions crystallized into the reform career of practicing medicine among the poor. The idea had come in stages. When she was six, she had told her father she wanted to live next door to poor families. Gradually she realized she could do that by being a doctor. She had read about such doctors in popular fiction—in a now-forgotten novel called *Jericho Road* and in Charles Dickens's *Bleak House*. Another likely inspiration was the village doctor, a close family friend who treated poor people as well as the more prosperous. Also, Harry Haldeman, Anna's elder son and thus Jane's stepbrother and her brother-in-law—John had lost that fight to Anna—was a doctor. The idea of women becoming doctors was just emerging in the mid-1870s, and this may have been part of its appeal to her. The general view (which later changed) was that a woman doctor was not a daring idea, given that women had nursed the ill for millennia.

More daring was Jane's determination to earn a Bachelor of Arts degree. Hardly any young women—less than three-quarters of 1 percent—went beyond high school in the mid-1870s.[29] Nearly all the colleges were for men; coeducational universities were just beginning in these years. Young women who wanted more education tended to go to female seminaries (the term referred to women's postsecondary institutions that were not colleges) or "colleges" (the term was abused) that awarded collegiate certificates, which had less rigorous requirements, especially in classical languages and mathematics, than the B.A. institutions. Jane's older sisters, Mary, Martha, and Alice, all had attended Rockford Female Seminary in Rockford, Illinois, a day's carriage ride from home. John had briefly served on its board of trustees. But when Jane was in her teens, the big news, publicized in the *Atlantic Monthly* and elsewhere, was about a women's college opening in Massachusetts, Smith College, that was to offer women "real" B.A.'s, degrees equal in difficulty to those men earned. Smith was scheduled to open its doors in the fall of 1877, just when Jane would be ready to enroll. It was reputed to have fine offerings in science, which she knew she would need to learn to prepare for studying medicine. Moreover, for an ambitious girl, going to glamorous Smith was important just in itself. Jane set her heart on going.

John Addams said no. Jane described his reasons in *Twenty Years*: "My father's theory in regard to the education of his daughters implied a school as near as home as possible." Afterward he intended his daughters to travel in Europe (as Alice did in 1875) as a substitute for "the wider advantages" of attending an eastern college. His refusal stung Jane in a way she did not quite convey in *Twenty Years*. Still, the words she chose— "I was greatly disappointed"—were among the strongest personal feelings she revealed in the whole book.[30] Whether she stormed about the house in anger, as seems unlikely, or sank quietly into a morose depression is hard to say. But her beloved father's refusal to allow her to pursue her dream to discover the "wider life" was a bitter pill.

||||||||||||

Jane did her duty—to be sure, she had no choice since she had no money of her own—and went to Rockford Female Seminary in the fall of 1877. Her plan was to excel academically and show that the school was too easy for her, so that her father would let her go to Smith the next year. She did not admit the anger she felt in *Twenty Years*, but she admitted it to her nephew when she was in her seventies. She told him she felt "resentful."[31]

The fact that the school was evangelical did not help. Its zealous founder, Anna Sill, intended to train women as missionaries for Christian service overseas. She had modified her rhetoric as necessary to ensure that the school appealed to the leading citizens of Rockford, who merely wanted their daughters given a sheen of culture before they married, but the school remained an intensely proselytizing institution. Every weekday morning Sill gave a sermon to students on a Bible passage they were then expected to memorize (and to be able to recite later that day to any teacher they might meet). They were also expected to pray every evening, to attend the church of their choice in town every Sunday, and to participate in Sunday evening prayer meetings at the school. Girls who had not yet "come to Jesus" were expected to convert and be baptized, and teachers and students put great pressure on the few who remained as yet unsaved, even praying publicly for them by name in morning chapel.[32]

Being unconverted and determined to remain so, Jane was a thorn in the side of the school and particularly in Sill's side. In these years Jane was a deist, like her favorite writer, Emerson. She thought God might be everywhere. She did not believe he had come down to earth as Jesus Christ, died for her sins, and been resurrected. Determined to follow her father's advice not to say she believed what she did not believe, she stalwartly resisted all urgings to convert, despite the pain she felt in taking a stand in opposition to her new community. Jane remembered being "unspeakably embarrassed" when a teacher sometimes visited her room to attempt to convert her. Later, however, she concluded the experience was useful. She wrote in *Twenty Years*, tongue in cheek, that "this clinging to individual conviction" at Rockford was "the best moral training" she received there.[33] Her ability at seventeen to resist such intense pressure was an early sign of her fierce desire to be true to her conscience and of the strength, the inner moral steel, she brought to the task.

Rockford had other gifts to offer Jane, though she did not know it at first. One was an inspiring teacher, Caroline Potter, the pedagogical mainstay of the seminary's curriculum. Whether a student chose to take the scientific, classical, or literary track, she was required to take Potter's literature and history courses. The result was that for four years every student had Potter for at least one and often two semesters.

Today history and literature are taught as criticism; the student's ability to judge her own and scholars' interpretations is sharpened. In the nineteenth century these subjects were taught as the wellsprings of human wisdom and, sometimes, of human folly. Students read not only history but also essays, biography, novels, plays, and poetry about great men like Napoleon and Moses for what they could teach about character, which was thought to be the force that shaped history. Character was a broad concept. A man of character was decisive, courageous, creative, engaged with his times, unwilling to compromise his integrity, responsible, and determined. Carlyle's *Heroes and Hero Worship*, read by Addams in her teens, was all about such men of character. Potter's entire curriculum was an intense and lengthy seminar on the heroic, and Jane was entranced.

Potter did not teach only about great men. She taught about women too. Like most girls of her generation, Addams had few, if any, female heroes in the Carlylean sense, whether living, dead, or imaginary. In high school she had adored reading *Little Women* and found the character of Jo, who loved books and writing and wanted to do "something heroic," enchanting, and she had thought Little Nell in Dickens's *The Old Curiosity Shop*, who was devoted to her elderly father and willing to sacrifice herself for his sake, "just perfect."[34] The real-life activist Lucy Stone intrigued her, but Addams knew little about Stone beyond a few articles in the newspaper. For a young woman with an ambition to be great, this was thin gruel. Now Caroline Potter laid a feast before her.

One of the texts Potter assigned was Margaret Fuller's *Woman in the Nineteenth Century*, a book published in 1845 that influenced many in Potter's generation. A recent biographer of Fuller's described it, in its various parts, as a wide-ranging discussion of the debate over women's nature and status, a philosophical text about ideal manhood and womanhood and about how these ideals conflicted with current reality, and a polemic advocating for social reform.[35] Drawing on the Bible, Greek, Roman, and Scandinavian mythology, classical Greek and Shakespearean plays, and the writings of the Europeans Johann von Goethe and Charles Fourier, Fuller showed that the current division of society into rigidly separate, gendered spheres did damage to both men and women but especially to the latter. "What Woman needs," she wrote, "is . . . as a nature to grow, as an intellect to discern, as a soul to live freely and unimpeded, to unfold such powers as were given her when we left our common home [Eden]." She added, "For human beings are not so constituted that they can live without expansion. If they do not get it in one way, they must in another, or perish." To accomplish such expansion, a woman must discover both her masculine side (her energy, power, and intellect) and her feminine side (her ability to create harmony, beauty, and love).[36]

Caroline Potter was a Fuller disciple. Excited by the changes that had come for women in her own lifetime and by the promises held by the blossoming woman's rights movement, Potter aimed to prepare girls, she wrote a friend, to "direct . . . this splendid accession of power." She looked for girls who were ready, if she found the right course of study for them, to "exhaust [their] strength in [its] pursuit." She also looked for originality and the willingness to act "upon the demand of the occasion."[37] She did not want to see learning pursued simply for its own sake; action, including creative thought, was required. She warned a group of alumnae in 1883: "If the mind of woman becomes chiefly a repository of learning, then she will lose her vital power."[38]

Jane read Fuller's text with attention and excitement. Its pages were full of references to heroic women she had never met before: the divinely wise Egyptian-Greek goddess Isis, Shakespeare's assertive Portia, the brilliant French novelist George Sand, and the truth-telling Greek priestess Cassandra. They all became topics in her essays for Potter and other college writings. Fuller's book and others she read in Potter's classes touched some part of her that her father's example and the male heroes in books had not; she was discovering that women could be great. As her ability to imagine herself a woman of power quickened, she began the slow, painful, thrilling process of giving birth to herself.

She closed her first year at Rockford with a stellar 9.3 out of a possible 10 grade point average and wrote her parents a letter—the document does not survive—announcing the news. Anna responded encouragingly, expressing her pleasure that Jane "feels happy . . . that her school work has been well-done." She told her to leave her bedding at Rockford in shape "to send for" in case she did not return next year. Anna, herself an aspirant to all things glamorous, was probably in sympathy with Jane's desire to go to prestigious Smith College. John, the taciturn and distracted businessman, gave no such encouragement. In fact in his letter he made no mention of Jane's excellent grades but simply expressed pleasure to hear she was in good health, sent her some local news, and closed by saying he had "no time to say more."[39] That summer he again refused Jane's plea to go to Smith.

||||||||||||

In her sophomore year Jane was drawn further into Potter's magic realm. She began writing short items for the student publication, the *Rockford Seminary Magazine*, for which Potter was founder and faculty adviser. The magazine was published by the two student literary societies at Rockford, also founded and advised by Potter. Every entering student was required to join one, and Jane joined the Castalian Society. In her second year the societies faced off in a debate, and she had her first chance to marshal arguments about women's heroic potential. Potter set the debaters the proposition that Frenchwomen (the cases to be compared were George Sand and Madame de Staël) "have more influence through literature than politics."

Assigned to argue in favor, Jane did so with gusto. She began by summing up the assumption behind the proposition—an assumption that was widely held and no doubt discussed in Potter's classes—that those who wished to be heroes should either write great literature or participate in politics. Adopting the grandiloquent style of the Victorians she was reading, Jane wrote: "If a man makes up his mind to do something worthy of remembrance, or utter one thought so illuminated that his name shall not be forgotten as soon as his body is turned into dust, he must either enter the region of literature or politics."[40] The same, she added, was true for women.

Dismissing as a failure de Staël's attempts to advance a constitutional monarchy through the convening of salons, Jane turned to George Sand to prove the power of literature to change the world. She laid out with an uncharacteristically fervent pen the events of Sand's life, including her marriage, at age eighteen, to "an ordinary commonplace despotic baron, the last creature in the universe that the quivering soul of genius should have wedded." The boldly unorthodox Sand, realizing her mistake and unable to divorce her husband because of French law, abandoned the marriage, Jane explained, and "evolved from her own heart and brain her own law of life." She wrote novels attacking the French marriage system and declared "the social independence and equality of woman [in] her relations to man, society and destiny." And when the Revolution of 1848 came, "this splendid, fiery woman" became "the world's peacemaker, the apologist of mankind." Jane then extracted the relevance of Sand's life to her own generation. Today's woman "wishes not to be a man or like a man," but, like Sand, "she claims the same right to independent thought and action."[41]

The argument Jane was making had been assigned, of course, but there was nothing halfhearted about her efforts. It almost seems as if the example of the passionate Sand—and perhaps the one-sided nature of a debater's role—had released some inhibition in the usually calm and steady Jane. It is clear that she thrilled to Sand's daring, her confident reliance on her brilliant mind, her resolute individualism, and her feminist vision for women. If, as appears likely, Jane could not admit yet to herself that she aspired to be like Sand, then at least she felt she had discovered a hero she could admire with her whole heart.

The mood did not last. Just then Jane was less determined to nurture the passions of her heart than the rationality of her mind. She still intended to pursue a medical career and therefore to study science with the limited resources Rockford had to offer and by means of whatever opportunities she could create for herself. She and a friend had cofounded a science club her first year, as a place to do rudimentary laboratory work they could not do in class. In the summers she and her stepbrother George, who wanted to be a scientist, caught, killed, and stuffed birds, pounded rocks, and examined earthworms under a microscope. Her vacation reading included Darwin's *On the Origin of Species* and *The Descent of Man*. She told herself that science offered "intellectual adventure" and tried to persuade herself, as she wrote a friend, that she would rather get her inspiration from "a dodecahedral crystal" than from "a Genius," but the opposite was closer to the truth. She admitted as much in a sophomore paper: "Science demands from its devotees only an exertion of the brain, and not a complete surrender of life and all its pleasures."[42] She was wrong, of course. Science could call forth such sacrifices. She really was speaking about her own feelings.

Evidently, Jane wanted a career that demanded self-sacrifice, even martyrdom, that close cousin of heroism. Martyrs embraced suffering as destiny, while heroes passed through suffering on their way to victory; martyrs consistently denied the self, while heroes celebrated it; martyrs did not seek power, while heroes did. The martyr was the aborted hero. Martyrdom was also the Christian's and the woman's greatest crown. Jane adored the heroic, but having been trained in Christianity and the female duties of self-sacrifice and having known personal suffering from childhood, she felt martyrdom's appeal.

In a sense she had approached attending Rockford in that spirit, always mindful that she wanted to be at Smith instead. But at the end of her sophomore year she reached the decision, uncoerced by her father, that she wanted to return to Rockford the next fall. No doubt the school had become a beloved place to her, associated with good friends and bold ideas, but with characteristic attentiveness to the question of her own growth, she made a moral assessment of her standoffish attitude and decided it was keeping her from fully developing her talents. In an editorial she wrote for the *Rockford Seminary Magazine* she advised her reader to avoid "locked up faculties" (she borrowed the phrase from Emerson's essay "Experience," a favorite of hers) by taking up her duties as a citizen in the community in which she finds herself. Whether that be "in the wide world or a school, . . . [her] responsibility is the same."[43] Emboldened by the self-empowering curriculum that Potter offered and the freedoms inherent in a women's institution, Jane was finally ready to see what she could accomplish if she really tried.

That summer her ability to conceive of female greatness deepened. A hint of what she was thinking survives in a letter she wrote her friend Ellen Gates Starr. She and Ellen had met their first year at Rockford, but after Ellen, unable to return for a second year because of family finances, had taken a job teaching school in Chicago, they kept up their friendship through correspondence. Ellen was far more interested in religion and matters of faith than Jane was, and in her letters she kept prodding Jane to explain what she believed. Finally, Jane answered that she had been pondering her sense of distance from God—the God she had once imagined as a gentleman on a throne surrounded by saints and angels—and had been noticing that praying to Jesus Christ did not help her feel closer to him. Slipping into midwestern vernacular, she wrote, "Christ don't [sic] help me in the least" come closer to "the Deity."[44]

But she had found something that did, the idea that God was female. Her reading planted the seed. Earlier that year she had come across a passing reference to a nature goddess "whose life and power were something deeper and more primordial than knowledge" in George Eliot's novel *Romola*, and she had read about the Egyptian-Greek goddess Isis, "of divine wisdom never yet surpassed," and about other goddesses in Fuller's *Woman in the Nineteenth Century*.[45] Now she wrote to Ellen these daring words: "Lately it seems to me that I am getting back of all of it—superior to it, I almost feel. Back to a great Primal Cause, not Nature exactly, but a fostering mother, a necessity, brooding and watching over all things, above every human passion & and yet not passive, the mystery of creation. I make a botch trying to describe it & yet the idea has been lots of comfort to me lately. The idea embodied in the sphinx—peace."[46] Her words reveal her longing for a spiritual life and the inherent appeal of a God that was female, but also the hole in her heart where her mother's love should have been.

|||||||||||

Back at Rockford for her junior year, Jane followed through on her editorial and flung herself into the life of the school. In addition to making excellent grades that year (she earned a 9.8 out of 10 grade point average), she was elected class president and president of the Castalian Society. By then she had learned from reading other college magazines that the literary societies at men's colleges held campus oratorical competitions. Eager to create public speaking opportunities for herself and other Rockford students, she decided to create an event for her class, most likely with Potter's encouragement.

Jane's enthusiasm for oratory was fed by many sources. In 1872, when she was twelve, her father gave a rousing, well-crafted speech in Freeport supporting the Republican president, Ulysses S. Grant, for reelection that Jane likely attended. She probably read noteworthy speeches reprinted in the *New York Tribune*. The books in her father's library had taught her that male heroes from every century distinguished themselves as orators. And in Latin class at Rockford, she had studied the oratory of Cicero, Horace, and Tacitus. Her junior year she spent the fall semester reading in Latin the fabled speeches of Cicero, considered by some to be the greatest orator in the history of the world. In the realm of books, all the great orators were men, which was discouraging. But if Jane read about Lucy Stone and other women's rights advocates who were giving lectures across the country in the 1870s, then she would have caught a glimpse of the oratorical possibilities for women.

Potter made sure her students learned the theory too. In her history and literature classes, she taught them the art of persuasion. Their textbook covered the different figures of speech, including comparison, metaphor, personification, allegory, metonymy, synecdoche, apostrophe, and irony. It also stressed the importance of establishing an emotional connection with the audience: The orator tries to persuade others by presenting his views "in a language" that makes those views appeal to the "free impulses" of his audience.[47] Jane learned that if she wanted to be a skillful orator, she would need to master the figures of speech and would have to learn how to express the feelings of her audience, so that, in turn, they would be willing to hear what she had to say.

Because Addams went to college in the 1870s, when rhetoric was still a required part of most college curricula in the Midwest (it was already disappearing in the eastern schools), she had a chance to study the subject. Putting that knowledge to use in later years, she was to become one of the nation's most accomplished and popular orators. Caroline Potter, who lived until 1933, must have been very proud.[48]

The public speaking event that Jane and her classmates dreamed up was a first for Rockford but a tradition at some men's colleges: a junior class oratorical exhibition. The citizens of Rockford came to the college chapel, which was festooned by evergreen boughs and stands of flowering plants, to hear members of the class present five orations (the categories—Latin, scientific, ethical, Greek, and philosophical—were traditional).

Jane had a prominent role, giving two speeches. As class president she opened the evening with the class address, and as the only member of her class who had studied Greek, she gave the Greek oration, although she delivered it in English, since few in the audience knew Greek. The latter was a clumsy exercise in allegory, in which she used the Greek myth of Bellerophon, mentioned in *The Iliad*, to argue that social reformers should use their idealism to slay the delusions of "prejudice and fanaticism" abroad in the land. The class speech was more impressive. It too was about social reform, but this time she chose for her figure of speech the metaphor of "breadgivers."

Her speech has been a puzzle to many. Some have read it as endorsing the idea that women should devote themselves to taking care of their families, but that was not Jane's meaning. She and her classmates had been reading in Potter's class John Ruskin's 1865 book on the nature and duties of men and women, *Sesame and Lilies*. There Ruskin explained that the phrase "breadgivers" is a translation of the Anglo-Saxon word for "lady" and "refers not to the bread which is given to the household but to the bread broken among the multitude." When Jane announced in her speech without further explanation that educated women of her day "planned [to be] 'breadgivers,'" she knew that her classmates, although maybe not the rest of the audience, would understand that she meant they would do charity work among the poor. Such efforts were also called philanthropy or social reform; the terms were used interchangeably.[49] In her class address she was confidently predicting her classmates' future or, at least, her own.

|||||||||||||||

Jane began her senior year feeling that peculiar mixture of confidence and trepidation that the last year of college generally arouses. Among her many triumphs, she had been named editor-in-chief of the *Rockford Seminary Magazine*, which allowed her the greatest satisfaction a writer can know, the pleasure of seeing her words in print on a regular basis. She reorganized the magazine's departments and, after a fund-raising fair, achieved a balanced budget. Pleased with her financial success, Jane teased in an editorial: "So why not become a capitalist?"[50]

Furthermore, by some unknown process that may have been as simple as popular acclamation, she had been chosen to represent Rockford Female Seminary in the Illinois state intercollegiate oratorical contest at Knox College that fall. Neither Rockford nor any other women's collegiate institution in the state had ever competed before. Jane, the only woman in a field of nine orators, did not do well, placing fifth. To be sure, the competition was stiff. Placing second was William Jennings Bryan, who was to achieve fame as a gifted orator and as a presidential candidate three times (although today he is mostly remembered as the lawyer for the prosecution in the Scopes trial). But Jane's friends teasingly scolded her when she returned for having "dealt the cause of woman's advancement a staggering blow."[51]

Academically her work remained excellent. She was to graduate valedictorian of her class, with a grade point average of 9.8, and a collegiate certificate. Her plan was to go to Smith the following year and do whatever course work she needed to earn a B.A., after which she would travel in Europe, then earn a degree in medicine from the University of Edinburgh. "This year is a solid dig," she wrote in a letter to Ellen Gates Starr, "to make up all the odds and ends for Smith. . . . My former vague dream is growing into a settled passion."[52]

But if her plans had not changed, something else had. In her senior year a new note of hesitation and fearfulness crept into her college essays and editorials. In several essays she praised heroes from history for *not* having a purpose in life since this prevented them from having to "sink under disappointment" when they failed to achieve it.[53] Then there was her new assumption that an outside agent was in charge of a person's future. The challenge, she wrote in a November editorial, is to "know . . . what niche in the world has been left for us to fill." In another, she remarked of her class of 1881, "We can only hope that each in her 'small corner' will accomplish that where-unto she may be sent."[54] Who was leaving Jane a niche to fill? Who was sending her to her "small corner"? To whose authority was she submitting? She wrote as if she expected the future to have an absence of freedom, a lack of choice. Even her sentences were tied in knots.

She also began to praise the virtue of obedience and the ethic of duty to the family, two subjects she had hardly mentioned in earlier Rockford writings. In an editorial she admired the Roman soldier who was guarding the gates of Pompeii when Mount Vesuvius erupted and who died at his post because he had received no orders to leave. In her commonplace book of favorite quotations she recorded George Eliot's observation about duty to family in *The Mill on the Floss*, a book she read over Christmas vacation, that "pity and faithfulness and memory are natural. . . . [They would] punish me if I did not obey them."[55]

The changes in her thinking all suggest that she was worried about the future and what her family, particularly her father, would expect of her. Perhaps he had already told her he did not want her to go to Smith the following year. More likely he had said nothing, but she had divined that for now—presumably he still wanted her to travel in Europe someday—he wanted her home, wanted her to be there at the breakfast table every morning and to be there to kiss him good-night every evening. Faced with his desire and her own, Jane was caught between what she longed for and her duty. Her dreams of independence had hit the wall of her reality: She was a woman and a daughter.

Jane Addams, graduation photo, 1881

The day of commencement arrived, and John Addams was a beam-ing father. A friend of his who was also there later told Jane, "I shall never forget . . . the contented, happy smile on his face as he talked of you."[56] As her class's top student Jane gave a short, uninspired valedic-tory speech. But like everyone in the class of seventeen girls, she also read her senior essay at the gathering. She had poured her heart into writing it.

Her speech was about Cassandra, the priestess at Troy who proph-esied to the soldiers the truth about their pending defeat and was mocked, scorned, and declared mad—and then became mad as a conse-quence. She explained why Cassandra had failed and how other women could avoid making her mistake. Here Jane was dreaming of a new possibility—that a woman have an authoritative voice in public debate. If so, how? Cassandra had relied on "female intuition," which, because of its long association with family life, was not respected in the public forum. It would be better for the women of today, Jane argued, to study reason, logic, and facts—that is, science. This, combined with her gift of intuition, would best prepare a woman for civic life.

Jane was making an abstract argument about her personal dilemma. Without an M.D. degree, she feared she would, like Cassandra, be disbelieved and laughed at if she claimed an authoritative voice. She realized only too well that men, and sometimes women too, perceived femininity as limiting because it was linked in their minds to powerlessness. She intended to claim her power, as Potter and Fuller had taught her she could. But there was another problem of powerlessness beyond the societal one she explored in the speech. She knew that in her determination to earn a B.A. at Smith and then an M.D. degree, she was on a collision course with her father. With her future unknown, these were the worries that absorbed her as she parted from her friends and teachers and climbed into her father's carriage for the journey home.

||||||||||||||||||||||||||||||||||||||||||||||||||||||||||||||||||||||||||||||||||||||||||||||||||||||||||||||||||||||||||||||||||||||||||||||

CHAPTER TWO

FREEDOM SEEKER

Wʜᴇɴ ᴅᴏᴇꜱ ᴀᴅᴜʟᴛʜᴏᴏᴅ begin? The question is urgently important to a person in her twenties, to whom adulthood signals the arrival
of that condition that childhood denies and college offers only in a cir-
cumscribed world—true independence. In the summer of 1881, twenty-
year-old Jane Addams, her well-earned collegiate certificate in hand,
was confident she was now an adult and ready to decide for herself how
best to pursue her dream of becoming a doctor and working among the
poor. Mindful of her father's reluctance to give her that freedom, she set
herself the task of persuading him.

She failed. John Addams told her she could not go to Smith College
in the fall. His kindly and protective reasons, which she explained in a
letter to a friend, were that she had strained her health at Rockford from
all the hard work (it was true that she had worn herself out) and that it
would be best if she stayed home and grew stronger first. But her father
had available to him other, more powerful reasons—arguments about a
daughter's duty to her family and the moral dangers of selfishness—and
it appears, although Jane does not mention them in her letter, that he
used them, just as she had sensed he would.

What happened that summer is captured in the story of a typical college-educated daughter that Jane told repeatedly in speeches throughout the 1890s. The daughter returns home from college eager to begin her adult life of "independent action" and to be of some use in the world. Her parents, however, dismiss her ambition as "a foolish enthusiasm," arguing that "she is restless and she does not know what she wants." When the daughter insists, the family is "injured and unhappy" and charges her with "setting up her will against [its will] for selfish ends."[1]

These words, from a speech Jane gave in 1898, sound neutral yet establish what she understood by then. The parents were being selfish in not encouraging their daughter's self-development. But in 1881 she was not so sure. She makes that clear in the speech too, as she tells about the daughter's response to her parents: "She hides her hurt. [H]er zeal and her emotions turn inward, and the result is an unhappy woman, whose vitality is consumed by vain regrets[.]"[2] She was hurt that her parents did not know her better, did not honor the depth and seriousness of her longing, but her training in self-sacrifice kept her from rebelling.

Nor could she feel singled out. Several Rockford classmates with similar ambitions wrote letters with similar news. One said that her father wanted her to "rest, not go away to work or study for a while. It is hard to be patient."[3] Another, who, like Jane, wanted to go to Smith College and medical school, reported that her father refused to pay for her to go to either. A third, who wanted to earn a B.A. degree, sent word that she would have to teach school next year instead, in order to help pay the costs of her brother going to medical school. For women of Jane Addams's generation, family duty commonly trumped personal ambition.

Duty made a daughter's self-denial noble. Left unstated, unless the daughter was rebellious and ready to bolt, was the father's financial power. Jane Addams had no money to pay for the costs of attending Smith. And her devotion to him was another velvet cord that bound her.

|||||||||||

Events that summer made it even more difficult for Jane Addams to rebel. The first involved the son of John's good friend and business colleague at his Freeport bank, Luther Guiteau. Charles Julius Guiteau, now forty years old, had long been a source of grief to his family. Having lived in many places and tried many jobs, he was generally broke. Irascible, egotistical, and hungry for fame and wealth, he had been disowned by his devoutly Christian perfectionist father, who thought him possessed of the devil (by the son's own fault) and therefore insane. But Luther, who died in 1880, had refused to commit him to an institution.

And so Julius—his family called him by his middle name—who in fact was mentally ill, was in Washington, D.C., the summer of 1881, trying but failing to get a job in the federal government. President James Garfield had been inaugurated in March, and Julius, who had worked on the 1880 campaign, or at least had harassed the campaign headquarters, thought he was owed employment. When no job emerged, he became Garfield's enemy and decided to remove him. On the morning of July 2, Julius, described in the newspapers and in history books ever after as a "frustrated office seeker," shot and seriously wounded the president of the United States at point-blank range in a D.C. train station. Julius, pistol in hand, was immediately arrested. President Garfield lingered for two months before dying in mid-September.

John Addams learned of the shooting from a Freeport news reporter, who, reading about it on the telegraph wire, dashed to the bank, seeking the scoop of his life. John took the horrifying news calmly, telling him that "he felt no particular surprise as he had known [Julius] to be a very erratic man from his youth and [he was] just the person to execute some sensational act."[4] John was worried that reporters would descend upon his friend's widow, who was Julius's stepmother; her daughter, Flora, who was a friend of Jane's; and the younger son, Luther, Jr., who worked for John at the bank. Taking Luther, Jr., with him, he broke the news to

Mrs. Guiteau and Flora and brought them from Freeport to stay with his family in Cedarville until things settled down.

For the Addams family, the tragedy hit especially close to home. Their family too had a mentally unstable son. When Jane Addams was eleven, her brother Weber, aged nineteen—who, having dropped out of college, was managing his father's cattle stock farm—had had a mental collapse, been judged "temporarily insane," and been committed, at the family's request and by the county court, to a state mental hospital. The cause was thought to be "exhaustion."[5] In reality it was the onset of paranoid schizophrenia, a disease that often first strikes when a person is in his or her late teens or early twenties. Those with the disease are typically agitated, voluble, and irritable, characteristics Weber was described in later court records as possessing.

Since then Weber had not had an "attack" or at least not one that caused his family to ask the court to institutionalize him again. Now twenty-eight, he was married, lived in Cedarville with his wife and child, and was still working for his father. But John lived with the worry that Weber would suffer another breakdown, especially if he continued to be, as we may imagine he was, difficult.

In the summer of 1881 John was a sorrowful man. In addition to grieving that Julius's tragic act had damaged the nation and worrying about Weber and Jane, he felt the burden of his responsibility to the Guiteau family. He knew he would be asked to testify as a character witness at Julius's criminal trial in Washington, D.C. Jane, watching her father in those difficult days, could only have wanted more than ever to obey and please him.

Perhaps it was Anna who proposed a family vacation to distract them from all the grimness. They decided to travel north by train to northwestern Michigan, to stay in Marquette, on the shores of Lake Superior. While there, John could visit some copper ore mines that he was considering investing in. But the vacation became its own tragedy. Climbing about a copper mine, he suddenly fell ill. Although no one realized it at the time, his appendix was inflamed. Hurrying toward home, the family reached Green Bay, Wisconsin. John Addams, fifty-nine years old and too ill to go farther, died in a hotel room of appendicitis.

To lose a parent abruptly is a devastation. For Jane it was doubly so. Not only had she lost the lodestone of her life, but she also was now an orphan. The "relentless and elemental forces" of death had truly left her alone in the world. The last time someone in her family had died, when her sister Martha passed away, she had sat on the stairs for hours, seeking protection the wall seemed to offer. Now, with her sisters and brother married, she needed the family she had, stepmother Anna and stepbrother George. As she mourned her father, hope—the essential emotion that fuels ambition—drained out of her. Two weeks after the funeral she observed to Ellen Gates Starr, "How purposeless and without ambition I am."[6]

With her father's death, her duty to the family took a new form. Instead of obeying and pleasing her father, she would take care of Anna. As the youngest and only unmarried daughter, she had already been expected to care for both her parents. This was the underlying duty that going to Smith would violate. Now Anna—volatile, elegant, imperious—alone was her charge.

At least financially, there were no worries. With John's death, his wife and each of his four children (normally stepchildren did not inherit anything, and that was true in this case) received a portion of his extensive wealth. For Harry Haldeman, who was practicing medicine in Iowa and his wife, Jane's sister Alice, who as a nurse assisted him in his practice, this meant, thanks to Alice's inheritance, opportunities for further training. For Anna, it meant the freedom to leave Cedarville and enjoy the pleasures of a sophisticated East Coast city. Within six weeks of John's passing, Anna, George, Jane, Alice, and Harry settled in Philadelphia. They planned to stay two years, so that Harry could continue his medical courses by enrolling in the University of Pennsylvania, and Alice and Jane could enroll in the Woman's Medical College to receive their own medical training.

To the outside world, it looked as if Jane were moving ahead with her plan to earn a medical degree, but she did not see it that way. She had wanted to go to Smith before going to medical school (this was her plan, not a requirement, in these years a person did not need a B.A. to study medicine). Now, because of her inheritance, she actually had the money she needed to pay for Smith. But the power of financial independence was too new, and she could not seize it. She went to Philadelphia to care for Anna, and she enrolled in medical school because others in the family were studying medicine and she might as well do so too.

It was a miserable winter. Jane slogged her way through the first year of studies, feeling exhausted, while her crooked back, registering her stress, caused her much pain. Then, in February, 1882, Anna became ill—she had suffered from neuralgia in the 1870s , and it had apparently returned—and underwent surgery. Soon after Anna came back from the hospital, Jane completed her exams, then suffered a nervous collapse and was hospitalized. She felt she had doubly failed. Later she remembered that "my experience in Philadelphia of trying to fulfill too many objects at once [left me with] . . . an uneasy consciousness that I had not done what I came purposely to do, because I tried to do something else and failed in that."[7]

Her doctor was S. Weir Mitchell, a specialist in nervous diseases, which were at the time called neurasthenia, but he was not just any doctor. He was the most famous American doctor in a burgeoning new field and the author of the popular book *Lectures on the Diseases of the Nervous System: Especially in Women*, published the year before. His theory was that women with the disease were suffering from physical manifestations of moral failure; that the cause of the illness was self-absorption. To counteract it, he treated his female patients with four to six weeks of seclusion and rest, during which he banned visitors, books, good food, and letter writing from the sickroom. He also instructed his patients to be less selfish in the future.

Mitchell was considered a genius. In 1885, three years after treating Jane Addams, he would treat Charlotte Perkins Gilman—niece of the much-admired minister Henry Beecher and, later, an author and reformer in her own right—after she suffered a similar nervous collapse. Her misery under his treatment inspired her famous work "The Yellow Wallpaper," published in 1892. The reader watches as the first-person narrator, after suffering from a "temporary nervous depression," gradually loses her mind under the Mitchell-like regimen her physician husband has prescribed. The problem is not in her body, he informs her, but in her mind, which it is her responsibility to control. "He says no one but myself can help me out of it, that I must use my will and self-control and not let any silly fancies run away with me."[8]

Jane Addams thought Mitchell's diagnosis of herself was correct. She saw her illness as he did, as a moral defeat. Later that year she recorded in her commonplace book of quotations a comment she had heard in a sermon: "Strength to begin a life of self-sacrifice without strength enough to carry on, makes one lead a life of duplicity and falsehood." Believing that she lacked the goodness of character to be truly self-denying, she saw in her illness the likelihood of a lifetime of failure. "The sensitivity which one always feels after an illness," she observed years later, "the fear that because you have failed, you are going to fail again ... can scarcely be overestimated."[9]

This is how culture persuades a strong mind to give up its efforts to think for itself. It supplies, as if in a conspiracy, the same message from every side—not just from parents, novels, and church but from the scientific world too. The message for Jane, as for most young women of her class and education in the 1880s, was that she must deny her own freedom for the sake of others and that failing to do so was selfish and would lead to illness.

The illnesses of both Anna and Jane brought the family's sojourn in Philadelphia to a sudden end. That summer, back in Cedarville, Jane accepted responsibility for disciplining herself. She browbeat herself in her commonplace book for her self-absorption and continually reminded herself of the selfless female ideal she aspired to: "[T]alk too much of myself and motives, am in danger of self-pity." Try "to be for others." "Strive to be the highest, gentlest and kindliest spirit." Despite her poor health, she flung herself into doing the housekeeping at the Addams home and worried that she was not a cheerful enough influence on Anna.[10]

In aspiring to selflessness, she was embracing suffering, which appealed to her. She later wrote, "[T]he path we all like when we first set out in our youth is the path of martyrdom and endurance."[11] But selflessness is not simply a self-destroying cultural ideal. It is also a real human virtue, an ethical goal worthy of achievement. Jane, who later was often described by others as possessing the highest and kindliest spirit, set out in her twenties to become that kind of person. She was not innately good; rather she achieved her goodness through tremendous self-discipline.

||||||||||||

Rockford Female Seminary now reached out to Jane to remind her of her career ambition. The school's board of trustees, recognizing that she had earned more than enough credits to receive a B.A. and, having decided to begin awarding the new degree that June, invited her to return to receive it at commencement, along with two seniors from the class of 1882 and a few other alumnae. That event, combined most likely with a conversation with Caroline Potter, who no doubt attended the ceremony, stirred Jane's hopes to go to Smith again, not for the B.A. per se but for the better scientific and generally more prestigious education. By this time, too, she must have realized she had the financial means to make it happen. Only her duty to Anna stood in her way.

For the dutiful, the only way to rebut the claim of one duty is to invoke the claim of another. That summer Jane recalled her duty to benevolence, the class ethic that her father had taught her and that her privileged education had reinforced. In her commonplace book, she wrote: "People with wealth and a start of right ideas from their father have no right not to make the very highest use of life, [having gained] the ... higher intellectual things of life."[12] Now it was selfish to stay in Cedarville with Anna and unselfish to go to Smith. Feeling fully persuaded where her duty lay, she planned to enroll in September.

A letter from her sister Alice derailed her plan. Harry, it turned out, had devised a surgical solution to her back problem. He had tried it on one patient and now wanted her to come to Iowa, rather than go to Smith, so that he could do the operation. Courageously, Jane went. She must have been deeply frustrated by the limitations her crooked back imposed. The surgery was painful, and recovery difficult. Harry used heated wires to fuse together the spinal disks damaged by the tubercular virus. Afterward he strapped her, immobilized, to her bed for two months while her back healed.

With so much time to think about what she was not accomplishing, Jane found herself, she wrote Ellen, sunk in "melancholy."[13] Finally, after more than four months, she returned to Cedarville encased in a heavy plaster cast, which was later replaced by a leather, steel, and whalebone corset. Harry did not think she should plan to attend school soon as it would be too hard on her back; instead he prescribed a trip to Europe to reduce the stress on her nerves. In the nineteenth century such physically arduous trips were, by a peculiar logic, thought just the thing for exhausted and ill people. Jane loved the idea. Europe was the place she most wanted to visit.

Abruptly another family crisis erupted. At the end of March 1883, two weeks after Jane returned to Cedarville, a long-feared event happened: Weber Addams's mind again gave way, and for a week Jane and his wife, Laura, tried by themselves to cope with his irascible and paranoid outbursts. Then Alice hurried from Iowa, and the family asked the county court to commit Weber. Eleven years after his first attack, he was again declared insane (the cause "undue mental exertion") and taken to the Illinois State Hospital for the Insane in Jacksonville where he would remain until July, when he returned home to Cedarville.

The family's sadness at Weber's suffering must have been mingled with gratitude that John was not alive to witness it. For Jane, who described the experience of coping with Weber's behavior to Ellen as simply "a peculiar kind of trouble," the pain was too deep to express.[14] Jane was touched by the shakiness of Weber's situation, writing Alice, who had returned to Iowa, "I feel as though he must necessarily be very uncertain of himself all summer."[15] She knew how painful self-doubt could be.

Jane never wrote about what it meant to her to have a brother whose mind was unstable. But she must have wondered about the cause. The medical theories of the day, the Addamses' family doctor, and the county court all agreed it was environmental. Her brother could not cope with the stress of heavy work. Should she worry for herself? The question had no answer, but her own nervous collapse in Philadelphia could not have reassured her.

Weber's mental breakdown and hospitalization did not change Jane's plans to go to Europe. She could rely on the state hospital to care for him. If this had been the 1830s, when Illinois did not have a state mental hospital system, Jane Addams might have canceled her trip in order to share the care of her brother with his wife, not knowing for how long or when she would be needed if another crisis occurred. For all her family's wealth, Jane knew at a young age how invaluable it was to have the state back up the family, ready to care for the vulnerable.

Free to go, Jane firmed up her trip. At first, she intended to travel with a classmate from Rockford, that classmate's sister, and their aunt, but then Anna, Anna's niece Sarah Hostetter, and a friend of Anna's from Freeport decided to come too. So there would be seven. Anna's son George did not come. Having graduated from Beloit College in May, he was spending the summer doing biological research in Massachusetts and was to enroll that fall at Johns Hopkins University in Baltimore, to earn his Ph.D. in biology.

For Jane, as for so many ambitious young Americans of her day, a trip to Europe was serious business, the best way to earn an informal certificate in high culture. Not even a college B.A. could accomplish what a trip to Europe could, as John Addams had understood in planning for his daughters to go. (Here, too, duty to her father's wishes aligned nicely with Jane's own desires.) Once a person had been to Europe, he or she could refer to that remarkable journey for the rest of his or her days, impressing others with his or her sophistication and worldliness.

Jane felt this appeal. But she felt something more. Burdened with a sense that she had failed in many ways, she needed a reason to believe she could put failure behind her, and Europe seemed to provide it. Inspired by her reading of European authors, from Dickens to George Eliot to George Sand to Cicero, she thought she would become a nobler person by going to the place from whence noble ideas came. She intended, she later remembered, to search "for those mountain tops upon which" she might "stand and dream [of] righteousness."[16] By "righteousness," she meant the nobler life. Now it was not Smith but Europe that would redeem her.

At other times, though, she thought she was just conforming to society's expectations of her, and it made her uncomfortable. She wrote to Ellen that she suspected she was "not following the call of my genius" by heading to Europe "in search of . . . this general idea of culture," which, she pointedly added, had never "commanded my full respect." Her fear, she explained, was that she would find it hard to "hold to full earnestness of purpose"[17] while abroad. In this mood, she found Europe a seductive distraction from her real work of philanthropy, which she still had not begun to do.

Encouragement to resist such expectations came from a book she read that summer by the British essayist Matthew Arnold. In *Literature and Dogma* he explained that the real meaning of Christ's message was to trust one's own moral judgment, to listen to one's conscience. For Jane, his words struck home. This was not the Rockford Female Seminary version of Christianity that she had fended off with such determination; it was the message her father had taught her as a child and that Emerson in his essays, in his secular way, had taught her too. She was also drawn to Arnold's promise that if a person trusted his conscience, he would experience Christ's "secret of peace." Peace—personal calm, a sense of restful centeredness—was what she felt was sorely missing. She wrote Ellen that her "experience of late has shown me" the need to rely on Christ's " 'secret,' as Arnold put it."[18] Now all she needed to know was what her own conscience believed.

There was one societal expectation, though, that she seems to have always resisted without wavering—the expectation that she would marry. Apparently she had no interest. In her letters from her teens and twenties, Addams mentioned the subject of love only once—and only because a cousin asked her what she thought. Her view was pessimistic. When "love does not beget love," she wrote in 1877, "it is apt to produce dislike or what is worse hatred. . . ." And when she praised George Sand in her college debate essay, she seemed untroubled by the fact that the novelist had abandoned her marriage. The love that she admired, she told her cousin, was a higher form—"Platonic love or rather sacred friendship."[19] Platonic love involved a meeting of souls rather than bodies. Her viewpoint was common among high-minded young people, including married (heterosexual) couples so it did not signal a lack of interest in marriage per se. Still, Jane saw sex as decidedly uninspiring.

As for boyfriends, there was only one. In her senior year a young man, also a senior, from nearby Beloit College had a crush on her and may have even proposed marriage, but if he did, she turned him down. The closest Jane ever came to explaining her failure to marry was in 1930. She noted the historical fact that women of her generation felt they had to choose between marriage and career, both because men did not want to marry career women and because the public did not approve of combining both. But when she described the first generation of unmarried career women, of which she was one, her language showed that singlehood was not her second choice but her first. "Changing conditions," she wrote, "produced . . . women selected by pioneer qualities of character and sometimes, at least, by the divine urge of intellectual hunger who were . . . devoted to their chosen fields. . . ."[20] In other words, she wanted to be free.

||||||||||||

A week after leaving New York Harbor, Jane's ship, the *Servia*, arrived off Queenstown, Ireland. On board, the group made their plans for the first year: to travel to Ireland, Scotland, northern England, London, then to Holland, before settling in Dresden, Germany, for the winter. In the spring it would be on to Italy, Austria, Switzerland, and France. Members of the party would peel off over time. By May it would just be Jane, Anna, and Sarah Hostetter. They would spend the summer in England, joined by George, on vacation from Johns Hopkins. Then George and Sarah would depart, and Anna and Jane, if their stamina held, would spend another winter in Europe before heading home.

The question of Jane's health remained. She later described herself as suffering from a "long illness" between 1881 and 1883 and noted that this illness left her "in a state of nervous exhaustion with which I struggled for years. . . . At best it allowed me but a limited amount of energy."[21] Although she was able after the first few weeks of travel to stop wearing the heavy leather-encased steel corset, fatigue continued to be her regular companion, a reminder that she was not well.

With the efficiency of Americans determined to absorb culture at a rapid clip, the group quickly explored Dublin and Edinburgh—the latter no doubt a wistful visit for Jane, with her fading dream of earning an M.D. at the university—visited the monument in Ayr to Anna's favorite poet, Robert Burns, paid their respects at Wordsworth's grave in the Lake District, and arrived in London. London, especially, took Jane's breath away. Polyglot and enormous, it was said to be the largest city in the world, with a population of 4.7 million. By comparison, New York City, with 1.2 million, was third, after Paris. Also, London was the capital of the British literary world that Jane had spent so many years exploring in her imagination, the home of William Shakespeare, Thomas Carlyle, and George Eliot. In its worldliness London reminded her of classical Rome, she wrote Ellen, "possessing the best of all nations, times and peoples."[22]

The traveling party to Europe, 1883. Jane Addams is in the back row, second from the left. Anna Haldeman Addams is in the front row, first on the right.

But London had a dark side, as Jane soon discovered. Just then the newspapers were stirring up concern about the problem of working-class poverty and printing excerpts from a recent anonymous pamphlet, *The Bitter Cry of Outcast London*, about the living and working conditions among the city's poorest inhabitants. The author, in fact, was a city missionary and clergyman named Andrew Mearns. He had spent much time in the bleakest neighborhoods. In his pamphlet he vividly described buildings in miserable repair, severe overcrowding in housing, children suffering from neglect, and families suffering from starvation and documented the criminally low wages for which they worked. He spoke of people's "emaciated starved bodies" and "staring eyes." He closed the pamphlet with a compelling question: "Will you venture to come with us and see for yourselves the ghastly reality?"[23]

Jane's answer was yes. A city missionary staying at the boardinghouse where she and her party were staying offered to take anyone interested to the East End, where London's poorest workers lived, and Jane accepted her offer. The missionary led Jane and others to see a special sight, the

Mile End Road market at midnight on Saturday night. Decaying meat and fruit and vegetables too rotten to sell when the market reopened on Monday were sold there for pennies to anyone willing to buy.

The market was five miles long; the Addams party traveled its length on a double-decker bus, sitting on top for a better view of the rows of booths and stalls, the aisles crowded with thousands of people. Of all that Jane saw that night, one image stuck in her mind. The bus stopped at the corner of a dark street, and beneath the sputtering gas streetlamp she saw, gathered around two carts, people dressed in rags, their hands thin, white, and empty, clutching to reach the food "that was already unfit to eat."[24]

The sight was wrenching to her. Afterward she wrote to Weber that her "superficial survey of the misery and wretchedness" of the East End left her feeling "thoroughly sad and perplexed." She now became afraid she would see the same awful sight around every corner in London. Much later she remembered how her visit to the East End was one of those experiences that left her in a "deep depression" and feeling "over-whelmed by a sense of failure."[25]

She overreacted, to be sure. Anyone would have felt sad, but Addams felt deeply and personally unmoored. Her reaction is hard to explain, but she inadvertently provided a clue when she wrote in *Twenty Years* about what she felt at the time, without any self-consciousness that her reaction was unusual: "I carried with me for days . . . that curious sur-prise we experience when we first come back into the streets after days given over to sorrow and death; we are bewildered that the world should be going on as usual and unable to determine which is real, the inner pang or the outward seeming. In time all huge London came to seem unreal save the poverty in its East End."[26] Addams felt as if she had seen death, and it shook her profoundly. As it had done before in her life, death threatened her sense of connection to reality and destroyed meaning.

But despair was not her only reaction. She also felt she had failed. She tells us in her memoir about a series of thoughts that flashed through her mind as she sat there watching the reaching hands. The first thought was that she wanted to do something right then to save those people. However, she did nothing. Her inaction, in turn, made her think of a famous story by Thomas De Quincey, in which he told how he had been riding at night at the top of a fast-moving mail coach that would have mowed down and killed two lovers in the road if he had not finally managed, after wasting time trying to remember Achilles' great warning cry in *The Iliad*, to shout out. Why couldn't she act? she wondered. At that point she decided that her enchantment with literature was as crippling to her ability to act as De Quincey's had been for him. She had long had doubts about the pursuit of culture, and now here was the proof of its dangers. *It prevented a person from preventing death.* It was a strange message to extract from the sight of gaunt hands waving in the London night. The scarred human psyche is a mysterious thing.

||||||||||||

Meanwhile, her European trip continued, a perfect example of what Caroline Potter had warned against—the pursuit of knowledge for its own sake. She saw Rembrandt's paintings in Holland, attended concerts and the opera in Berlin, and studied art in Dresden, even as self-revulsion and depression dogged her footsteps. Once, when she and Anna went sightseeing in Saxe-Coburg-Gotha, she made a small attempt to do something. Looking out her hotel window over breakfast one morning, she saw a line of women bearing heavy wooden tanks on their backs, crossing the town square. The tanks, open at the top, were sloshing as the women walked, spilling steamy liquid that scalded their faces and hands. They were transporting freshly brewed beer to another building for cooling. Indignant at these cruel conditions, Jane sought out the innkeeper and insisted he take her to speak to the owner of the brewery. The two of them found the owner, and Jane made her case, but the owner was unmoved. Her first attempt at action was not successful, but at least—unlike at the Mile End Road market—she had managed to act.

Addams was becoming obsessed with the suffering of the poor. Terrified in London that she might see them around every corner, she now hoped she would. She remembered: "During the following two years on the continent . . . I was irresistibly drawn to the poorer quarters of each city."[27] Their pain, she wrote in *Twenty Years*, now seemed to her the world's pain. In fact, carrying her own pain from death, failure, and illness on her back, she had discovered that the urban poor of Europe carried similar burdens. Across the barrier of class, with all the material and educational differences that barrier implied, she felt as one with people whose misery was more obvious than her own.

Jane had always wanted to live among the poor and thought that medicine offered her the best way to do that. But in Rome, where she, Anna, and Sarah traveled in the spring, she found in the history of the early Christians a new model for cross-class living. While visiting their underground burial grounds, the catacombs, a true place of death, she was startled and enchanted to see on the ceilings and walls images of cheerful spring flowers, and shepherds and lambs. It seemed, she later remembered, that "the Christian message was one of inexpressible joy." Reading more about them, she learned that they "longed to share the common lot" and were willing to "sacrifice themselves for the weak, for children and the aged."[28]

Once again, as when she had read Matthew Arnold's *Literature and Dogma*, she found herself drawn to the religion from which she had previously fled. Once again she was gaining a fresh interpretation of its meaning, one that had nothing to do with human sinfulness, the need for personal redemption, a belief in Jesus Christ as the Son of God, or even a personal faith in God. Perhaps she had this new understanding in mind when she wrote, somewhat elliptically, in *Twenty Years*: "Before I returned to America I had discovered that there were other genuine reasons for living among the poor than that of practicing medicine upon them."[29]

Meanwhile, her sense of failure continued to haunt her. In June she wrote Ellen from Geneva, Switzerland, "I wish everybody were as thoroughly convinced as I that failure through ill health is just as culpable and miserable as failure through any other cause." Despite her family's careful schooling in writing cheerful letters, her mood of depression peeked through. She wrote: "I have been idle for two years just because I had not enough vitality to be anything else and the consequence is that . . . I have constantly lost confidence in myself and have gained nothing and improved nothing. A sad record, isn't it[?]" Ellen was sympathetic, arguing in one letter that too many demands on Jane's mind and body, "demands that do not come to most people," had come to her.[30] But Jane did not accept the idea that fate had simply dealt her an unfair hand. She believed she had the responsibility to heal herself.

The European trip continued. Jane and Anna, joined by George, summered in Great Britain and, after George left, wintered in Berlin, enjoying more rounds of museums, cathedrals, and opera. In the spring they were in Paris, feeling increasingly eager to head for home.

By mid-June 1885 they were back in Cedarville. Alice and Harry, traveling from their new home in Girard, Kansas, were there to greet them, as were Weber and his wife, Laura, but events soon revealed that all was not well. Shortly after Alice and Harry left for Kansas, Weber had another breakdown. This time Jane moved quickly. Within two days of his attack she had petitioned the county court, which ordered him committed to the Elgin State Mental Hospital. Any hope the family had had that Weber would lead a normal life was fading.

Jane and Anna spent the winter of 1885–86 in Baltimore, where George was continuing in biology in graduate school at Johns Hopkins University. The situation was difficult for Jane since her constant companionship with Anna increased her depression and sense of loneliness. Her stepmother delighted in doing all the social things that Jane found pointless and exhausting: paying and receiving calls, attending and hosting parties and teas. Again she condemned herself for her uselessness. She wrote Ellen: "I am filled with shame that with all my apparent leisure I do nothing at all." Jane was trapped in a life she did not want, and she did not know what to do about it. Years later she described a

Jane Addams in Baltimore, 1885 or 1886

frustrated young woman in words that captured how she felt: "Her life is full of contradictions, she looks out into the world, longing that some demand be made upon her powers, for they are untrained to furnish the initiative."[31]

Meanwhile she read books. Religion interested her especially. Ellen's letters from Chicago about her deepening faith and a long visit they had had in the fall were keeping religion at the front of her mind. She had also not forgotten Matthew Arnold's idea that Christianity offered the peace that comes from being true to one's conscience nor the joyous example of the early Christians living in a community that ignored the barriers of class. She felt herself to be at a spiritual crossroads. She had been trying through her own efforts to be a morally perfect person, as her father had been, and failing for many years now. As she later put it, her efforts at "self-dependence" had been "broken into" by "many piteous failures." And she had been living with Anna, and suffering from the emotional turmoil that Anna's difficult temperament created and from the sense of isolation that came from having no like-minded people to talk to. She longed, she remembered, "for some blessed spot where unity of spirit reigned."[32] Although she wanted desperately to act, she did nothing, feeling so unsure of herself.

Then she read the newly published English translation of Leo Tolstoy's *My Religion*. She later called it the book that changed her life. What gripped her was the discovery that Tolstoy, the famous and accomplished novelist, felt himself to be a great moral failure, and that even so, at age fifty, he was able to redeem his life by becoming a Christian. He had not let his inability to believe in himself keep him from trying to be a morally good person. Reading the book, she wrote, "made clear [to me] that men's poor little efforts to do right are put forth for the most part in the chill of self-distrust."[33] She thought she could emulate Tolstoy's example.

His book also introduced her to the idea of nonresistance. Well trained in Sunday school and at Rockford, Addams could recite verbatim Jesus' teachings about forgiveness and love and had long ago memorized Matthew 5:38–39: "You have heard that it hath been said unto you, an eye for an eye, a tooth for a tooth: but I say unto you, that ye resist not evil" and "whosoever shall smite thee on thy right cheek, turn to him the other also." But Tolstoy made the old words come alive. They meant, he explained, not that suffering was exalted but that you should do good to those who injured you. Christ called his disciples, he wrote, to "observe the rule of non-resistance to evil." This meant "never oppose violence" and "never do anything contrary to the law of love."[34]

The idea of nonresistance captured Addams's heart and mind. She had few enemies at the time. In the hothouse of her narrow private life the idea meant mainly to be good to those who were angry. For reasons she never explained but may well have had to do with her tempestuous stepmother, she ached for the absence of strife; the thought that there could be gentle and restful peacefulness between human beings drew her like a magnet. She was forever to credit Tolstoy with teaching her about nonresistance (though she agreed with him that the term was too passive-sounding for an assertive moral practice), and beginning in the mid-1880s, she placed the idea at the center of her life philosophy. Her gentleness had its roots here, and was not the result of genes but of choice.

At the same time, another book helped her see another familiar idea, democracy, in a new light. The author was one of her father's heroes, the Italian revolutionary Giuseppe Mazzini. During the winter of 1885–86 in Baltimore, while attending a public lecture series at Johns Hopkins on the united Italy movement, she read Mazzini's classic text, *The Duties of Man* and an essay that had been published with it, "Thoughts upon Democracy in Europe." Mazzini's argument was that serving humanity was a morally higher duty than serving one's family or one's country and that it was a particularly Christian duty to serve humanity because Christ had loved mankind. Moreover, Mazzini too, in his vaguely poetic way, embraced the idea of cross-class social relations. He suggested that to attain democracy, a man "should commune as intimately as possible with the greatest possible number of his fellows."[35] Addams loved his vision. A new passion for democracy began to grow within her.

The balance scales in Addams's mind were now tilting in one direction: toward conversion to Christianity, the unfinished business of her childhood. When she returned to Cedarville that summer, she was baptized at, and joined, the Cedarville Presbyterian Church. By 1886 the church no longer required its members to assent to its denominational tenets, and Addams was able to join on her own terms. In her mind Christianity was an institution that stood for "universal fellowship" and gave "thrilling" expression to democratic ideas.[36] By rejecting the version of Christianity in which she had been raised and that she had resisted for so long, Addams managed to make converting to Christianity the first independent act of her twenties.

That fall, having joined Anna and George in Baltimore again, her mood was much better than the year before. She wrote Alice, "I am feeling so well this fall . . . vigorous [and] happy . . . in a way [that] I had imagined I should never feel again."[37] She began to spend more time with her sisters and their families and less with Anna and George. And the following spring she refused George's proposal of marriage. It was her second act of independence.

Stepsiblings did sometimes marry in those days, and Anna was entirely in favor of the idea. But George was an eccentric personality, and Jane, while having a sisterly fondness for him, was not in love with him. Anna was furious, however, when Jane rejected the proposal. To make matters worse, after Jane's refusal, George's already fragile mental state began to deteriorate, and Anna blamed Jane for this. The alienation between Jane and her stepmother deepened. Meanwhile Anna drew George closer, with tragic consequences. The following fall he returned from Germany, where he had gone to study, to take care of his mother and, abandoning his scientific work, was to live as her reclusive and mostly silent companion for the rest of his life.

In the spring of 1887, as Jane disentangled herself from her stepfamily, her hope that she could do something was strengthening, but she still had no definite plan beyond living in a spirit of democratic and universal fellowship among the poor. How did one do that exactly? As a Protestant she had only the example of Protestant urban missionaries, some of them women, who lived in the poorest parts of cities in order to provide charity and convert their neighbors to evangelical Christianity. But that model did not appeal to her; she had resented the attempts of others to convert her too much to take up proselytization, and, in any case, her Christian faith was too unorthodox.

And there was another problem that held her back: her doubt whether young educated women like her should properly concern themselves with the poor or with societal problems at all. She had been confident enough at Rockford, when she argued in her junior exhibition speech that she and her classmates would become "breadgivers," philanthropists, and in her senior essay, when she urged her generation of women to train their minds to be better reformers. But immersed in a world of societal proprieties and living with Anna, an assiduously proper woman, she was disoriented by everyone's expectations of her. "This then was the difficulty," she wrote about herself and other young women in the 1880s, "the assumption that the sheltered, educated girl has nothing to do with the bitter poverty and the social maladjustment which is all about her and which, after all, cannot be concealed."[38]

Two books dismantled this last obstacle in her path. The first was another Christian book by Tolstoy. Published in the United States in 1887, *What to Do?* was about the Russian novelist-aristocrat's first encounter with urban poverty, when he assisted with the census of Moscow in 1881. What he learned, and admonished his readers to grasp, was that a Christian living in comfort was an economic parasite and that he had a responsibility to address the problem of the suffering of the working poor. For Tolstoy, that meant ceasing to employ others and instead working with his own hands to meet his own needs. He turned over his wealth to his family (who continued to live prosperously off the labor of the estate's serfs), stopped writing novels, wore peasant clothes, slept in a peasant-style bed, and worked in his own fields.

Addams did not consider pursuing Tolstoy's solution, but the experience of reading his book, she wrote, "profoundly modified my religious convictions." His example taught her that being a Christian required drastically reshaping one's life. It was what Jesus Christ had also said, words from the Bible that she had heard often in Sunday school and church and had had to memorize at Rockford: "If any man will come after me, let him deny himself . . . and follow me. . . . For what is a man profited, if he shall gain the whole world and lose his own soul?"[39] Perhaps what made Tolstoy's example so gripping was his willingness to overthrow his class status. Jesus held no privileged place in his society. Tolstoy did. Addams identified with that, and found his willingness to turn his back on it, at least in a material sense, profoundly impressive.

The second book that helped her was John Stuart Mill's *The Subjection of Women*, which had been reissued in 1885 with *On Liberty* in a newly combined American edition. Mill wrote movingly of a prosperous woman's despair over her lack of challenging work to do: "There is nothing, after disease, indigence, and guilt, so fatal to the pleasurable enjoyment of life as the want of a proper outlet for active faculties."[40] Jane had experienced two of those conditions and knew that Mill was right—uselessness was a soul-destroying experience. She would later use the quotation in a speech.

Mill not only described her experience, he had a solution for it. Mill argued that women should have complete latitude in choosing their work, based on their gifts and experience. Furthermore, he called the idea that women were fit only to be wives and mothers "an eminently artificial thing" produced by "forced repression" and "unnatural stimulation."[41] One of the world's most articulate philosopher advocates for freedom, Mill had written a book that liberated women's minds from enslaving assumptions. Reading *The Subjection of Women*, Jane Addams, like the many early women's rights reformers who read the book when it first was published in 1869, felt mental chains fall away. She was not required to lead a life of numbing leisure. She could listen to her conscience. It was her choice what she wanted to do. Period.

Ready to act now, she still needed a specific plan. This time it was a periodical that helped her. Sometime in the summer or fall of 1887 she read an article in the *Century* magazine about a new kind of philanthropic organization called a settlement house. The experiment was taking place in London's East End, the very part of the city where she had been shocked by the sight of the hungry poor four years before. Led by an Anglican clergyman, Samuel Barnett, fifteen young men, most of them graduates of Oxford University, had moved there and were living in their own elegant building, right in the midst of a crowded, low-income neighborhood. While working in the city during weekdays, the residents, as they were called, spent their free time, the magazine reported, trying to make "the lives of the East End poor more wholesome and beautiful than they could be without such help."[42] The settlement house, which they named Toynbee Hall after Arnold Toynbee, the recently deceased economic historian and social critic (and uncle of the later famous historian of the same name), offered lectures and clubs, such as the Shakespeare Club, the Adam Smith Club, and the Natural History Society, and classes in singing, drawing, and reading.

Jane loved the idea. She wanted to visit London and see Toynbee Hall. She and Ellen had already been planning a trip to Europe; they could just add it to their itinerary. But the idea remained Jane's secret. Afraid that her dream would seem ridiculous, she did not tell Ellen. In December 1887 Jane and another college friend, Sarah Anderson, took a boat from Hoboken, New Jersey, for Southampton, England. They planned to celebrate Christmas in Paris and then travel to Germany to meet Ellen, who was already in Europe, chaperoning several students from her school. Tucked in Jane's trunk was the address for Toynbee Hall.

||||||||||||

With her two college friends, Jane was once more pursuing culture; Europe was being a seductress again. With money no obstacle, Jane was failing to conquer the moral challenge uniquely faced by people of wealth, the temptation to postpone taking life seriously. The appeal of traveling with friends, seeing wonderful art and theater, and enjoying the sights and sounds of foreign countries was too strong. Sarah stayed in Paris to take care of personal business, so Jane met up with Ellen in Munich, where they remained for a week.

Ellen was an interesting choice for a friend. She and Jane had in common their love of great literature, their love of writing and all things beautiful, and their sense of religion as urgently important, but their temperaments were different. Ellen was zealous in her passions, an enthusiast and a critic, freely expressive of her feelings, be they impatience, admiration, anger, or love. Jane was emotionally cool, self-contained, steady. Thus each had a quality the other envied and needed to nurture in herself. Their friendship had taken root their first year at Rockford Female Seminary, but after Ellen had been unable to return because of her family's tight finances, it had consisted mainly of letters and visits.

Ellen Gates Starr around age eighteen

In Munich they delighted in each other's company. In the mornings they visited art galleries, looking for prints for Ellen's school, and in the afternoons they talked for hours, studied Italian, and paid visits to people they had met. Jane wrote to Alice that she had "seldom in my life had a happier week than [this week Ellen and I] have had together."[43] Each was finding in the other the quality she felt she most lacked, the strength of will to make herself a better person. Jane wrote a friend how much she admired Ellen's "patience to work out [the best] in her own character." And Ellen wrote Anna Addams saying she wished she were willing to invest "the moral effort and self-discipline . . . required to develop a character like [Jane's]."[44] Their friendship was built especially on this bond: their shared ambition to improve.

After Munich, joined by Sarah, the friends went on to Italy. After lingering in Florence for a time, they went to Rome, where Jane visited the catacombs again, and they took in the Vatican, an unforgettable sight. Then it was back to Florence to watch the Easter celebrations, and on to

Madrid, Spain, where they went to a bullfight. It was an experience Jane never forgot, not so much the bullfight itself as her reaction to it.

Having studied the history of Spain and the history of bullfights, Jane thought of the bullfight as a purely cultural event. Sitting in the immense amphitheater as ten thousand people roared their delight when the first bull entered the arena, she thought about all the historical meanings of the scene. She knew that the Spanish sport was thought to have evolved from the Roman practice of forcing the "pagan" Christians to face raging bulls in the Colosseum, and that the riders on caparisoned horses looked much like knights in a medieval tournament. And so, as the bulls killed the horses that the picadors were riding, and then the matadors killed the bulls, she watched, oblivious to the blood and suffering, with cool, intellectual fascination. Ellen and Sarah, revolted by the gore, told Jane they wanted to leave. She agreed but remained glued to her seat as they walked out. They waited for her in the foyer of the amphitheater, and when she finally appeared, she found them "stern . . . with disapproval of my brutal endurance."[45]

That night self-revulsion followed. Suddenly Jane was horrified that she had watched such suffering without a twinge of sympathy. Once again she blamed her love of culture for cutting her off from engaging with brutal reality. And then the larger guilt of her years of inaction piled on, and she blamed culture for that too. She had been selfishly exploring the high civilizations of Europe instead of listening to her conscience; she had been living among people of her own class, rather than finding a way to do as Mazzini and the early Christians instructed—to serve humanity and put the ideal of universal, democratic fellowship into action. Ashamed but determined, she told Ellen that night about her dream of starting a settlement house. To her delight, Ellen liked the idea. They agreed that Jane would join Ellen in Chicago and, using income from Jane's inheritance, they would execute the plan.

To have a partner to do this daring, difficult thing was what Jane Addams needed most of all. During her twenties she had been realizing that part of her difficulty was her isolation, post-Rockford, from friends who thought as she did. Marcus Aurelius, the Roman emperor-philosopher who was a favorite of hers and whose *Meditations* she must have read, summed the point up well when he said: "How great a weariness there is in living with those who are out of tune with you . . . [who do not] share your principles." The solution, she saw, was to create a life with those who did. In 1883 she wrote Ellen: "I am more convinced every day that friendship . . . is after all the main thing in life, and [that] friendship and affections must be guarded and taken care of just as other valuable things."[46] The insight quarreled with her natural bent toward self-sufficiency; reaching it marked a revolution in her thinking. But until Ellen agreed to start a settlement house with her, she had not been able to begin. Now she could.

The next step, of course, after a planned visit to France, was to visit London and see Toynbee Hall. But because of Ellen's responsibilities to chaperone some more students in Italy, Jane would have to make her first visit to Toynbee Hall without her.

Toynbee Hall stood on Commercial Street in a crowded down-and-out neighborhood that was adjacent to the London docks. In a district of just a few square acres lived eight thousand people of English, Irish, Welsh, and eastern European Jewish backgrounds, often six to eight in a room, scraping by on low and unreliable wages. The hall, built to house the new settlement in 1884, was a handsome, gracious set of three interconnected brick buildings that stood around a quadrangle, looking like a college at a British university. In effect, university-educated, upper-middle-class men had inserted themselves, by dint of some lovely architecture, into a completely alien, hand-to-mouth world.

Their intentions, propounded by Samuel Barnett, were to mingle socially with workingmen on an equal footing and perhaps be of some help. Barnett always emphasized that the idea was to work "with, not for." A frustrated Anglican minister, he had despaired of converting his working-class neighbors to his faith and decided instead to put into practice the latest ideas of what was known as the social Christian movement—which called for economic cooperation among workers and social cooperation across class lines.[47] But British class relations could not be so easily restructured; those who met at the settlement house still felt, on one side, benevolent noblesse oblige and, on the other, strategic deference. At the same time, something fine was going on. For those workingmen and boys (women and girls were soon added) hungry to know something of the arts, literature, and history, Toynbee Hall offered a feast. As for those whose only social life was the hard-drinking one of the pub, the settlement house was a place to make friends around new interests.

Jane Addams was enchanted. Here was a way to live among the poor that was Christian in motive, did not require her to abandon either gracious living or her love of culture, yet offered "universal and demo-cratic fellowship" of the kind she longed to enjoy. She wrote Alice that Toynbee Hall "is a community of University men who live there, have their recreation clubs and society all among the poor people yet in the same style in which they would live in their own circle. It is so free from 'professional doing good,' so unaffectedly sincere and so productive of good results in its classes and libraries that it seems perfectly ideal."[48]

Visiting Toynbee Hall with the intention of starting something simi-lar in the United States was the third independent act of Jane Addams's twenties. The fierce ambition that her stepmother had recognized in her early and that had fueled Jane's college achievements had gnawed at her even as she tried to bury it. By the late 1880s she finally understood that she must give it wing.

She expressed that realization in a letter to Alice, written within months of her return to the United States. She wrote her sister to con-gratulate her on an unusual accomplishment for a woman of their day, her appointment as a trustee of her church. Jane then quoted a passage from a poem by Robert Browning they both knew: "There's power in me and will to dominate / Which I must exercise, they hurt me else: / In many ways I need mankind's respect, / Obedience . . ." To Browning's insight she added her own explanation for the source of Alice's and her drive to power, even as she acknowledged the difficulty of ignoring it:

"It seems almost impossible . . . to express inherited power and tendencies [while] constantly try[ing] to exercise another set [of behaviors]."[49]
Her language was impersonal, but her point was not: She and Alice had
inherited their father's ambition and desire for a wide public reputation
and when they tried to tamp it down to fit the small scope allotted to
women, they could not do it without causing themselves harm.

Her new solution to the trap was psychologically deft. Before, when
she embraced the traditional female role of self-sacrifice and submis-
sion, she had lost her freedom to exercise her will. By identifying with
her father, whose (white) masculinity and wealth authorized him to
act independently, she could assert power. But there was a problem
embedded in her solution that could not be ignored forever. She was
not a man but a woman. She was still struggling with the dilemma that
her Cassandra speech had captured so well. Could a woman possess
authority in the public realm—exercise power—in her own right? She
still had grave doubts that she could.

‖‖‖

CHAPTER THREE

ACTIVIST

TEN MONTHS AFTER telling Ellen Gates Starr about her vague dream, in January 1889, Jane moved to Chicago to begin launching what was now their, not just her, plan. Reading her letters from those early months, when she was dashing about, talking up the project with people who might support it as volunteers or donors, one feels as if a racehorse had burst out of the gate, free at last to pour every ounce of energy into running. She was all business, writing not about her moral failings but about the people they talked to and the enthusiasm they were finding for the settlement idea.

The two friends were at least partly prepared for the work. Ellen, thirty, with one year of college and a great deal of self-education, had been teaching at a girls' secondary school for ten years and along the way had learned Italian and French. She also knew many young women from prosperous Chicago families, her former students, who had time on their hands and were longing for something useful to do. Jane, twenty-nine, had a B.A. from Rockford Female Seminary and some experience managing things, albeit on a small scale, having been editor-in-chief of the school magazine, president of her class, and president of her literary

society. She had dabbled in philanthropy during the 1880s, paying charity visits in Baltimore, and she knew several languages, having studied
French, German and Italian. She had even recently done a little fund-
raising for the seminary from her Rockford classmates.

The plan she and Ellen had devised—borrowed and adapted from
Toynbee Hall—was that young people with backgrounds like their own
would pay rent and board to live at the settlement house for a time, thus
becoming settlement residents. As neighbors they would form social
ties with the working people in the neighborhood and, along with other
nonresident volunteers from across the city, would organize clubs and
classes in their spare time. Charity—caring for the sick and elderly,
assisting in family crises—would be provided in a neighborly way but
would not be the house's main task.

They had two purposes in cofounding the settlement, both of which
were also Toynbee Hall's but modified to suit American circumstances.
The first was to provide the women and men of their generation, over-
cultured and isolated in their class, with a way to live up to the high
ideals they had been taught. As Addams put it in a speech she gave to
Rockford alumnae later that year, young people yearned to "confirm
by the deed those dreams of sacrifice and unselfish devotion of which
[their] heads were full."[1]

Second, they wished to repair the damage done to egalitarian social
relations by massive industrialization and, in the United States far more
than in Great Britain, massive immigration. Chicago illustrated the
developments perfectly. Between 1840 and 1890 its population exploded
from forty-five hundred to one million, turning the place from a swampy
lakeshore trading post into an industrial giant and the second-largest
city in the country. As the owners of businesses prospered and the ranks
of the upper-middle and upper classes expanded, some families became
hugely wealthy. At the same time, the number of working people living
in overcrowded neighborhoods burgeoned. Many were immigrants. By
the time Addams arrived there, a staggering 78 percent of the population was either foreign-born or the children of foreign-born, most of

them from the farming, or peasant, classes of Europe and therefore without industrial skills, and all of them seeking better lives. Paid low wages, these workers lived on the edge of poverty as they struggled to learn English and adjust to urban living.

This situation of a widening and dramatic "gap between rich and poor," as it was called, was shocking to the American middle classes. They read about it in magazines and books and heard sermons about it in church and synagogue. One best seller, Henry George's *Progress and Poverty* proposed redistributing the wealth by taxing only the productivity of land. Others, including Addams's favorite British authors, all of them widely read in the United States—Thomas Carlyle, George Eliot, John Ruskin, and Matthew Arnold—addressed mainly the social distance and urged readers (i.e., the prosperous) to treat the poor as their social equals. As Arnold put it in an essay about democracy, "[m]en . . . are made equal . . . by the humanity of their manners."[2] This idea was central to the settlement house movement.

One aspect of Toynbee Hall was harder to imitate—its political agenda. In 1884 the British Parliament had given workingmen the vote. To set these new voters an example, Barnett encouraged settlement residents to be elected to citizen bodies in the district, such as the school board. But a settlement of women residents, being unable to vote, could not do this. Addams's solution was to cofound the first coeducational settlement house in the world. That spring she was pleased when more than half of those who heard her speak at a reception were men, because it allayed, she wrote her sister, "our fear re [becoming a] home for single women. . . ."[3]

If Jane's lack of the vote was a limitation, she did have two other important qualifications for starting a settlement house. One was her wealth. Clearly, she and Ellen would not have been able to pursue the plan if she had not had the income from her inheritance to finance it—to rent a house, to purchase furniture, to pay for heating and other expenses. She knew she could not fund the effort over the long haul, that donors would need to support it, but she could get it started. Her wealth, while not large, also protected her from having to earn a living; she could give all her time to the project.

Her other main qualification was her purposeful idealism. Her large vision was to create a place that would nurture universal and democratic fellowship among peoples of all classes. It was a distinctly social, not political, ideal. Democracy, she told an audience of Chicago clubwomen in 1890, ought to involve not only "political freedom and equality" but also "social affairs" and a democratic "theory [of] the social order."[4] It was a grand aspiration, and she was shortly to learn more about the obstacles she faced, including those within herself. But her ambitious, dogged commitment to achieving social unity was essential to what was to come. There is something to be said for aiming high and holding fast, as long as you are also willing to learn.

What they needed was a house. Intending to rent one in a neighborhood of immigrants from countries whose languages they spoke, Ellen and Jane explored the Nineteenth Ward, on the near west side. Italians, Germans, and some French Canadians were concentrated there, albeit among sixteen other nationalities, including Irish Catholics and Russian Jews. The 527-acre ward was home to 44,380 people, with a major north-south artery, Halsted Street, running right down the middle. To the west, the neighborhood became gradually more prosperous. To the east, toward the Chicago River, was the industrial district, where the working poor lived and were employed. Since Ellen's days were tied up with teaching, it was mostly Jane who explored the neighborhood. Driving in a carriage down Halsted Street one day, she saw what she was looking for, a building as refined as Toynbee Hall, plunked down on the edge of that crowded industrial neighborhood.

The house had been built in 1856 as a summer home for a wealthy real estate magnate and philanthropist, Charles Hull. It was a relic of the neighborhood's former life as countryside. Hull died that spring, and his cousin Helen Culver, who had long managed his properties, inherited his extensive estate, which included much of the Near West

Side and this house. It needed some fixing up but had many fine fea-
tures. Italianate in style, it had high ceilings, marble fireplaces, and a
handsome curved and cantilevered staircase that dominated the central
front hall.

That summer Addams paid one thousand dollars to have spruced up
the part of the house that was available to rent—the second floor, which
had five rooms, and the drawing room downstairs (the rest was occupied
by stored school desks). She had the floors repaired and polished and
the rooms painted: the upstairs in terra-cotta tints, the downstairs drawing room in ivory and gold. Culver agreed to pay for a new furnace. In
May of the following year, once they were occupying the whole house
and once Culver had learned more about the philanthropic nature of
the enterprise, she would agree to give them a four-year lease rent free.
It was a generous and important subsidy for their work. Soon after, in

The drawing room of Hull House, circa 1890s

gratitude to their first major donor and with her permission, and in recognition of the name the neighbors had already given the house, Addams and Starr would name the new settlement Hull House.

Thrilled to have their own home for the first time and to be starting their adventure at last, Addams and Starr, along with their housekeeper and third settlement resident, Mary Keyser, moved in on September 18. Addams remembered, "Probably no young matron every placed her own things in her own house with more pleasure than that with which we first furnished [Hull House]."[5] They hung framed photographs and lithographs of art, drawings of the cathedrals of Europe, and portraits of their intellectual mentors, George Eliot, Ralph Waldo Emerson, and Thomas Carlyle, on their freshly painted walls. They had achieved their first goal—to create a place of beauty for themselves and the neighborhood to enjoy.

Jane Addams was used to living amid beautiful things. She was not used to living amid what lay just outside the house's doors—urban poverty. The neighborhood's garbage overflowed the large wooden boxes that were emptied by the city's removal services far too rarely; human waste decayed in open sewers, the result of a general lack of plumbing. Here and there a rotting horse carcass could be found, its owner having left it where it dropped. In the warm weather of September, the smells were pungent. Disease spread easily under such conditions. As for the families, their lives were marked by overcrowded living, insecure employment, periodic hunger, and sometimes homelessness. But Jane was not interested in any of these material conditions. She was focused on people's morale. As she explained in a letter to her stepbrother George, she and Ellen were not living on Halsted Street to "stem poverty" but to "fortify" their neighbors' spirits.[6]

By a matter of weeks, theirs was the first settlement in the United States. A second, the College Settlement, also founded by women, opened in New York City in October. Addams and Starr had first heard about it back in February, and Addams, wishing to be friendly, wrote the woman who was organizing it to establish relations, but her competitive feelings leaked through in a letter she wrote to her sister Mary: "We are modest enough to think ours is better, is more distinctly Christian and less social science."[7] Her claim referred to the social Christian motives and cooperative methods she and Starr had seen at Toynbee Hall and wished to imitate. They did not wish to "study" their neighbors.

When she said her settlement was more "Christian," she did not mean that she and Starr would try to convert anyone to Protestant or any other kind of Christianity. They did not want to run a mission house, not only because Addams hated proselytizing but also because they were living in a neighborhood of diverse faiths. In making this decision, however, Starr and Addams were bucking the expectations of certain circles. One perplexed writer for a local evangelical Christian paper observed of Addams: "I don't quite understand her religious position. She seems to be a Christian without religion."[8]

||||||||||||

At first, when Addams and Starr paid social visits, they felt uneasy. Addams, speaking in the third person, a habit of her father's she adopted in her speeches and writings, recalled that "the first settlers felt as if they were going into a strange country [where they would] . . . encounter people more or less unlike themselves." The crowded streets felt overwhelming. "[W]hen you go and live in [such] a neighborhood, you feel a little swallowed up."[9] For their part, the neighbors thought it peculiar that two wealthy young women wanted to live in the Nineteenth Ward. One man, Jane remembered, shook his head and said "it was 'the strangest thing he had met in his experience.'" Small boys threw stones at the Hull mansion and broke windows. Some of the Catholics and Jews, believing the women were the usual Protestant missionaries there to convert them, stayed away.[10]

But necessity and curiosity drew people in. The working mothers came first, eager to leave their small children at the morning kindergarten a volunteer started, and the older children were quick to discover the social clubs and afternoon classes in the arts. Soon, with the help of

Jane Addams, early 1890s

volunteers, there were weekly social receptions, organized by ethnicity at the neighbors' request, and evening classes in college topics, including favorite books. Starr taught a class on George Eliot's *Romola* and Addams taught one on Mazzini's *The Duties of Man*. Most precious to Addams, though, were the many conversations she had. She and Starr spent a great deal of time listening as people told them their stories. "We hear about experiences," Addams wrote in 1890, "sad and amusing, humbling and inspiring, but always genuine and never wearisome." She called such conversations "the part of the life . . . which the [settlement] residents care most for."[11]

She learned, to her surprise, that the working poor were far more generous than people of her own class. They opened their crowded homes to friends and relations who needed help, and they cared for the children of sick friends even if it meant losing their jobs. And she learned about the instability of their employment. Seasonal industries, including the garment trade, whose factories and sweatshops dominated the neighborhood, hired and laid off their workers four times a year. Statewide, only 20 percent of all industrial workers were employed full-time in 1886. In Chicago in 1892, on average, women at the lowest end of the wage scale were laid off for roughly a third of the year.[12] And she learned that when her neighbors lost their jobs and could not afford heating fuel on their meager wages, they faced physical suffering. The winter of 1890–91 was particularly hard. Addams gave money to people she knew to help with their rent, food, and heating bills and was soon low on funds herself.

She spent a lot of money on Hull House too. In the settlement's first year, she paid 58 percent of its total expenses of $8,634, even though her annual income from her inheritance was only about $4,000. These numbers tell the story she never told in print: that she was spending assets as well as income. In the second year the house's revenues from gifts and student and resident fees increased but so did its expenses. Addams again paid the deficit, which was $2,364, or 26 percent of that year's annual budget of $9,173.[13] It would be several more years before she stopped subsidizing the house's debts. She would never stop giving away money to friends in crisis. Her wealth gradually dissipated. By the mid-1890s she had given away almost all her inheritance except one small farm (one can almost hear her father saying, "No matter what, don't sell the farm!"). For the rest of her life, from age thirty-five or so, Addams lived off the income she earned from lecturing and writing. She never took a salary from Hull House.[14]

One reason Addams did not hoard her money was her antimaterialism, her belief that matters of the soul were of much greater importance than matters of the body. This was a strong conviction by the time she moved to Halsted Street. Hull House was all about the human spirit. Jane Addams intended its programs—its social clubs, classes and public lectures in the humanities and the arts, and music concerts—as well as the elegance of the building itself, to spark the imagination and feed the universal capacity for joy. Her interest in human fellowship arose out of the same passion. In truth her work at the settlement reflected what she had learned in her unhappy, if materially comfortable, twenties: money did not alleviate inner misery, and the resources of the spirit—

books, Christianity, friendship—could save a person from sadness. It was some time before she understood that poverty too could shrivel a person's soul.

Because the neighborhood around Hull House was full of workers, including women and children, Addams learned about them and their jobs. It was a new world to her, eye-opening, shocking, interesting. They worked mostly in the garment industry, but also in the bookbinding, metalworking, cigar, printing, glass, and candy industries.[15] Those in the skilled trades, mostly men, were paid better than those who were unskilled, a group that included men, women, and children. Working conditions were unhealthy and often involved laboring ten to twelve hours in crowded, dirty, and dank places and using dangerous machinery.

She also learned about the workers' response to their conditions: labor unions. Those in the trades formed trade unions, men and women usually organizing separately. Unskilled workers, so easily replaced by the employer, were harder to organize, but efforts were made. Trade unions were controversial. Employers often locked striking workers out of the workplace and hired new workers to replace them. Strikes were frequent, even if they often failed. In Chicago, in the single year of 1890, there were some eighty strikes over such issues as union recognition and the eight-hour day.[16] Sometimes violence arose from confrontations with police.

Addams got involved with the labor disputes in her first year on Halsted Street. Her motive was not a reformer's desire to improve working conditions but a mediator's desire to resolve disputes peacefully and fairly. Committed to nonresistance, she wanted to prevent not only violence but antagonism of any sort. Inexperienced in industrial relations, she thought that disputes could easily be solved if the employer and his workers learned more about each other's point of view. She expected industrial employers to be like her father, the industrial capitalist she knew best.

She soon learned otherwise. One by one, three Hull House club children who worked at a nearby factory were injured at the same machine because it lacked a protective guard, and one of them died from his injuries. Distraught, Addams sought out the owner and was shocked when he refused her request to install the needed guard. It was her experience at Saxe-Coburg-Gotha with the beer carriers all over again. The next time she changed her strategy. When twelve girls from a factory asked her to help them negotiate with their foreman over a wage cut, she asked a judge of the Cook County District Court who had experience with labor arbitration, an idea that had been spreading in the United States since the 1880s, to resolve the dispute. They reached a settlement. From then on, Addams was an advocate for voluntary arbitration.

Addams also cooperated with labor unions in their efforts to improve wages and working conditions. Again, her motive was not so much to help them improve their material lives as to cooperate with the constructive efforts going on in the Nineteenth Ward. It was the "with, not for" philosophy of Toynbee Hall; she was putting into practice Christian love, informed by Tolstoy's theory of nonresistance. "The design of the settlement," Addams wrote in 1894, "is . . . co-operation with all good which it finds in its neighborhood."[17] The first union organizer to whom she reached out was a young bookbinder named Mary Kenney. Skeptical at first, Kenney found Addams willing to be useful in the ways Kenney asked, and a friendship and lifelong partnership in labor activism began.

While she cooperated with unionized workers and was intrigued by the labor movement's enthusiasm for cooperation, Addams was perplexed by the serious critiques of capitalism workers offered, including various types of anarchism and socialism embraced by the radical wing of the labor movement. Although she listened with fascination to the lectures and discussions at the weekly meeting of the Hull House Social Science Club, where speakers of every political stripe proposed solutions to social and economic problems, she was more interested in hearing the range of viewpoints than in making up her own mind. By then she had read Karl Marx's *Capital*, but she had not liked it. She had no real interest in economic theory.

Then, in the settlement's third year, a new resident arrived: Florence Kelley. An educated upper-middle-class American from Philadelphia, she had embraced Marxist socialism while studying in Germany, married a fellow Marxist socialist Russian Jewish medical student, moved with him to New York City, and had three children. A year older than Addams, Kelley was something entirely new to Hull House—a political activist and a writer.

Kelley's upbringing encouraged her to become both. Her father, William Darrah Kelley, a Republican and U.S. congressman for almost thirty years, had immersed her from a young age in his political world and encouraged her interest in labor questions. By the time she came to Hull House, she was a seasoned advocate, having lobbied successfully alongside women trade union groups to amend laws in Pennsylvania and New York in order to create safer working conditions for women and children. She also wrote prodigiously. Before she came to Chicago, she had published twenty-five articles in national and international publications and two pamphlets, mostly on labor issues, and the first English translation of Frederick Engels's *The Condition of the Working Class in England* (1887).

But her personal life had reached a point of crisis. Her husband was abusive, and she feared for herself and her three children. In late 1891 she fled to Illinois, to seek a divorce in a state where she could get custody of the children. Hiding them with a friend in a Chicago suburb so that her husband would not take them away from her, in early January 1892 she found a place for herself at Hull House.

Brilliant and combative, Kelley brought her Marxism with her to the nightly dinner table conversations. Perhaps she told her fellow residents what she told a group of college alumnae in 1887: that she hoped they would join her and the "proletariat" in its struggle "to end [the] capitalist system." What mattered, she explained, was that in "the great strife of the classes . . . that is rending society to its foundations," people asked themselves the question, "Where do I belong?" It was, she told them, "the imperative question for women of our generation."[18] She did not convert Addams to Marxism, but, like the Marxists in the neighborhood, she repeatedly reminded Addams, so absorbed in the morality of interpersonal relations, that the American capitalist system lay behind the troubling social conditions.

Kelley's most important and immediate influence on Addams was in the field of politics. Within a few months of coming to Hull House, Kelley was working on education and labor reforms with women activists in Chicago, primarily members of the Chicago Woman's Club and the Illinois Woman's Alliance. The club, whose members had to be nominated and whose numbers were restricted, was a prestigious organization of mostly prosperous Anglo-Saxon women interested in culture and reform; the alliance was a new cross-class group of club and trade union women, including immigrants, formed in 1888 to support reforms to benefit workingwomen. Soon the two groups began to press the city council for a new elementary school in the crowded Nineteenth Ward and for better garbage removal services citywide. They also pressed the state for improved labor legislation. They used research, petitions, newspaper publicity, mass rallies, and personal lobbying of legislators to strengthen the state's compulsory education law and Chicago's sweatshop laws.[19] Jane Addams took note. Apparently women did not need the vote to wield political influence.

Women in other states were doing similar work in the 1880s and 1890s, as Kelley's experiences in New York and Pennsylvania showed. It was a new and striking development. Before the Civil War, women had lobbied Congress, state legislatures, and city councils on issues like Indian removal, slavery, temperance, and women's suffrage, but after the war their political efforts expanded. There were more women involved, new issues like women's suffrage, and new women's organizations that were not limited to single issues—organizations like those in Chicago as well as women's trade unions. Nothing like this political uprising of women had been seen in the history of the world (in Europe in the nineteenth century there were laws prohibiting women and workers from forming organizations or participating in politics). A powerful optimism about the ability of voteless women to influence local and state public policy was taking hold in the United States.

As Addams watched Kelley and other Chicago women doing politics, she continued to puzzle over exactly how to fit Hull House and herself into the picture. Although she still wanted men to be residents, only one man had moved in, joining the seven women now living there. In a speech she gave to a men's club in early 1892 she mused that while a settlement of women could provide a neighborhood center to "keep intellectual and social activity alive," there were "certain activities of citizenship which society thus far has insisted on thrusting upon men and which a women's settlement must perforce leave unperformed."[20] Some months later, in August, in a speech she gave at a Christian reformers' conference in Massachusetts, she dipped her toe in a little bit further. When describing the settlement's activities, she added "civic" to her usual categories of "social," "educational," and "humanitarian." She felt a bit self-conscious about the addition. "I have added civic," she said, "if indeed a settlement of women can be said to perform civic duties." But if she was hesitant, she was also wistful. "I am sorry," she said, "we have not more to present in the line of civic activities."[21]

Her education continued. In early 1893 Kelley, the Chicago Trades and Labor Assembly, the Illinois Woman's Alliance, and the Chicago Woman's Club launched a lobbying campaign for state legislation to protect workers who worked the small businesses called sweatshops that did contract work for the factories, often in private homes. The reformers wanted laws that required employers to limit women to working eight hours a day (instead of ten or twelve) and to end the employment of children under fourteen. Jane Addams supported their agenda but was reluctant to join them. Later she wrote that at the time she "very much disliked the word ["lobbying"], and still more the prospect" of doing it.[22]

A sweatshop in the 1890s

Her dislike of lobbying sprang from something deeper than mere inexperience. For one thing, she had moral qualms. Because of her commitment to nonresistance, she neither believed in nor was comfortable with antagonism, and lobbying risked arousing antagonism. Whoever disagreed with her might become angry with her.

Another obstacle was intellectual: her broad-mindedness. An excellent listener and empathizer, she was eager, as her nephew Weber Linn observed, to understand an issue "from everybody's point of view." One settlement resident remembered: "One cannot talk to her for five minutes without realizing that hers is the great gift of synthesis, of bringing things to unity, by 'patience, subtlety, and breadth.'"[23] At the same time, she enjoyed lively debate. She laughed with delight when Florence Kelley, who was described as like "a lioness at bay" when she was arguing, and another resident at Hull House, the equally brilliant Julia Lathrop—like Kelley, the daughter of a lawyer—sparred, as they often did.[24] But to be the assertive debater? Addams did not have the taste for

it. Lathrop, whose interests lay in the direction of government administration, was a member of the State Board of Charities and another of
Addams's close friends among the residents.

Then, too, Addams did not like the idea of lobbying because her
father had disliked it. He had been determined to legislate according
to his own conscience and disapproved of those who tried to turn him
from his settled convictions. Finally, there were her confused feelings
about women and politics. If only men could vote, should not lobbying
be restricted to them? She had not shaken off this old idea even though
she was watching women be political activists all around her.

Still, Kelley and Kenney, both active in the alliance, had become
members of a new committee of twenty-five called the Anti-Sweatshop
League to push for the legislation, and Addams found herself a member too. Full of doubts, she plunged in. The Anti-Sweatshop League's
first assignment was to arouse support of "all elements of the community" for the proposed legislation, the Workshop and Factories Act.
Throughout the spring Addams and the others exhausted themselves,
speaking "literally every evening" to trade unions and benefit societies,
church groups, and social clubs.[25] The other assignment was to lobby.
Addams joined Kelley, the members of the city's labor federation, the
Illinois Woman's Alliance, and the Chicago Woman's Club in Springfield, the Illinois capital, to press legislators to vote for the bill.

They met with startling success. The manufacturers were caught off
guard by the legislation and didn't organize quickly enough. The bill
sailed through the state legislature and was signed into law in July by
the newly elected populist governor, John P. Altgeld. It banned children under fourteen from working in manufacturing establishments,
and women and older children were limited to working an eight-hour
day and a forty-eight-hour week. Illinois, the third-largest manufacturing state, had become the first in the country to adopt a law limiting
women to working eight hours (although the state supreme court would
declare it unconstitutional two years later). Enforcement powers were

given to the office of state factory inspector, a new position that the governor soon appointed Florence Kelley to fill. Other major manufacturing states had such officers, but only Illinois had Kelley.

Addams learned many things from the experience of lobbying and, more broadly, from being part of a cross-class political campaign. She discovered that politics was not just about voting but about people from all classes working for citizens whose political voices were not yet strong. This basic lesson of democracy was just becoming imaginable in the 1890s. For Addams, with her enduring longing for universal and democratic fellowship, the experience must have been especially joyous.

Finally, she learned the wisdom of ignoring personal qualms. In the 1880s she had allowed her doubts to rule her. After cofounding Hull House, she began to set her doubts aside and act. She did this by relying on her friends for inspiration and on her belief in cooperating "with the good." In 1893, Jane Addams started down the path that would lead to her becoming one of the nation's most influential and effective political activists. But she might never have become that person if she had not swallowed her distaste for lobbying, ignored her skepticism about women's political potential, and, joining others, forged ahead. In time, her ideas about women and politics would catch up with her actions.

|||||||||||||

In 1893 the settlement house movement was thriving in the United States. Addams and Starr were among many of their generation who longed to bridge the social gap between rich and poor by strengthening ties across class lines. There were now nineteen settlements, mostly in Boston, New York, Philadelphia, and Chicago.[26] Of course there was a practical side to the appeal: Settlements provided college graduates with cheap, interesting, and communal places to live in major cities. At first all residents were volunteers, in keeping with the Toynbee Hall model. That remained true at Hull House, but gradually residents at most other American settlements became (poorly) paid staff whose work was assigned. This tended to increase the turnover. At Hull House residents stayed longer, on average, because they had greater freedom.[27]

For women of Addams's generation, settlements in the early years were especially enticing. The houses offered women a chance to be part of an exciting new social movement and to lead a life that was both independent *and* centered on a community. By 1910, although most settlement houses were coed, three-fourths of all residents and three-fourths of head residents were women.[28] During those years settlement houses incubated the talents of, and provided crucial institutional homes for, American female social activists, including Addams.

For her, the trajectory was to be to the top. A crucial next step, and perhaps the moment when she first emerged as a national leader of the settlement movement, took place in the summer of 1892, when she gave two impressive speeches about settlements that received widespread press coverage at a national conference on applied ethics in Plymouth, Massachusetts. She received the attention because of the masterful job she had been doing since 1889 of promoting the settlement in the national progressive religious, trade union, and secular reform press, usually by encouraging friends of the house to write articles about it. She had yet to publish an article herself although one of her speeches had appeared in print.

The following summer Chicago hosted a world's fair, and she had a second opportunity to lead. Some twenty-seven million visitors flocked to Chicago from around the country and the world to attend both the fair and a series of congresses held in conjunction with it. What better moment to put the settlement house movement on the international map? Addams and several other head residents organized the Congress of Social Settlements, which was held at Hull House. Some of the papers Hull House residents gave at the congress became part of a book they published two years later, *Hull-House Maps and Papers*, a landmark sociological study of the neighborhood that also featured color-coded maps about the ethnic living patterns and weekly wages of the eastern half of the Nineteenth Ward.[29]

It was in the summer of 1893 that Hull House and Jane Addams became thoroughly famous. The fair brought a surge of people to the city, and Hull House was on everyone's list as a place to visit. Endlessly, residents gave tours of the settlement's three buildings. An art gallery had been built in 1891 with a gift from a trustee of the Art Institute, and the summer of the fair the settlement opened its second new structure, which it called the Gymnasium Building. This housed a gymnasium/auditorium, a coffeehouse, a "diet kitchen" to supply nutritious broths, gruels, and custards for the sick, and men's club rooms. With its three buildings and twelve residents, including seven men—more men had finally arrived—Hull House was the largest settlement house in the United States, a distinction it would retain for decades to come. In only four years Addams had built a remarkable institution.

Ellen Gates Starr, though a vibrant presence at the settlement, was not an equal in all that had been accomplished. She took no part in the

Hull House exterior, circa 1892. The Butler Art Gallery is on
the left and the Hull mansion is on the right.

settlement's management. Practicalities were one reason. Since she had to earn her living from the beginning, she did not have the free time that Jane did in the early years. Ellen soon quit her girls' teaching job, but the various low-paying sources of income she scrapped together over the years—tutoring, part-time teaching, and lecturing—kept her income limited and unstable. Most important, she did not have the talent or inclination to run Hull House. Her niece observed: "While an enlivener and an inspirer, Ellen Gates Starr had no slightest capacity for administration."[30] What she enjoyed most about settlement life were the friendships. She took special pleasure in knowing Florence Kelley, who often made her roar with laughter. But Kelley's political interests did not rub off on her at first. For most of the 1890s Ellen taught art and culture and searched for a meaningful religious faith.

By 1893 Jane and Ellen's relationship had changed. They were still good friends and in fact would always remain so, but the feeling of special closeness was gone. Ellen's zeal and tempestuousness, as well as her willingness to criticize Jane frankly, had begun to wear on the even-tempered, conflict-avoiding Jane; and Jane's phlegmatic open-mindedness was proving equally wearing on the opinionated, freely judgmental Ellen. Jane once said to Ellen that she knew Ellen loved her but that she did not think Ellen liked her. Ellen once said of Jane that if she saw the devil coming down the street, she would admire the curve in his tail.[31]

One of the things that Ellen criticized was Hull House. With her high standards for excellence, she saw the settlement's flaws more than its strengths and worried that, given all the accolades it was receiving, there was too much resting on laurels. In the summer of 1892 she had written her cousin Mary Allen, "The success of Hull House outwardly and visibly is something of a snare. [The praise] serves as an excuse for [our not doing and being] the things we ought to do and be." She also criticized Jane's tendency to distribute her love widely, rather than invest her heart deeply in one person. Ellen once complained that Jane's affection for her also "includ[ed] the 19th ward."[32]

Mary Rozet Smith around age seventeen

Both women began to look elsewhere for close companionship. Ellen soon "fell in love," as she put it, with Mary Allen, whom she visited every summer.[33] For Jane, the special person became Mary Rozet Smith, a wealthy woman who was twenty when they first met, nine years younger than Jane. She was a former student of Ellen's, had volunteered at Hull House from its first days, and shared the cofounders' passion for bridging the social divide. Over the years Mary visited sick neighbors with Jane, led a boys' club, and, though she lived with her parents, often spent a night or two a week at Hull House. (In the years to come she was to be a generous major donor to Hull House and serve on its board of trustees.) Like Ellen, Mary loved to read—her interests were biography and history—had a lively sense of humor, and was a delightful conversationalist, but the similarities ended there. Where Ellen was intense, Mary was calm; where Ellen lost her temper, Mary did not. Her niece recalled her as "dignified, gracious," and "never angry."[34] Mary's great gifts, Hull House resident Alice Hamilton recalled, were for listening, for drawing a person out, and for giving comfort. She was also, according to many, beautiful, adding to her appeal. Jane had needed Ellen's bracing enthusiasm to start Hull House; now she needed Mary's unflappable and generous constancy.

And Mary? Earlier she had been engaged to be married—her family to this day has the diamond engagement ring her fiancé gave her—but the young man, a soldier, had gone west, and, apparently seduced by the charms of the fading frontier, never returned. The young man's disappearance had devastated Mary, but she soon found new interests, and first among them were Hull House and Jane Addams.[35]

||||||||||||

In the summer of 1893, as the world's fair, with its hundreds of buildings, exhibits and congresses, was glittering and as Hull House was revealing itself to be the settlement all other settlements admired, the people of the Nineteenth Ward were suffering. A serious economic depression, marked by a large number of bankruptcies in the early part of the year and the crash of the New York Stock Exchange in May, was beginning to take hold. Some people's wages were cut; many lost their jobs. By September one-third of the factories in Chicago had closed their doors, and the unemployment rate had risen to a stunning 40 percent. Those seeking jobs or assistance with food, clothing, and heating bills, whether they were from the neighborhood or elsewhere in the city, came to Hull House. Ellen wrote a friend in August, "We are sunk under a mass of the unemployed morning, noon and night."[36] Jane found listening to their stories hard to bear. She wrote Mary Rozet Smith using the third person, as she often did when speaking of herself: "It takes something . . . in these hard times to keep up one's spirits."[37]

She had seen borderline poverty before, the poverty of those who barely managed to live from paycheck to paycheck, but in the fall of 1893 she saw "dire poverty" for the first time. She paid many relief visits and found herself "dealing directly with the simplest human wants."[38] And she saw severe mental suffering. She learned that people feared three things the most: debt, the shame of appearing as paupers to their children, and dying of hunger. Under severe psychic pressure, some people simply lost their minds.

The misery of the workers and their families deeply unsettled certain of Addams's ideas. Three years of living on Halsted Street had already begun to corrode her belief that the human spirit was unaffected by poverty; now the depression completed the process. In that crucible of economic tragedy she forged a new understanding: Human beings required the material necessities and the ability to work for them in order to maintain their sanity and self-respect. And she learned something else startling and important, something that contradicted her father's and most successful capitalists' deepest conviction—that men were responsible for their poverty. Surrounded by workers—men, women, and children—who had been reliable and good workers, who badly wanted to work and were unable to find jobs, who wept because there were no jobs to be had, she learned that poverty was *not* always the individual's fault, was *not* always due to laziness, and did *not* always mark a failure of character.

The depression also recast her feelings about herself. Her material ease now embarrassed her. As she visited with neighbors, she recalled, "I was constantly shadowed by a certain sense of shame that I should be comfortable in the midst of such distress." Her efforts to share the fruits of culture now seemed pointless—"futile and superficial," "a mere pretense and a travesty."[39]

That winter Jane Addams took up a material agenda—to do everything she could to help the unemployed. She and the other residents, she remembered, "all worked under a sense of desperate need, and a paralyzing consciousness that our best efforts were most inadequate."[40] Hull House set up a free health clinic and a relief bureau to screen relief applicants from across the city for private charities. Addams proposed that the settlement host a homeless shelter for women and children, the city's first, but the settlement residents, who made collective decisions about house projects at their weekly meetings, voted down the plan. The shelter, they argued, was a charity, not appropriate work for a settlement house. Undeterred, Addams worked with women's clubs around the city to organize and fund a shelter and a sewing workshop, where women could earn money for food and clothing.

As homelessness and hunger worsened, it was obvious to some that the local government needed to do something. For weeks Chicago's union leaders had been calling for the city to create public works jobs for the able-bodied. But the view among those in office was that this was not a responsibility of government. One Chicago alderman said that, "[c]ity officials [have no legal] obligation . . . to . . . furnish employment to . . . citizens."[41] The governor of New York State, Roswell P. Flower, under similar pressure, was more blunt: "It is not the province of government to support the people." A group of economists sympathetic to the workers' situation dismissed the economic theory that justified such a limited role for government. "Laissez-faire [capitalism is] an excuse for doing nothing while people starve."[42]

Addams had been raised by her capitalist father to believe that the free market brought prosperity to all, but she had to admit that the theory did not explain why the depression had happened or offer a constructive solution. But what did? Given all the suffering around her, she remembered, "I longed for the comfort of a definite social creed" that could explain the "social chaos."[43] She also wanted to know the causes of poverty and the way to prevent it in the future. As for the present, she was coming to believe that local government had a responsibility to protect its citizens from the worst effects of capitalism's collapse. Perhaps there is nothing like a depression to teach that lesson.

She toyed with embracing Marxist socialism as her new "creed." The Marxists in the neighborhood, sensing her confusion, pressed her harder to agree with them that the depression was caused by the capitalist class's pursuit of overproduction and that class conflict was a necessary response. But while she listened and read, she found she could not accept certain Marxist ideas.

One she had trouble with was Marx's theory that people's class position inescapably determined their political consciousness. Addams's strongest belief was that no one, including a wealthy woman like her, was condemned to the narrow perspective to which she was born, that she, or anyone, could understand someone from another class by listening carefully and with empathy to his story. Marx's theory denied the power of learning from experience and the possibility of human growth. Furthermore, Marxism declared the achievement of universal and democratic fellowship, the central passion of her life, to be impossible. Another problem was Marxism's reliance on violent class struggle to bring about social change. As a believer in the power of assertive nonresistance Addams could not agree.

There was another issue. Behind Marx's solution of class struggle lay his belief, or more accurately his and his colleague Frederick Engels's belief, that capitalists as a class controlled the industrial workplace and that workers as a class were at their mercy. It was a reality of the 1890s Addams could not yet see. But history would not leave her uneducated much longer. That spring, during and after a massive strike in Chicago, she would learn that a large imbalance of power between the classes could polarize society, arouse violence, and raise the question of what the government should do about it.

|||||||||||

The Pullman Strike was a consequence of George Pullman's response to the depression. As the market for railroad sleeping cars collapsed in the summer and fall of 1893, he cut his Chicago workforce, half of whom lived in housing he rented to them, by 75 percent. He then gradually rehired most of them (and restored his rent income) but cut their wages by an average of 30 percent. At the same time, to increase his rent income (he refused to charge less for rent), he told his foremen to require workers who did not live in Pullman housing to move there or lose their jobs. By May two-thirds of the workers were living in Pullman town (located within Chicago's city limits but company managed) and turning over nearly all of their paychecks for rent. Their families were starving. They sent a small committee to try to negotiate with Pullman, but he refused to meet with them. Trade unions were illegal in Pullman, but the workers had behind-the-scenes support from the new cross-trades railroad union the American Railway Union (ARU), which Eugene V. Debs had founded. When Pullman learned the workers were preparing to strike, he locked them out.

At first, hopes were high that the dispute could be settled quickly. A few months earlier a group of citizens, including Jane Addams, had formed a new cross-class organization, the Civic Federation of Chicago, to apply political pressure to city government to end corruption and improve municipal services. Now the federation pulled together the Conciliation Board, which was made up of leading citizens from the business, labor, academic, and reform communities, Addams among them, and chaired by a businessman. The board did not seek to arbitrate the dispute itself but to persuade the parties to agree to voluntary arbitration by a neutral third party (that part of the plan was never really explained).

The board met daily during the early part of the strike, seeking solutions; Addams, having ties to business and labor, became the de facto leader of its efforts. Its position was neutral: to persuade the parties to come to the negotiating table. Eventually she convinced the Strike Committee to meet with George Pullman, but Pullman would not meet with her even to discuss the question, and the effort collapsed.

Meanwhile Chicagoans became increasingly polarized in their feelings toward the strikers. Initially, the *Chicago Tribune* had presented sympathetic stories about the sufferings of the Pullman workers to its middle-class readers, but as the strike wore on, and the Pullman Palace Car Company reiterated its right to manage itself as it saw fit, the paper began to run nasty headlines about Debs, calling him a "dictator."[44] The

New York Times was only slightly less restrained. Middle-class readers, on the whole, turned hostile to the workers' cause. After members of the ARU national convention, meeting in Chicago in June, voted to strike in sympathy with the Pullman workers, railroad cars owned by many companies, not just by Pullman, stopped moving, and much of the nation's economy ground to a halt. Letters of complaint poured into the White House. The railroad companies, represented by the American Railway Association, persuaded President Grover Cleveland to send in the National Guard to occupy Chicago's stockyards and the Pullman factory; unemployed troublemakers—not Pullman workers—became violent, possibly at the instigation of the American Railway Association. Debs was arrested and jailed, and the strike was broken. New workers were hired by Pullman, and the factory reopened. The strikers were now unemployed.

Like most Americans, Addams found that summer's experiences shocking. But unlike nearly everyone else, she refused to choose a side. She thought that to do so would amount to a betrayal of her devotion to the possibility of human unity. Still, she saw "the sharp division into class lines" and the resulting "distrust and bitterness." The strike, she concluded, had drawn back the curtain on tensions already present, dispelling "the good nature which in happier times envelops the ugliness of the industrial situation."[45] She had always known the United States was divided into social classes; the strike taught her that these divisions not only betrayed the democratic ideal but also permitted hatred to fester. The stakes were higher than she had thought.

Another painful experience was enduring people's anger at her for not giving at least tacit support to their side. Her impartiality made her look to them as if she were on the other side. Many of her wealthy friends, one resident at Hull House remembered, thought her a "traitor to her class," while the workers felt she had betrayed them by not publicly endorsing the strike. Hull House resident Alice Hamilton, who did not live there at the time but heard later about Addams's reactions during the strike, wrote that the strike was "for her the most painful of experiences because . . . she was forced by conviction to work against the stream, to separate herself from the great mass of her countrymen," and she "suffered . . . from spiritual loneliness."[46] In these circumstances, no one could mistake Addams's neutrality for wishy-washiness. Staying neutral during the Pullman Strike required integrity and courage. She paid an enormous price for being true to her ideals.

In the wake of the strike, an effort arose to reform labor policy. The strike had created a political opening. Trade unions, long advocates for voluntary arbitration, joined middle-class reformers like Addams and others involved with the Civic Federation of Chicago, to call for the creation of state and federal boards to arbitrate labor disputes on a voluntary basis. Addams joined this effort. With the federation, she helped organize a national conference convened in Chicago the following fall to explore the idea. She gave a speech at the event, lobbied for a law to create such a board in Illinois, and was named to a national commission to press for federal legislation. (There is no record that the commission ever actually got off the ground.) She no longer doubted her ability to be political.

But her deepest longing remained for a new understanding across class lines, for a feeling of community based on humanness. She had seen before and especially during the strike that trade unionists believed in the brotherhood of all men and that this was not understood by those outside the labor movement. In a paper she wrote a few months after the strike ended, "The Settlement as a Factor in the Labor Movement," published in *Hull-House Maps and Papers* the following spring, she encouraged that new understanding. Her goal was to persuade people from prosperous backgrounds—capitalists, middle-class people, settlement workers—to sympathize with labor. She set before her readers the enticing vision of "the larger solidarity which includes labor and capital" based on a "notion of universal kinship" and "the common good."[47] Remarkably, in the wake of a national trauma that had stirred much hatred and fear of unions, she argued that the labor movement could teach the nation about the idea of democracy.

She did not ignore the evil aspects of the strike. She saw the hatred on both sides and the self-righteousness that fueled it. She thought such single-minded zeal naive and dangerous. "Life itself teaches us nothing [is] more inevitable than that right and wrong are most confusedly mixed, . . . that the blackest wrong is by our side and within our own motives [and] that right . . . has to be found by exerting patience, discrimination and impartiality." If each side is convinced it is completely in the right, and the other side completely in the wrong, then the result must be a struggle between adversaries, the "sole judge" of which "must be force." It would be better, she argued, for citizens to join the flow of history. Democracy was spreading from the political to the social realms of life. People should step outside their narrow, selfish viewpoints and consider what might be best for society as a whole; they must develop a "social conscience."[48]

Her tenacious hold on her vision was remarkable. The hostilities aroused by the strike deeply pained her. Yet somehow she still saw the good that might come out of the tragic clash. Instead of abandoning her belief in universal fellowship because devastating events had proved it wrong, Addams deepened her understanding of what achieving such fellowship required. It wasn't just that she didn't get discouraged or bitter or despairing (or at least she left no trace of these feelings in her paper); it was that she took what she had learned from trade unionists and from the horrible experience of the strike, turned these things over in her mind, passed them through the sieve of her thought, and returned them to the world, strained of narrow-mindedness and selfishness and imbued with fresh hope about the good embedded in the strike's reality. In this paper, more than in any other writing she had done before, she positioned herself as an interpreter across divisions of misunderstanding and as a prophetic visionary of future possibilities. These two roles of interpreter and prophet became as much a part of her reform method—and of her greatness as a moral leader—as her more recognizable role of political activist. In all three, she practiced a deeply thoughtful hope.

She believed she understood the cause of the strike, that it had resulted from antagonism. The clash arose, it seemed to her, because of feelings of anger between the employer and the employees. Instead of being sympathetic and compassionate, both sides were selfish. She knew that labor was fighting for safe working conditions, shorter hours, and adequate wages, yet she did not think that gaining them was a matter of social justice. In her world it was all a problem of feelings.

However, other theories were circulating, and she soon found herself caught up in a debate about class power and the necessity of opposition. While writing the paper, she and a friend of hers, John Dewey, a new philosophy professor at the University of Chicago, had a heartfelt conversation about the subject of antagonism. Dewey argued, Kantian that he was, that tensions in society led to antagonistic struggles and that such struggles could serve the developmental direction of history. Addams gently but firmly disagreed. Dewey, writing to his wife, summed up what Addams had said: "[A]ntagonisms of institutions were always [due to the] injection of the personal attitude and reaction."[49] In fact on this subject Jane Addams's understanding *was* limited, as Marx had predicted it would be, by the perspective formed by her narrow life experience. Growing up white and female in a private world of plenty and never having worked in a factory, she was blind to the forces of economic power; the only kind of antagonism she recognized was personal.

But Addams was not finished with thinking about the Pullman Strike. She began to work on a new essay about it alone. This was "A Modern Lear," a speech she gave first in March 1896, to an audience of five hundred at the Chicago Woman's Club, later around the country, and eventually published. In it she noted the selfishness of the employer but also argued for the first time that the workers had a right to better wages, better working conditions, and shorter hours. In one of the most passionate sentences she ever wrote, she said, "The aroused conscience of men [requires] . . . the complete participation of the working classes in the spiritual, intellectual and material inheritance of the human race."

She called it a matter of "social justice." And she spoke of Pullman's "power" to build the town of Pullman and about his failure to recognize the legitimacy of democratic political power—i.e., "the consent of the men who were living" there.[50]

"Power" was a word Addams had previously used to refer to character. Growing up, she had dreamed of achieving that kind of personal power, but she had no conscious experience with other kinds of power. Sheltered within her family, she had not seen the power the family's wealth gave it economically and socially, nor seen the other kinds of power her father's influence as a politician created. She lived on the safe side of impersonal power, oblivious and innocent. Why did she see it now?

The answer is found in a commencement speech she gave at Rockford College (her alma mater had finally changed its name) in June 1895, while she was writing an early draft of "A Modern Lear." Addressing the popular assumption that woman's absence from public and business scandal was due to her inherent purity, she wrote: "I have a warning to give [female] college graduates, a warning against self-righteousness." Women were fully capable of corruption; they simply had not been given the freedom to be corrupt. "Perhaps the reason women have not made politics impure, have not corrupted legislatures and wrecked railroads is because they have not had the opportunity to do so, as they have been chained down by a military code whose penalty is far worse than the court martial."[51] Chained down by a military code? A penalty worse than the court-martial? Addams was not mincing words here. She was describing a social system, a "code," that denied women the freedoms men possessed simply because they were women.

The graduates and parents in her audience may have found her military metaphor obscure, but for Addams it was freighted with meaning. In 1895 she had just begun to think about the idea of militarism; it was to become a theme of her second book, *Newer Ideals of Peace*, published in 1907. There she explained that militarism meant, among other things, a devotion to the principle of hierarchy, to the idea that a superior had the right to rule over an inferior. As Addams well knew from reading John

Stuart Mill's *The Subjection of Women*, the principle, when it was applied to the sexes, was called patriarchy, from the Greek for "rule by the father." Patriarchy was the value system that ranked men superior to women; it was the "military code" that kept women enchained.

When a person understands that the principles of patriarchy and hierarchy can be challenged, that "the way things are" is not the way things must be, it is a moment of blinding insight. Many pieces of the puzzle fall into place. For Addams, it meant, among other things, the end of her faith in the ethic of benevolence, her belief that the superior person ought to take care of the inferior person and that the inferior person ought to be grateful. This was no small thing. Benevolence had been the unquestioned ethic of her childhood, the ethic that her kind, well-meaning father had followed when he prevented her from going to Smith College, the ethic that had first fueled her desire to "help the poor," and the ethic that George Pullman invoked to justify his paternalistic power over his workers' lives.

Seeing through benevolence and seeing patriarchy's power, she saw through a great deal else. Her new understanding filtered into her speech on the Pullman Strike. She compared George Pullman with King Lear and compared the workers with Lear's daughter Cordelia. Lear's "paternal expression was one of domination and indulgence," she wrote. He did not believe that his daughter "could have a worthy life apart from him."[52] Pullman, she argued, made the same mistakes.

Addams's interpretation of the Pullman Strike reframed her world. At thirty-four she dismissed her beloved father's ethic of benevolence as old-fashioned and lost her innocence about economic power. Using her imagination to cast off her class blinkers, she perceived the connections between different kinds of oppression. Marx, it turned out, had been wrong after all: An upper-middle-class person *could* perceive how those in the working class experienced the economic power of the industrialist. And when she turned to look at politics—the business of redistributing public power—she saw it with new eyes.

|||||||||||||

We all live our lives immersed in a political world. It is only a question of whether and when we want to reach out and connect to it. Addams had gotten involved with state politics in 1893, but municipal politics held little interest for her until she became the guardian of her sister Mary's two younger children in the summer of 1894. As the public tragedy of the Pullman Strike was unfolding, she endured the private tragedy of Mary's death from an unidentified illness at the age of forty-nine. Because their father had for years failed to support the family (they had spent down Mary's inheritance and were in debt) and possibly for other reasons, the younger children, Esther Linn, aged thirteen, and Stanley Linn, aged eleven, came to stay with their aunt at Hull House. But not for long. Addams, suddenly aware in a visceral way of the health threat the rat-infested, garbage-strewn neighborhood posed to children, regretfully sent Esther and Stanley away to school and began for the first time to think seriously about the sanitation problem. She felt ashamed, she later wrote, that she had not tackled it sooner for the sake of the neighborhood children.[53]

Two results followed. First, as part of a Civic Federation campaign, a new reform-minded mayor appointed Addams, with pay, to inspect the work of the individual contractors hired to remove garbage from the Nineteenth Ward; the ward's wooden boxes often overflowed because of their casual approach to their work. Instead of removing garbage three times a week, they removed it twice a month. Second, she learned that the garbage removal contracts were political spoils, handed out by one of the ward's two aldermen, John Powers, who also happened to be one of the most powerful and notoriously corrupt aldermen in the city council. In the spring of 1896, Addams joined a Hull House effort to defeat him. The energetic Florence Kelley led the campaign, with the support of the citywide Municipal Voters' League, an offshoot of the Civic Federation of Chicago, and a group of local young men called the Nineteenth Ward Improvement Club. The reformers put forward a "clean" candidate and lobbied the men voters of the ward to vote for him, but their efforts failed, and Powers was reelected.

Afterward Kelley and Addams pondered why the forces of good government had lost. They knew a big factor was Powers's skills in machine politics, including his willingness to provide the ward's voters, 60 percent of whom were immigrant men struggling to establish themselves, with jobs, free railroad passes, and free meals at his saloon, and his willingness to buy their votes. But the campaign had also failed, they believed, because nonvoters led it. Some of the ward's voters told Kelley they resented "attempts at political leadership" by women.[54] Kelley and Addams were deeply frustrated that not one woman could vote for the reform candidate. In sum, they saw how badly women's disenfranchisement hurt the community. They decided that women's suffrage was an issue they needed to tackle. The disenfranchisement of half the adult population of the United States, a supposedly democratic country, had to end.

By the mid-1890s the organized woman's suffrage movement had been under way in the United States for nearly three decades but had little to show for it. As of 1896, women had the full vote in only four western states—Wyoming, Idaho, Utah, and Colorado—and two territories, Washington and Montana. The good news was that the movement's two national organizations, both founded in 1869, the National Woman Suffrage Association, which favored the federal amendment strategy, and the American Woman Suffrage Association, which favored state-by-state reform, had united in 1890 to become, de rigueur, the National-American Woman Suffrage Association (NAWSA). Resources could now be concentrated, but a long struggle lay ahead.

The president of the NAWSA, Susan B. Anthony, had wanted for some time to recruit the much-admired Jane Addams to the cause. In 1895 she invited her to speak at the national convention but without success. Two years later Addams was ready. In 1897 the Massachusetts branch of the association, learning Addams would be in Boston to give

Jane Addams, circa 1897

her speech about the Pullman Strike, invited her to a suffrage reception. Much to their delight, she not only attended but spoke.

Addams had always agreed with the idea that women should have the vote. She once said that both her parents (she meant her father and her mother; Anna was opposed to suffrage) supported it, and in college she had written an editorial favoring it.[55] What had changed for her was her new sense that she could be engaged politically and also that women voting would benefit citizens as a whole. Suffrage had moved from an abstraction to a passion.

For her first suffrage speech, Addams had many arguments to choose from. She might have told her audience of mostly prosperous women that working-class women needed the vote to kick corrupt politicians out of office. Or she might have been really daring and said that women could not overthrow the "military code" that restricted their freedom if they did not have the right to vote. Instead she chose the argument that spoke to prosperous women like her most directly: Women needed the vote in order to develop as citizens and fulfill their "civic duties."[56]

||||||||||||

Although now thoroughly interested in political action, Addams in her speeches and writings remained focused on the question of personal growth. In a speech she gave a few months after her suffrage speech she pointed out that the "ultimate end" of education and political equality "must be the development of human nature in scope and power and happiness, in a word of character, including powers of life and enjoyment."[57] This belief—so classically Greek, so eighteenth-century Enlightenment, so evangelical Christian in its emphasis on human potential and on (ultimate) happiness—had brought her to Halsted Street, and it had not changed; nor would it. Behind every political action Addams took in the future and behind every argument she would make for political action in the years to come lay this conviction. It was her credo.

Addams's own ethical growth forms the hidden theme of her writings in the 1890s, when she was learning so much about herself. Despite her democratic ideals, expressed through her egalitarian social etiquette, she had arrived on Halsted Street with an unexamined belief in her class-based superiority and the attitude of noblesse oblige that came with it. In this she was just like her father. But after writing "A Modern Lear," and rejecting the ethic of benevolence, she began to see more clearly what life on Halsted Street had really been teaching her all along: Class-based superiority was a myth. The most "civilized" or "cultured" person, she concluded, was not the person who was widely read or who had visited the most cultural institutions but the person who understood all sorts of people—poor or middling or rich, Anglo or not, white or not, Christian or not, sober or not, able-bodied or not, healthy or sick, young or old. "The cultivated person is the one who [uses] his

social faculties, his interpretative power, the one who ... put[s himself]
into the minds and experiences of other people."[58]

Her moral revolution did not stop there. Seeing through benevolence,
she began to doubt the belief that undergirded it—another tenet of her
childhood—that moral absolutes existed. She had edged up to it in her
1894 paper on the settlement and the labor movement when she wrote
that "right and wrong are most confusingly mixed." But it was in "A
Modern Lear," the speech that captured her transformed thinking in so
many ways, that she freed herself completely from this old belief. First
she dismissed George Pullman's ethics, noting that he "must have been
sustained [in his resistance to his workers' demands] by the consciousness of being in the right. ... He could not see the situation from the
social point of view." Second, she praised Abraham Lincoln, her father's
political friend and a hero to many of her generation, for his willingness
to abandon the "absolute right."[59]

But if moral absolutes could no longer be her guide, what could?
Lincoln offered her the answer: a new, more deeply democratic ethic.
He sought, she wrote in "Lear," to "discover what the people really
want," to "move with the people," and to seek the "best possible." For
Addams, "the people" meant the labor movement. Through the people,
she explained, it was possible to connect with "the Zeitgeist, ... the
great moral life springing from our common experiences," what she
called "the genuine feeling of the age."[60] She now believed that the
people's desires should instruct her conscience. This was cooperation
with the good taken to another level, and it amounted to a new theory
of leadership for her. She was describing a new kind of hero, not an
isolated Carlylean figure but a person guided by those he led.

It was a short step from there to Addams's next radical conclusion.
Again, she reached it in "A Modern Lear." A society's morality—her
own morality—was not fixed and absolute; each generation needed to
shape its own, in response to the new circumstances it faced and the
new hopes to which it aspired. She needed to do so too. Her conclu-

sions about benevolence illustrated the point. The ethic was suited to her father's generation, but it was now old-fashioned. Her generation's ethic—her own ethic—was social justice. "The social passion of the age" today, she wrote, is to emancipate the worker.[61] Carefully, with surgical precision, Addams was removing from her moral philosophy those inherited ideas that were putting her at odds with her times and the people she lived among, the workers and their families. Listening with an open mind, she let Halsted Street teach her what no book could.

In this way Addams took up the workers' reform agenda: freedom from wage-induced poverty and work-induced suffering; freedom to prosper economically and grow as human beings. The question for her now was how that agenda should be accomplished. The general mainstream view, the product of preindustrial times, was that each worker should free himself by pulling himself up by his famous bootstraps. Workers argued and taught Addams that in an industrial economy, in which large employers had great organizational power and a fiercer drive for maximum profit, workers needed trade unions and government on their side. Trade unions had long sought legislation to protect young children from labor and obtain shorter hours for the overworked. Belonging to a trade union, Addams wrote in 1899, "leads men to appeal to the state and to use the tools democracy offers." The public and therefore the government have "a duty toward the weak and defenseless members of the community."[62]

The workers were arguing to expand the government's responsibilities. They understood that morality evolved. Addams was impressed. Labor tries to "secure each advance in ethics by a step taken in politics," she wrote. "We would not have the state remain motionless, enchained to the [stage] of civilization attained at the moment the state was founded."[63] Her new goal was labor's goal, the creation of a democratic state that would protect a wider variety of the vulnerable people—not just the charity cases but hardworking families whose employers cheated them of their health, prosperity, self-development, and leisure.

The argument was of its times. Trade unionists had been early advocates of a democratic state, but now Americans in other classes, and especially the prosperous middle class, also believed that a more democratic state should come. A portion of an entire generation of clubwomen, teachers, settlement house volunteers, social workers, businessmen, ministers, and professors agreed with labor that the citizens needed to organize together to make government—by which they meant their city, county, and state governments—more responsive to the demands and needs of the people. (At the turn of the century only the radical few were ready to argue for federal action.) In the second half of the 1890s, Americans pressed their governments to adopt reforms, often with success (although in the South, African Americans faced mounting obstacles because of Jim Crow laws and violence). The democratic wing of the progressive movement arose in the cities and states in the 1890s, and by 1899 it was poised to become a major force in American history.

||||||||||||||||||||||||||||||||||||||||||||||||||||||||||||||||||||||||||||||||||||||||||||||||||||||||||||||||||||||||||||||||||||||||||||||

CHAPTER FOUR

POLITICAL
ETHICIST

As the new century loomed on the horizon, Jane Addams was not yet a leader of a broad, national base of reform-minded citizens, but she was certainly famous. For almost ten years, earning her living as she went, she had periodically traveled the country, giving speeches to women's and men's clubs, settlement house gatherings, women's colleges, universities, churches, trade unions, ethical societies, and adult education classes, and receiving extensive coverage by the local press. Her name circulated nationally because the Associated Press wire service often sent out a few paragraphs about something eye-catching she did, like work as a city garbage inspector; editors used them to fill holes in their page layouts. The groups she spoke to also had national publications that were eager to publish her writings, often as reprints or in excerpts.

But she had never served on the board of a national reform organization, let alone been president of one; the only legislature she had ever lobbied was the Illinois General Assembly; and the only legislation for which she had ever lobbied was on child labor and sweatshop reform. She had met a president of the United States once, in 1898, when she tried, unsuccessfully, to persuade President McKinley to name Florence Kelley to the staff of a federal commission, but she had never attended or addressed a national party convention or published a piece in a broadly popular magazine like the *Ladies' Home Journal* or written a book. To be sure, her ambition—her burning desire to make a difference, to contribute her talents to the world, and to attain public honor—had flourished. But as she entered her forties, it was stretching its wings and preparing to soar.

||||||||||||

Where does the idea of writing a book come from? For Addams, as for most authors, it arose partly from her longing to create for others the experience she enjoyed as a reader and partly from a growing sense that she had something more complex to say than could be said in a short piece. She knew writing a book would be difficult. When she wrote to congratulate her friend Henry Demarest Lloyd in 1894 on publishing his critique of industrial capitalism, *Wealth Against Commonwealth*, she noted that she had "a great deal of respect for anyone who writes a good book."[1] At the time she was serving as a behind-the-scenes editor for the book by the residents *Hull-House Maps and Papers*, but while this was deeply satisfying, it hardly scratched her authorial itch.

In the fall of 1897 the nudge she needed came in the form of an invitation to give a five-part lecture series in February at Iowa (now Grinnell) College. The theme she chose, the necessary end of benevolence, had been percolating in her mind for some time. It seemed that everywhere she looked she saw the dangers that ethic posed to democracy. Once she had seen it in George Pullman's relations with his employees, she began to see it in other relationships: between the household employer and the servant, between the charity worker and the beneficiary; between the prosperous citizen and struggling union member, between the educator and his adult student; between the educated, supposedly incorruptible reformer and the uneducated voter who supported the corrupt alderman; and, most personally, between a father and his adult daughter. In the second half of the 1890s she wrote speeches and essays about all these relationships. Her conclusion in each case was that benevolence was a selfish, arrogant, and antidemocratic ethic that needed to be retired from contemporary life. She reworked this material for the Iowa College lectures and, then, for several other lecture series. In 1902, Macmillan published the final result, *Democracy and Social Ethics*, her first book.

In each chapter, she discussed a different relationship but made the same point: Benevolence was no longer relevant to the rising spirit of democracy. No category of people should feel superior to another category of people. Every person should represent his or her own interests and develop his or her own talents. "[T]he creative power in the people themselves . . . will come out if it only has a chance."[2]

Addams approached her task of persuasion sensitively. She knew that most of her readers—prosperous people who could afford to buy books—were content in their benevolence, comfortable in their superiority. In the introduction, she was fairly hard-hitting. "[W]e consciously limit our [social] intercourse to certain kinds of people who [*sic*] we have previously decided to respect," she wrote, allowing us to grow "contemptuous" of our fellow human beings. But in the rest of the book she was gentler. Rather than accuse her readers directly, she let them discover themselves in her sympathetic descriptions of each pair. It was a way for those who felt superior to see their inherited ethical ideas in a new light and also to see differently those people they thought of as inferior and whom they felt free to judge. Without such efforts, she noted in the introduction, feelings of harsh disapproval or disrespectful pity festered. "We have learned . . . that much of the insensibility and hardness of the world is due to the lack of imagination which prevents [understanding] the experiences of other people."[3] She avoided references to class. Still, class prejudice, except in the case of the father and daughter, was her subtext. Her subject was really paternalism in all its forms.

This would have been enough to accomplish in one book, but Addams, with her passion for helping others grow, wrote a second book, interwoven with the first, about how citizens in a democracy could learn social ethics by living more democratically. In each chapter she found a fresh philosophical or metaphorical way to urge readers to break out of their narrow, class-defined family and social rounds and their private trajectories of ambition and come to know a wider range of people socially. It was charming and ironic: She, a lifelong book lover, had written a book endorsing the need to put down her book, or any book, and learn from life.

She never said specifically what people should do, wanting readers to make their own discoveries. But she was clear about the importance of their trying to bridge the social divide. Knowing how much her own life had changed, she thought the stakes were high for everyone. "We are under a moral obligation in choosing our experiences, since the result of those experiences must ultimately determine our understanding of life." She added: "We determine our ideals by our daily actions and decisions. . . ."[4]

Aware that her readers would balk at the idea of violating the conventions of their social class, she addressed that point. Social change only happened, she argued, when people who disagreed with the status quo spoke out. She had absorbed the idea long ago from Emerson. "Progress must always come," she wrote, "through the individual who varies from the type and has sufficient [moral] energy to express this variation." She made the same point more bluntly in a 1901 lecture: "If you are different than [sic] others you need to act on that difference, if society is to advance."[5] There was something here of the self-reliant hero but with a difference. Addams thought the source of such boldness was not genius, as Emerson believed, but wide experience carefully interpreted. And, although she had not found it easy, she herself had sometimes stood apart from the majority, notably during the Pullman Strike.

Democracy and Social Ethics was essentially the work of a moral philosopher. It sought to undermine the social side of the class system by persuading people to change their lives in ways that would change their ethics. But the political activist was not entirely missing. In the chapter

on industrial relations, Addams criticized "successful men" for failing
to push for legislation that would "raise the standard" of workers' lives
and praised the labor unions for taking up that task, including their
efforts to end child labor. Although she did not argue for any specific
policy change aside from endorsing child labor laws, she claimed that
"public agitation" was necessary "to secure help from the state."[6]

The book was for the most part enthusiastically received. After
reading it, U.S. Supreme Court Justice Oliver Wendell Holmes wrote
a friend that Jane Addams "gives me more insight into the point of
view of the working man and the poor than I had before." Another
male reader, surprised that a woman had written a good book, praised
it to Addams's face as a unique achievement for someone of her sex.
He told her, "[N]o other book by a woman shows such vitality—such
masculinity of mental grasp & surefootedness." The poet Harriet Monroe managed to compliment Addams for her accomplishment without
insulting their shared womanhood by remarking on her "mountaineer
venturesomeness." William James, the famous Harvard philosopher-
psychologist, loved the book, calling it "one of the great books of
our time."[7]

Addams, like every first-time book author, was horribly nervous
about whether the book was any good. When the first copy arrived, she
took it off by herself to look at, expecting to be greatly disappointed.
And she was, although she tried to tell herself this was normal. She
wrote a friend soon after, "I have had some terrible qualms since it has
been issued but perhaps that is inevitable." A few weeks later, after she
received some "friendly" reviews and "heart-warming letters" and knew
the book was selling well, she wrote to Mary Rozet Smith, to whom
she had dedicated the book: "I feel a little better about it, but it is all I
can do not to tear out the leaves."[8] She longed to revise it and thought
she could do so when the book went into its second printing six weeks
later, but the editor did not ask her for corrections. When the book
went into a third printing, Addams, this time alerted by her editor,
naively seized the chance to substantially rewrite the book, prompting

a scolding from him about the great expense such extensive changes would involve.[9] Presumably they were never made. Addams was learning the hard lesson every author must learn: Once a book is between hard covers, it is finished. The author must move on.

|||||||||||

Meanwhile, a national tragedy stunned the nation. The week before her lectures at Iowa College began, on February 15, 1898, an explosion sank the U.S. warship *Maine* in Havana Harbor, Cuba, killing 266 of the men on board. Spain, Cuba's occupying colonial power, was blamed— wrongly, as it turned out—for the *Maine*'s destruction (the ship's cargo of armaments had accidentally ignited). The public was outraged. Newspapers stirred the pot by running graphic stories about Spain's cruel treatment of Cubans. In Congress, politicians intent on looking out for the nation's large commercial interests in Cuba, which was the reason the *Maine* was in Havana Harbor in the first place, stoked the outrage.

War came quickly. In April the United States declared war on Spain in support of Cuba's revolutionaries. Immediately President McKinley, urged on by the business community that had helped win him the presidency, widened the purpose of the war to include removing from Spain's possession its colonies of Puerto Rico, Guam, and the Philippines. Troops were marshaled and shipped off with dispatch to all four islands, two of which were in the Caribbean and two in distant Pacific waters. All these territories were tempting plums for the United States to pick, being good places for commercial and naval ships to refuel and good sources for cheap factory labor. The United States had earlier resisted the temptation to imitate the European nations and become an empire, but, having become a world economic power, it could resist no longer.

Americans were divided about the war. Mindful of the revolutionary origins of their own country, many supported it because they sympathized with the revolutionaries in Cuba and the Philippines, where a

revolt against Spain was also under way, while others argued that violence should not be used. Still others insisted that the nation's true
motive was imperialism, that in the words of William Jennings Bryan,
the nation was entering upon "a career of empire."[10]

Bryan's charge proved true. After a short war, from April to August
1898, a peace agreement was reached, and on December 10, 1898, the
United States and Spain signed the Treaty of Paris. It granted Cuba
independence because Congress had mandated that; it also granted the
United States the authority to annex the Philippines, for which the
federal government paid Spain twenty million dollars, as well as Guam
and Puerto Rico. The Filipinos were furious at the U.S. betrayal of
their nation, but imperialists like Theodore Roosevelt were delighted.
Roosevelt, a former governor of New York State, had resigned his position as assistant secretary of the navy to fight in the war in Cuba, and,
thanks to the vivid reporting of journalists covering the war and his
soon-to-be-published book on his adventure, his national political star
was now ascendant. The imperialists moved quickly to consolidate their
position. President McKinley, arguing that the Filipinos were unable to
govern themselves, issued the Benevolent Assimilation Proclamation in
January 1899. Soon after, an American soldier on patrol at night shot
an approaching Filipino soldier who did not halt upon command, the
Filipinos fired back, and the Filipino–American War began.

Many Americans had been shocked when the United States went to
war with Spain over Cuba. Once the war with the Philippines began in
early 1899, a national opposition movement emerged, and in October
the American Anti-Imperialist League was formed in Chicago. Quickly
growing to thirty thousand members, it soon became the largest antiwar
organization in the nation's history. Its two goals were the immediate
cessation of hostilities and a congressional pledge to support Philippine
independence.

Addams at first watched from the sidelines. She had been interested
in the peace movement since at least 1893, when she joined the Chicago
Peace Society, and had chaired the local committee that hosted the Con-

gress of Arbitration and Peace at the World's Columbian Exposition (world's fair) in Chicago, but before 1898 she had mainly nurtured peace in local ways through private means.[11] She had mediated labor disputes, arguments between friends, and family quarrels. To her, peace meant the opposite of anger.

But the war in Cuba deeply troubled her. She had read Tolstoy's most recent Christian book, *The Kingdom of God Is Within You*, when it was published in English in 1894. She later described it as his "masterly exposition of the doctrine of nonresistance."[12] In his earlier book *My Religion*, which she had read in the 1880s, he had stressed that the only way to overcome evil was with good, with love. The new book expanded on this theme and had a long section about war. His view that war was an effort to overcome evil with evil—that it was mankind committing suicide—was unequivocal.

Tolstoy's ideas, she later wrote, were on her mind when she attended the Chicago Jubilee charity ball on October 18, 1898. The ball, a gala affair attended by thousands, including President McKinley, was to celebrate peace with Spain and the heroic deaths of the slain and to raise money to support the wounded. Afterward Addams wrote Mary Rozet Smith that she was feeling "quite blue, not play blue but real depths," and concluded, "I will have to be more of a Tolstoyan or less of one right off."[13] The day after the ball, she shared her qualms in a speech mostly about social settlements to two thousand women at a meeting of the Illinois Federation of Women's Clubs. Our peace jubilee, she said, honored "our heroes" and the battlefields in Cuba, but "we have said nothing of the liberated Cuba." We have "forgotten the aim of the war," she said, and have come "to love the war . . . for itself."[14]

Six months later, in late April 1899, after the Filipino-American War had begun, the anti-imperialists in Chicago, many of them her good friends in the city's municipal reform movement, organized a mass meeting to object to the new war. Addams was one of seven speakers and the only woman to address the crowd of three thousand.

In her speech she took hold of the subject of war by the handle she thought the most important, that of ideas. While the meeting adopted resolutions to end the war and give independence to the Filipinos, Addams called for expanding the meaning of democracy to include having respectful relations between nations. To meet the present situation fully, she said, we must extend "our patriotism into humanitarianism." She invoked historical trends. More and more people around the world, but especially working people, who bore the greatest burden from war, felt morally repulsed by the idea of conquest, and this "rising tide of moral feeling" was slowly "making war impossible."[15]

It was her favorite point—that morality evolved with the times, that each generation improved on the ethics of the previous generation in response to the demands of its own age. The idea had now moved to the center of her thinking, where it would remain. In *Democracy and Social Ethics* she had claimed that the nation was moving toward a new, more humanitarian social ethic. In her speech she said that the world was. In both cases, despite her use of the present tense, she did not mean to describe reality or even claim that the trend she described would spread quickly. Rather she spoke as a prophet, painting a vision in order to inspire those listening to make it manifest.

At the same time, Addams was not an unrealistic dreamer. The biggest obstacle to progress, she said, was human nature. "[B]rutal instincts ... [are] latent in every human being," she told the massive crowd. War then made things worse. During war "the humane instinct, which keeps in abeyance the tendency to cruelty, ... gives way." She was not speaking only of men; she knew women could be equally cruel. Living on Halsted Street had taught her over and over about the harshest realities of life, about rape, murder, men beating women and, more rarely, women beating men. Her friends often said about her that she faced life as it was.

She also acknowledged the Filipinos' feelings. Being well read in history, she understood the reaction the nascent Filippino nation had had to being ruled by Spain and was having to its new ruler, the United States. We may claim we are "protecting the weak," she said, but when a nation occupies another nation, it weakens the other nation's govern-ment, arouses "smart animosity on the part of the conquered," and prompts its most able citizens to leave.[16]

Strangely missing from her speech, other than the passing reference to "protecting the weak," was any acknowledgment that the American posture of benevolence—that out-of-date ethic so much on her mind—was undemocratic and an insult to the Filipino people. Her silence sug-gests that, despite her ideals, she could not quite see the Filipinos the way she saw Americans. One senses in the omission the stretch that she was making to think about foreign policy at all, but, in any case, her sympathetic imagination had failed her. It was likely she had never met a Filipino and certain she had never been to the Philippines. Her theory that experience was key to widening one's moral compass was evidently true. Lacking it, she could only lean hard on the democratic ideal and her knowledge of the history of conquered nations.

|||||||||||

In the same year the Filipino-American War began, 1899, many Ameri-cans were troubled by another violent means that men used to achieve their goals—lynching. First British colonists and then Americans had been lynching one another for criminal and lesser offenses for cen-turies. A lynching meant that a group of people committed murder collectively—no legal process was involved—by whatever means but often by hanging or burning. As the nineteenth century closed and white men intensified their efforts to use violence to keep African American men from voting, the numbers of lynchings increased and the motives were more frequently racist.

In the 1890s across the country but mostly in the South and West, white men, with the support of white women, lynched more than two thousand people, the great majority of them African American males. Sometimes the charges were for an actual crime committed, such as murdering a white man, and sometimes for pursuing racially dangerous behavior, such as insulting a white person. But often the charges were

Mr. McManus, African American, lynched, and the crowd
of men who attended his lynching, Minneapolis, MN, 1882

trumped up or did not even exist. The most frequent false criminal
charge was that a black man had raped a white woman. The white and
black press reported different versions of these events. Many northern
whites were concerned, not about racism but about the fact that there
had been no trial or sentence, that lynchings were lawless. President
McKinley even spoke about it in his first message to Congress. Addams
too was drawn into the debate.

The person who drew her in was a Chicago journalist, Ida Wells-
Barnett. In the late 1890s Wells-Barnett was battling to keep the issue
of lynching in the public eye by publicizing the facts. Born in Mississippi in 1862 into slavery, and a journalist by trade, Ida Wells was living

in Memphis by 1892 and owned one-third of a black newspaper there. That year she lost to lynchings a close friend and two acquaintances, all of them falsely accused of rape by the same white mob. After she had written a fierce editorial for her paper and fled north into exile because of threats on her life, she made it her passionate cause to inform the nation of the truths about lynching. That same year she published a thorough investigative report on lynching in the South and began lecturing widely to call attention to the injustice. In 1895 she married a Chicago lawyer, Ferdinand Barnett, and moved to Chicago, where she continued her national campaign.

Yet another horrible set of lynchings took place in the spring of 1899, even as the Filipino-American War was under way overseas. During a period of six weeks, twelve black men were murdered by crowds of white men in two neighboring towns in Georgia. Investigating, Wells-Barnett found that "[t]he real purpose of these savage demonstrations is to teach the Negro that in the South he has no rights that the law will enforce."[17]

At the time, Addams's focus when it came to matters of race was on the injustices of social segregation in the North. During the 1890s she had sought ways to bring African Americans and white Americans together in Chicago, a highly segregated city. While there were hardly any African Americans living in the settlement house's neighborhood, Addams worked on her own social class. In 1893 an African American medical doctor, Harriet Rice, joined the all-white group of Hull House residents. In 1894–95, Addams endorsed the admission of the socially prominent, prosperous African American woman Fannie Barrier Williams to the Chicago Woman's Club, telling a reporter that if "all social barriers were abolish[ed]," everyone would benefit.[18]

In the summer of 1899, after Addams learned that the newly formed National Association of Colored Women's Clubs was to meet in Chicago, she contacted Wells-Barnett. The two had not met, but Addams knew that the journalist, who had been living in Chicago for five years, had organized a black women's club and often spoke to white women's clubs. She asked Wells-Barnett to extend an invitation to the officers of the association to lunch at Hull House. The officers came and dined.[19]

Wells-Barnett, delighted to make the acquaintance of the prominent social reformer, soon enlisted Addams in her cause. On December 12, 1899, Wells-Barnett hosted a mass meeting of mostly black, but also some white, women at her South Side church, Bethel AME, to protest racial lynchings. Several prominent white women active in municipal reform, including Addams, spoke.

It was her first speech against lynching, a subject about which she knew little. Disturbed, as most northerners were, by the violence, she rebutted the reasons southern white men, an audience not present in the room, gave for going outside the law to murder African Americans. White southerners said lynching was intended to stop black rapists by teaching them a lesson. Addams accepted the premise that the rapes had taken place but not the conclusion. "Let us assume," she said, "that the Southern citizens who take part in and abet the lynching of Negroes honestly believe that that is the only successful method of dealing with a certain class of crimes." In those days the word "rape" was avoided in polite society. "We would send this message to our fellow citizens of the South who are . . . trying to suppress vice [i.e., rape] by violence: that the bestial in man can never be controlled by public cruelty and dramatic punishment[.]" Lynching, she added, is a "savage method of dealing with criminality."[20]

Addams knew both her assumptions were not always true and said so. Sometimes, she said, lynchers "convince[d] themselves" they were doing right or embraced a justification later "to cover and support their deeds." Moreover, she acknowledged, "I have said nothing of the innumerable chances of punishing an innocent man [in order to] avoid confusing the main issue"—i.e., lawlessness.[21] But she said these things in passing; the main issue about lynching, she said, was that it was outside the law.

Wells-Barnett agreed that the lawlessness of lynching was a serious problem but felt profoundly that the racial injustice involved was even more serious. She was hugely disappointed in Addams's speech because it failed to acknowledge that the majority of lynchings were punishment for racially charged misbehavior, not for an actual crime. Yet it is not clear she said anything afterward to Addams. Perhaps she told herself the speech would be forgotten; perhaps, despite her general fearlessness and bluntness, Wells-Barnett hesitated to criticize someone she considered "the greatest woman in the United States."[22] In any case, thirteen months later, when Addams published the speech, slightly edited, in the national social reform journal the *Independent,* Wells-Barnett decided she had to speak up. A few months later the *Independent* published her rebuttal, "Lynching and the Excuse for It."

Wells-Barnett praised Addams for highlighting the contempt for the law that lynching showed but called her decision to focus on how best to deal with black rapists "unfortunate," "unwarrantable," and "baseless." Four-fifths of the men who were lynched were not even accused of rape, she said. They were certainly not the "moral monsters" they were being painted to be. In good journalistic fashion, Wells-Barnett supplied the reader with the statistics for the past five years: Only 96 of the 504 victims had been charged with rape, while 229 had been charged with insulting or "wronging" a white person. The record, she noted pointedly, is "easily within the reach of everyone who wants it." Her source, she added, was the *Chicago Tribune,* which for the past fifteen years had published on January 1 a record of all the lynchings in the previous year.[23] It was one of Addams's local papers. Clearly, she had not done her homework and was properly rebuked.

Of course arguments based on facts were not Addams's forte in 1899. The equally interesting question is why she did not grasp how offensive it was to African Americans, the audience in the room, that innocent African Americans *in any numbers* were being killed. Part of the answer seems to be that Addams, being white, was thinking about the lesson she needed to teach white southerners. That in itself is interesting. Apparently she, like many white northerners in the decades after the

Civil War, felt superior to white southerners when it came to race relations. It seems that her feelings of benevolence blinded her to the true
moral issue involved.

But there was also another reason for her failure, and once again it
illustrated the wisdom of her own advice to learn from experience.
Most likely she wrote the speech using knowledge gained from whatever
she had read and perhaps conversations with white southerners. It is
doubtful she knew any lynchers or southern African Americans personally. Certainly she had not been to a lynching. She had not felt the cold,
inhuman hatred in the white crowd as it cheered the sight of a limp
black body at the end of a noose, nor had she listened at a kitchen table
to African Americans tell how they had lost innocent family members
or friends to the violence or how they lived in constant fear of being
lynched. Instead the furthest her imagination could reach was to the
minds of the white men who did the murdering and the white people
who supported it.

It was true that she knew a former southern African American she
could have talked to, Ida Wells-Barnett. But apparently she did not
seek out Wells-Barnett to listen to her story, either before Addams gave
the speech in 1899 or before she published it thirteen months later.
Despite Addams's good intentions and her philosophical wisdom, her
sympathies were bound by her experience. Perhaps, after reading Wells-
Barnett's courteous but hard-hitting essay, she realized her mistake and
concluded that she should not speak in depth on subjects she had not
learned about first-hand, even when pressed by a friend and the times to
do so. In any case, although she continued to oppose lynching publicly,
she never gave an entire speech about lynching again.

||||||||||||

Shortly after her lynching speech was published, on September 6, 1901,
the same day that Jane Addams turned forty-one, she felt for the second
time in her life the unforgettable shock of learning that the president

of the United States had been shot. And once more, by a strange coincidence, she knew someone who knew the assassin.

President William McKinley had been shaking hands with the crowd at the Pan-American Exposition in Buffalo, New York, when he was shot and seriously wounded by a self-proclaimed anarchist. The would-be assassin was Leon Czolgosz. Born in the United States, he had become an enthusiast for anarchism only recently, after hearing the Russian-born anarchist Emma Goldman speak in his hometown of Cleveland. The detectives on the case suspected Czolgosz was not acting alone, especially when he told them that he had passed through Chicago on his way to Buffalo and met some anarchists there, including a man named Abraham Isaak. The detectives assumed immediately that Isaak had incited Czolgosz to commit violence. In fact, Isaak was a gentle, scholarly man who published the anarchist newspaper the *Free Society* and believed in the Tolstoyan nonresistant form of anarchism, a peaceful antigovernment individualism.

Now the nation's eyes turned to Chicago, already famous as a hotbed of anarchism. The *Chicago Tribune* editorialized, "How is society to guard itself against this Anarchist peril?"[24] Within hours the city's detectives arrested and charged Isaak, his wife and daughter, and eight other Chicago anarchists with "co-conspiracy to commit murder." They were denied lawyers and put in jail. Isaak's friends immediately appealed to Addams for help while also mocking the justice of the legal system in which he and the others were now innocently ensnared. "You see what becomes of your boasted law," they told her.[25]

Addams knew that the anarchists expected government to be cruel and unjust and that this expectation had been confirmed by Isaak's arrest. She was determined to show them American law was fair and impartial. She and a labor lawyer named Raymond Robins, who was also upset about the arrest, got the mayor's permission to meet with Isaak, whom both knew, to reassure him that he and the others would be treated fairly. Robins was impressed that Addams would risk her reputation in this way. "In all this great city," he later wrote, "just one person of position and influence . . . dared stand with me against the popular outcry. . . . [Jane Addams] stood like a stone wall."[26]

It was not clear how much their visit with the "co-conspirators" accomplished (they did get a lawyer eventually), but the fact that Robins and especially the more famous Addams had visited them at all was big news and widely reported in the national and even international press. British magazine editor W. T. Stead, writing from London, told her he feared that Isaak and the others would be lynched. Indeed, the day after Isaak and the others were arrested, on two different Chicago street corners, Isaak's supposed co-conspirator Czolgosz was hanged in effigy.

Addams paid a price for supporting the civil rights of Isaak and the other anarchists. People threw stones at Hull House's windows, and she received hundreds of abusive and hostile letters from Americans all over the country, which, as she recalled, "made my mail a horror every morning." Many were convinced that she was a champion of (violent) anarchism. Wealthy donors, including Mrs. Potter Palmer, were offended and withdrew their financial support from Hull House. Finally, in mid-September, a few days after President McKinley had died, the Chicago police decided that Czolgosz had acted alone and announced that the anarchists would soon be released. Addams, writing to a friend, said she looked forward to that moment, when "the troublous days [will] come to an end."[27]

In the Isaak case, as in her antilynching speech, Addams defended the principle that the U.S. government stood for the fair enforcement of the law. But this time her argument was morally central to the case. While most Chicagoans, across all classes, assumed Isaak's guilt given his anarchist loyalties, Addams, confident of his innocence, took a stand for legal justice. Her passion for fairness, as embodied in the law properly enforced, was rock solid. That her view was unpopular carried no weight with her. This was one of those times when the fact that she saw things differently from most people required her, as she put it in *Democracy and Social Ethics*, to "express her variation."

||||||||||||

By September 1901, Jane Addams had been living in Hull House for twelve years. During that time the settlement house had changed a great deal. The Hull mansion was now encircled, by dint of much fund-raising, by five buildings. In addition to the art gallery and the gymnasium-clubhouse building, there was a children's building, where the kindergarten, day care programs, and clubs and classes were housed; a cooperative apartment building for workingwomen; and a coffeehouse-theater building. Hull House's popularity among Chicagoans was legion, despite its sometimes rocky reputation as a radical hotbed. Every week some seven thousand people all of ages thronged to its

Julia Lathrop in the 1890s

clubs, lectures, classes, and meetings. There were now twenty (unpaid) residents, some of them in charge of a department, whether it was the clubs, or the coffee house, or the music school. Paid staff did the cooking, cleaning, and maintenance.[28] A five-person board had been created when the settlement was incorporated as Hull House Association in 1895; these good friends and major donors served long years and stalwartly kept the settlement flourishing.

Addams was the head resident and in charge, but because she believed that independence spurred creativity and a sense of responsibility, she held the reins of control lightly. Louise de Koven Bowen, a longtime volunteer and donor to Hull House, remembered: "Miss Addams had a rare way of . . . letting [people] work out their own plans; [afterward] she always commended them for what they had done, although in a very wise way, she [helped] them see . . . how . . . it might be bettered another time." This light touch meant that when she traveled and someone else—usually Julia Lathrop—filled in for her, Hull House continued to hum along.[29] When she was home, she was not so much the person to decide as the person to consult. Her days consisted of interruptions. A working mother might need to leave her child someplace while she went to work, or the leader of a women's trade union might need a meeting place, or a board member from the Civic Federation of Chicago might want a good progressive to fill the job of head of the Chicago Sanitary Bureau, or the founder of the new Jewish settlement might ask her to help him raise money by introducing him to one of Hull House's major donors, or a neighbor might ask if she could get a man's life sentence reduced. As an observer noted, "[i]n her own home, she is at everyone's beck and call."[30]

Famous visitors flocked to the house. Accomplished Americans were curious and impressed. Political journalist Walter Lippmann praised the settlement as "friendly, beautiful, sociable, and open" and the embodiment, in miniature, of what "civilization might be like." Economic journalist Henry Demarest Lloyd, a good friend of Addams's, called Hull House "the best club in Chicago" because, unlike any other club, it allowed men and women to associate "under one roof." Europeans were equally curious. Economic journalist Ida Tarbell, another visitor, recalled that Hull House was *the* place everyone visiting Chicago from overseas wanted to see.[31] Often these guests came to dinner. One evening those who dined included, in addition to Addams, Prince Peter Kropotkin, the nonviolent anarchist and founder of the Russian anarchism movement; the philosopher John Dewey; the German American conductor of the New York Symphony Orchestra Walter Damrosch; and the socialist mayor of Toledo, Ohio, Samuel L. "Golden Rule" Jones.[32] It must have been an interesting conversation.

To an outsider, Hull House was glamorous. To Addams, it was, first of all, her home and a residential community. What gratified her the most, she later wrote, was not "any understanding or response from without . . . [but] the consciousness that a growing group of residents was gathering at Hull House, held together in that soundest of all social bonds, the companionship of mutual interests."[33] Ten years after the settlement had opened, some of the earliest residents, including Ellen Gates Starr and Julia Lathrop, were still there, but not all. It had been a blow to Addams when Florence Kelley, after losing her job as state factory inspector, moved in 1899 to New York City to head the National Consumers League and take up residence at the Henry Street Settlement. But their companionship held. Kelley often returned to Hull House to visit as she crisscrossed the country on speaking tours, and she regularly sought Addams's advice.[34]

Addams also relished the idea that the Hull House group could lead "a life of upright purpose," as she put it, yet avoid the unappealing aspects of moral earnestness. A settlement, she wrote, should "make clear that one need not be . . . solemn in order to be wise."[35] It was a new insight and personal. A childhood friend recalled that Addams had been without much of a sense of humor in her twenties and had gained one from the ribald company of Ellen Gates Starr, Florence Kelley, Julia Lathrop, and Mary Rozet Smith. Friends from later years recalled Addams's "whimsical humor" and her "keen . . . wit."[36] Addams, recognizing she had grown in this way, responded completely in character: She philosophized about the moral significance of being able to laugh. "A sense of humor in life ... [is a] trait which we ... associate ... with the mature mind of wide and tolerant experience."[37] It was certainly true for her.

Yet her sadness was always there too, for those able to see it. Her nephew Weber Linn, who knew her well, thought she had "sad eyes but smiling lips."[38] A resident of Hull House described her as "sad-eyed, with a great weariness in her face."[39] A reform colleague wrote, "She did look sad, but how delightfully [sic] she looked when she smiled...."[40] Burdened by the childhood losses of her mother, sister, and father and by a lack of meaningful purpose, Addams had struggled with depression in the 1880s, but once she moved to Halsted Street, she faced more of a gray undertow of sadness. To restore her cheerfulness, she relied on the exuberant, irrepressible joy of the children who came to Hull House's after-school programs (these were lucky ones who did not have to work ten-hour days), the laughter of the community of residents she lived among, and, most of all, Mary Rozet Smith.

They were partners in the work of Hull House, of course. Mary shared Jane's devotion to the settlement; she was a frequent volunteer, a member of its board of directors, and a reliable and generous major donor. But they also shared a devotion to each other that both thought the equivalent of marriage. In 1902 Jane wrote Mary, away in Europe: "You must know, dear, how I long for you all the time.... There is reason in the habit of married folk keeping together." A few years later, after they had spent a month together in the summer, Jane wrote Mary wistfully from the road of "the healing domesticity" they had shared.[41] When both were in Chicago, Jane would scribble a quick note to Mary inviting her to come for dinner with an interesting guest or to attend a concert or play at Hull House. These letters, addressed to "Dearest" or "Darling," are the only traces left of their regular companionship when both were in the city.

Mary's presence mattered to Jane. In a poem Jane wrote to her on

Jane Addams and Mary Rozet Smith, 1890s

her birthday in 1900, Jane remembered how sad she had been growing up "because there was no Mary Smith to lighten all my woes" and how now, "with Mary Smith beside me, . . . no woes betide me."[42] When one or the other was traveling, Jane would write Mary about how she waited impatiently for a letter from her, "my best beloved," and how, when one came, it "cheered me mightily."[43] In 1902, just after *Democracy and Social Ethics* had been published, Jane was out of town on a lecture tour and feeling blue about the book's inadequacies. She wrote Mary, "I have . . . time here to think about you a great deal and you have been a great solace in the midst of terrible throes about the awful book."[44]

||||||||||||

The sadness Addams carried inside her mingled imperceptibly with the reasons for sadness all around her on Halsted Street, what one friend called "the sorrows of the neighborhood." Another friend thought that she looked sad "because the times in which she lived were sad." Addams spoke of her sadness rarely and obliquely. "We" are sometimes "filled with a sense of the futility of our efforts," she observed.[45]

The suffering in the lives of workingwomen and working children haunted her the most. She knew so many women and young children who worked ten- or twelve-hour days for tiny wages, whose health was broken by the difficult labor and poor diet that a life of poverty required, and whose creative spirit had been drained out of them by the rigors of work and lack of chance to play, read, and dream.

Addams was puzzled that the wider public was untroubled by this suffering. In every community, she observed, the tendency was strong "not to see the evil effect of child labor." There was an equal public tolerance for the long hours women (and men) worked. Sometimes her frustration simply, and uncharacteristically, exploded. To an audience of earnest Christians at the Chautauqua Institution, a prosperous group that studied the Bible and believed themselves to have a social conscience but mostly were not active politically, she spoke frankly: "We go along thinking that things in America will come through all right. If we could only get it into our minds that this is a stupid thing to do!"[46]

If it was stupid to trust that things would work out, the question remained what should be done. In the years since Illinois had adopted its first sweatshop law, Addams had joined others in lobbying the legislature to improve it, but with meager results. What next? Should the state campaigns for child labor legislation be coordinated and better supported? Could the American Federation of Labor, founded in 1886, do more for women trade unionists? Or would some other approach be needed? Reformers were always looking for ways to increase their impact. As the new century opened, creative ideas were percolating, sparked by the widening sense that these campaigns were of national importance. Addams was ready to cooperate.

|||||||||||

In the United States in 1900 child labor was widespread and growing along with industry, especially in the South. Millions of children worked with their families or alone in fields, sweatshops, mines, and cotton mills, laboring ten- to twelve-hour days, sometimes in dank, stifling conditions, with dangerous equipment, sometimes under the brutal summer sun, and without the freedom to leave.[47] They were in fact, despite the small wages they brought home to their parents, slaves.

The reformers—union members, women's club members, and settlement house workers—wanted strong child labor laws in every state. A strong law was one that barred children under fourteen from working in any industry, required them to attend school for the whole school year, and limited older children to an eight- or ten-hour day. By 1902 about half the states had strong child labor laws; the rest had either no laws or weak laws. In the South, where child labor was often unregulated, children as young as five were working all night in the cotton mills. In the North laws were weakly enforced. Parents lied about their children's ages so the children could drop out of school and work.

In Illinois in 1902 the same alliance of clubwomen and trade unionists, male and female, that had pushed through the state's first sweatshop law in 1893 now formed a coalition to improve the child labor provisions of the legislation. This time both had statewide organizations—the Illinois Federation of Women's Clubs and the Illinois Federation of Labor—through which to work. Addams did not serve on the bill-drafting committee, but she presented the proposed bill to the labor federation and gave speeches endorsing the legislation everywhere she could—to the neighborhood women's clubs of various settlement houses, to the Chicago women's suffrage league, and to the League of Cook County Clubs—that were publicized in the Chicago press.

When the lobbying began in early 1903, Addams led the campaign as chair of the Industrial Committee of the Illinois Federation of Women's Clubs. Her friend Raymond Robins, now the head of another settlement house in Chicago and also on the committee, watched her at work and took her measure. She was "simple as a child, with a heart of oak and a brain like a Damascus Blade, looking out from quiet steadfast eyes with reaching honesty and unfaltering constancy." To the delight of its advocates, the bill passed the legislature as the federation had drafted it. Addams was happy not only that she and others had done something good for children in the state but that they had done it in a way

Florence Kelley, 1900

that embodied how democracy ought to work. As she later observed, "Social advance depends as much upon the process through which it is secured as upon the result itself."[48] Democracy was about means as much as ends.

The next step—obvious in hindsight but novel at the time—was to create a national body to coordinate work on state child labor laws. Florence Kelley, among others, saw the need. As general secretary of the National Consumers League she had been supporting city and state groups across the country in their fight for strong state labor legislation using consumer boycotts of clothes without the union label as one means of leverage. She cofounded the New York Child Labor Committee in 1902, and she had come to Chicago several times to help with the Illinois campaign. In 1903 she and Lillian Wald, the head of the Henry Street Settlement and a good friend of Kelley's and Addams's, helped organize the National Child Labor Committee (NCLC).[49]

The new organization, formally launched in 1904 and headquartered in New York City, was not cross-class in its leadership, however. The committee consisted of thirty-five members, including a number of journalists, writers, professors, and ministers, all of them prominent and none of them working class. Its purpose, as publicized in the *New York Times*, was to make sure existing state laws were enforced, help strengthen those laws, and get new ones passed. The two main means were to educate the public investigating current conditions in key states and to support the work of newly formed state child labor committees and its close allies—women's clubs, consumers' leagues, and trade unions.[50]

Addams joined the committee, one of only four women, but did not join the board in its early years (she joined later, in 1911). Instead she chaired the Industrial Committee of the General Federation of Women's Clubs as it conducted a groundbreaking study of child labor legislation in all the states.[51]

Her other role was as the inspiring assembler and disseminator of persuasive arguments. Her speeches at the committee's annual meetings and at other national conferences were turned into pamphlets for the state child labor committees to circulate. In these she challenged the arguments used by manufacturers and legislators who opposed reform—that child labor taught children the value of hard work, that large numbers of widows relied on their children's labor, and that business needed cheap child labor to survive—but she mostly emphasized the positive moral case, the urgent need to nurture children's individual gifts. Imagine a time, she told one audience, "when city children are free from premature labor, . . . when they have a chance to use some initiative, to plan for their own futures in relation to the things that they like to do."[52] It upset her that Americans thought it was less important to nurture children than to keep the price of clothing cheap. We "are imperiling our civilization . . . by wantonly sacrificing to that materialism the eternal spirit of youth, the power of variation."[53] Hoping to shock her audiences, she claimed even unsupervised play would be better for the children than factory work. "I would rather that children were allowed to run in the streets than have them working in factories at a tender age."[54] In her mind freedom was always better than slavery.

The 1893 Illinois sweatshop law had also sought to improve working conditions for women. In 1903 the issue remained on the table, not only in Illinois, where the state supreme court had knocked down the eight-hour law in the bill, but nationwide. The national trade union organization, the American Federation of Labor, might have led the fight, but the AF of L was essentially a federation of men's unions, and it was at best inconsistent in how it treated women trade unionists. In 1892 it had hired and quickly fired its first national women's organizer, Mary Kenney, the union leader Addams had welcomed to Hull House two years before. Two more times in the 1890s it hired and fired a woman organizer. Less than 2 percent of the almost five hundred delegates attending the AF of L national convention in 1903 were women, despite the fact that at the time, to consider only one city, 16 percent of the members of the Chicago Federation of Labor were women.[55]

In truth the federation and its affiliated trade unions did not believe that married women should be working at all. The president of the AF of L, Samuel Gompers, published an essay in its magazine in 1906 titled "Should the Wife Help to Support the Family?" His answer was no. And most married women, from those living in dire or stretched circumstances to those in the leisured classes, conformed to the expectation that they not work. In 1900 only 5.6 percent of married women worked, while 44 percent of single women worked, as did 30 percent of those who were widowed (or abandoned) or divorced.[56] Institutions reinforced the cultural view. Sears, Roebuck refused to hire married women as clerks. School boards fired female teachers when they married.

Aside from such institutional obstacles in their path, married women stayed home for many reasons. Most women wanted to be home to raise their children or could not imagine being married and working. Often this was because they had husbands who expected them not to work, but another obstacle was the kind of work available to them. While women with skills could find satisfying, challenging jobs—like doctoring, lawyering, nursing, teaching (if single), trade union organizing, operating a small business, charity, or school, doing social work, writing, lecturing, newspaper reporting, or working in some of the highly skilled trades, like bookbinding and shoemaking—many women had no marketable skills and worked in whatever situation they could find. They held some of the most unappealing jobs, jobs that were repetitive, boring, and exhausting, required ten- to twelve-hour workdays, and were seriously underpaid. Addams knew many married women in her neighborhood, which was the kind of neighborhood where the few married women who worked were concentrated, who longed to stay home with their children rather than mop floors in office buildings late at night.

Whatever their situation, women *were* working, and like the men, if they worked in industry, they needed unions to negotiate better wages, shorter working hours, and safer working conditions. When they were barred from joining the men's unions, as often happened, they organized separate women's unions, but the AF of L refused them affiliation. By 1903 some of the most determined women trade union leaders, including Mary Kenney, were fed up. She had married in the mid-1890s, becoming Mary Kenney O'Sullivan, and moved to Boston, but was now widowed. Conversations among trade union women and settlement leaders in Chicago, New York, and Boston, including Addams, led to a plan: to re-create a national version of the now-defunct Illinois Woman's Alliance, the cross-class organization that had thrived in Chicago in the first part of the 1890s under Kenney's leadership and with which Addams had cooperated. There was also a British model they could adopt, or at least they could adopt the name, the Women's Trade Union League. A wealthy young man, William English Walling, formerly a resident and assistant factory inspector at Hull House and now a resident at the University Settlement in New York City, was dispatched to England to do research and report back.

Urged on by Walling, the Women's Trade Union League (WTUL) (later named the National Women's Trade Union League) was formed in the fall of 1903. The WTUL was the first national group dedicated to organizing women workers. It filled a crucial function in the trade union movement, not only by creating unions and supporting strikes, especially of unorganized women workers, but also by developing leaders. Trade union women held paid jobs as organizers for the WTUL and its branches, made lifelong friendships, and built strong reform networks.

The WTUL immediately confronted the delicate question of what mix of people to have on its board. The trade union women, mindful of the need to keep their voices dominant in an organization committed to labor organizing, insisted that the prosperous women, whom they called allies, agree to a crucial bylaw requirement: Women labor organizers would be a majority of the WTUL board and a majority of the membership of the league. (The issue was not so easily resolved, however, and was to be a source of tension in the league's branches for years to come.[57])

Thus the new national board was made up of five trade union organizers with settlement house experience and four settlement leaders with experience cooperating with trade unions, many linked by friendship. Jane Addams, who became vice president, was a friend of the board's secretary, Mary Kenney O'Sullivan, as well as of board members Lillian Wald, the head of the Henry Street Settlement in New York City, and Mary McDowell, the head of the University of Chicago Settlement. Wald and O'Sullivan had similar ties. The president, Mary Kehew—a Boston Brahmin with a long history of activism on behalf of women workers and a friend of O'Sullivan's—and Addams were given the top officer positions to lend prestige to the new organization. It was an experienced group, ready to undertake the tasks it had set for itself: to organize more women into trade unions and support women workers when they went out on strike. Local branches were established in New York, Boston, and Chicago and sought affiliations with their local labor federations. In Chicago, Jane Addams chaired the meeting at Hull House that organized the Illinois (later Chicago) Women's Trade Union League.[58]

Addams was happy to join the league's national board. It was the first national board she had ever sat on. The new organization's belief in the value of the self-empowerment of working people and its cross-class methods appealed to her. If the National Child Labor Committee was about an elite leadership coordinating state efforts, the Women's Trade Union League was about workers organizing at the grass roots, supported by the resources of prosperous women and coordinated by a board of organizers and allies. In a word, the league was more democratic. In *Democracy and Social Ethics*, Addams wrote that "unless all men and all classes contribute to [achieving] a good, we cannot even be sure it is worth having."[59] The league embodied her belief that the prosperous class should cooperate with the working class on behalf of the workers.

The WTUL was all about gender solidarity. Supporting women's strikes was a crucial part of the national league's and its branches' work. In 1904 it supported strikes in Aurora, Illinois; Troy, New York; and Fall River, Massachusetts. There was a sensible division of responsibilities during a strike. While the trade unionists worked with the strikers on their labor actions, the allies from the nearest local branch helped by raising money for strike funds, providing strike headquarters, joining the strikers on the picket lines in order to inhibit police abuse, bailing out the strikers if they were arrested, and publicizing the grievances to generate public support. The same sort of strategy was used in Chicago during the citywide Garment Strike of 1910–11, which was ultimately successful. Addams and Ellen Gates Starr walked the picket line and helped raise money for the relief fund. Addams also mediated the strike.[60]

Addams understood that some prosperous women would be embarrassed to be associated with the labor movement because they disap-

New York City garment workers at the time of a strike

proved of it. She explained to a Berkeley, California, audience in 1905 that she and other settlement women had joined the Women's Trade Union League because they wanted to "stand with" the union women, "to share their blunders with them as well as their successes." It was unrealistic, she said, to support only those movements that made no mistakes. "No moral movement has been without its perplexities," she told them. "To enlist in a cause which has none is to enlist in a dead cause, one with a tombstone."[61] As for the mistakes the allies might make, Addams knew the problems that arose from her class's tendency toward self-righteousness masked as benevolence. If her hopes were high, her expectations were realistic about what lay ahead.

|||||||||||

One of the striking things about Jane Addams was her synthesizing mind. While she worked toward specific goals like better state child labor laws and stronger women's trade unions, she also stepped back from the details and tried to see the picture whole, tried to identify the abstract truth that the details suggested. Recently, she had been pondering two questions—why democratic institutions failed their citizens so much of the time and what new ideal could make them more able to support their citizens and their development. She thought she knew what a person living in a democracy needed to do to be ethically responsible; now she was wrestling with the question of what democratic institutions, from settlement houses and trade unions to the administrative operations of government, needed to do.

Addams counted the U.S. entry into the Spanish-American and Filipino-American Wars as among the ways that democratic institutions had failed. It was therefore crucial to find ways for pro-peace citizens to express their views. In the next few years she, along with thousands of others, became even more involved in the peace movement. In 1900 she spoke to an enormous crowd at a mass rally in Chicago organized to support the Boers in their revolt against Great Britain's colonial rule; in 1902 she helped resuscitate the Chicago Peace Society; and in 1904 she gave three addresses at the Universal Peace Congress in Boston.[62] In addition, the convening of the world's first International Peace Conference at The Hague, the Netherlands, in 1899 added to the sense of forward motion that was building among enthusiasts, enhanced the movement's prestige, and made it easy to organize for peace.

But how exactly did issues of war and peace fit together with Addams's domestic reform agenda? And where was her thinking heading? In a new book, *Newer Ideals of Peace*, she set out in a single integrated argument her understanding of the social-political problems her nation and the world faced and the social-political vision they should now embrace. These ideas were to guide her reform work for the rest of her life.

Like *Democracy and Social Ethics*, this second book had been gestating for a long time. She had first used the title "Newer Ideals of Peace" for several lectures in 1902 and had a contract with Macmillan to publish the book by early 1903, but the writing came slowly, because of the vagueness of her ideas and the demands on her time, as she explained apologetically to her editor, Edward Marsh. To be sure, some of the book would be partly recycled material. Of the eight chapters, two would be edited versions of published speeches, and two of published articles; with small adjustments she brought them into the larger framework the book imposed. But she was writing half the book from scratch. For several years Marsh and her publisher at Macmillan, George Brett, and the series editor, Professor Richard T. Ely, who taught at the University of Wisconsin, had been pushing her to complete the manuscript. Ely invited her to do a twelve-part summer lecture series on "newer ideals of peace" at the University of Wisconsin–Madison the summer of 1906 with that goal in mind, and she agreed, telling him, "It will be the only way to get my book written."[63]

The other reason she was having a hard time writing was that she had set herself a big challenge. This was evident in the high quality of what she eventually produced. With its tightly conceived, many-faceted argument, *Newer Ideals* was the most intellectually ambitious book she would ever write. She intended it to be a work of theoretical sociology, suited for adoption in the college classroom—i.e., for the same audience as her Wisconsin lectures—although she also hoped for a popular readership. To write such a book, she set aside her love of story and vignette (she included a few) and the goal of arousing sympathy and instead marshaled the power of her strong, logical mind to analyze and synthesize a huge subject. The result was a cogent, conceptually bold book. At the same time, it did not present material with a strictly linear logic. The basic argument was present on nearly every page and was enriched in layers, in a circular way. In both content and rhetorical strategy, *Newer Ideals* was a tour de force.

As in her first book, Addams argued that an out-of-date ethic was lingering too long and blocking the spread of a newer, more democratic ethic, an ethic more attuned to a highly industrial age. Here she fleshed out the point she had first made in her 1899 speech against the Filipino-American War: that militarism was an old-fashioned ethic, while humanitarianism, which she also called "the new patriotism," or "the newer ideals of peace," was the rising new ethic. It was militarism that was making democratic institutions fail, and it was humanitarianism that would help them thrive. She might have titled the book "The Necessary End of Militarism" or "The Rise of Humanitarianism" or perhaps "Democracy and the New Patriotism."

In Addams's day the term "militarism" often referred to the belief that a nation could avoid war—i.e., keep the peace—only by having a strong military. But it was also used, notably by Herbert Spencer, an influential British sociologist whose books Addams had read, to refer to a certain spirit or worldview. Spencer equated militarism with barbarism, since the military served the primitive functions of defense and attack, and peace with civilization. In *Newer Ideals* Addams broadened the meaning of militarism. To her it meant relying on physical force as the ultimate solution to every difficulty, not just in international relations, but also in other ways: seeing enemies, whether overseas or around the corner, where there were none; distrusting the people; adopting laws that institutionalized that distrust; being content with "the passive results of order and discipline"; pursuing "conquest and repression"; basing a nation's patriotism upon war; and admiring excessively the courage and daring that war required.[64]

She saw militarism everywhere. She saw it in the way that city government disdained and distrusted immigrants as if they were "the conquered people." She saw it in the way that industry, distrusting labor unions, refused to negotiate, leading to unjust labor conditions and class warfare. She saw it in the way that male voters, distrusting women, refused to give them the vote, leading to the socially damaging result of public policies shaped by the views of only half the population. She saw it in the way that industry, disdaining the potential of poor children, employed them, leading to the narrowing of their futures. Most of all, she saw it in "the unrestricted commercial spirit," that, when it dominated a nation, she believed, led to war.[65] Addams had traveled some distance since the Pullman Strike, when she had been unwilling to side with the workers against the capitalist. Now she, along with many left-leaning workers and left-leaning prosperous progressives, believed that unregulated companies did serious harm to humanity. She did not express her views through sustained, hostile verbal attacks but in incisive sentences and through her political actions.

By "humanitarianism," Addams did not mean a kindly, helpful attitude toward those who suffered, its most common meaning. Nor did she mean the attitude of the eighteenth-century type of humanitarian, who, she wrote, "loved the people without really knowing them."[66] She meant something both more intimate and more "aggressive," an ideal that fully honored the "great reservoirs of human ability" of those usually seen as "inferior": workingmen and workingwomen, labor unions, immigrants, and women. (Because her experience was too limited, or her prejudices were too unexamined, she did not think to discuss two other excluded groups, African Americans and Native Americans.) Humanitarianism was inclusive, affectionate, and nurturing.[67] She was finding fresh, secular language to describe what she thought the early Christians meant by "love" and what Tolstoy meant by "nonresistance."

As humanitarianism spread, Addams argued, government would embrace the ideals of the workers. "The normal ideals of the laborer to [have] food and shelter for his family, a security for his own old age, and a larger opportunity for his children [should become] the ideals of democratic government." For example, workers often created mutual benefit societies; it would be better if the government created a system of insurance "to protect [everyone] against disaster" and "misfortune."[68] Workers wanted to end child labor. Therefore the government should investigate the harms of the practice. Addams was arguing, in essence, for expanding the government's roles, legislatively and through regulation, to make its work more in keeping with working people's ideals and experience.

Despite its title, the book did not have anything meaty to say about peace between nations or when world peace would be achieved. But its ideas about the forces shaping the possibilities of peace were thought-provoking. Addams rejected the oft-repeated platitude that as nations became more "civilized"—i.e., more educated—peace would follow. She believed working people around the world, and especially the United States, were gaining and spreading the humanitarian values that would lead to peace. Moreover, by "peace" she meant not the absence of war but "the unfolding of worldwide processes making for the nurture of human life." The change was coming because immigrants from many nations, and particularly those in her own country, were learning "to live together in forbearance and understanding" in cities like Chicago. She called this "a rising tide of moral feeling" among millions of people. Writing as a prophet, Addams saw the day coming when immigrant and native Chicagoans might, without dishonoring the varied cultures and customs brought from the old countries, "fuse together all nations of men into the newest and, perhaps, the highest type of citizenship." Writing as a realist, she added that this opportunity would be "wantonly" wasted if "race and national animosity" were aroused.[69] In sum, she was not saying that war would disappear soon but that a countervailing force was strengthening. She was not making a moral argument so much as describing how evolving morality reshaped history by revising ideas in the light of experience.

She was also unearthing a possible "moral equivalent of war." Harvard psychologist-philosopher William James had coined the famous phrase in his 1898 masterpiece, *The Varieties of Religious Experience*, which Addams read and loved. She used the phrase, crediting him, in *Newer Ideals*.[70] He had borrowed the idea, although not the phrase, from an essay titled "War" by Ralph Waldo Emerson, a favorite writer and a close friend of his father. Emerson and James both wanted peace to inspire in men (not women) the same heroism that war so easily aroused. But both also painted in broad strokes a "spiritual reform" in the "social realm" (James) that would raise men to the "height of moral cultivation" and create "a nation of lovers" (Emerson).[71] Who knows? Perhaps Addams had read "War" too, since Emerson was a favorite writer of hers. In a sense, *Newer Ideals* is one grand elaboration on what James and Emerson might have meant. She took the seeds of ideas planted in passing by two great philosophers, watered them with what she had learned on Halsted Street, and produced a veritable garden.

||||||||||||

"When will the book come out?" is every eager author's query. But for Jane Addams, the wait for the publication of *Newer Ideals* was particularly torturous. During the fall of 1906 she had kept one eye on the publication process and the other on an immigration bill moving through Congress that proposed, among other things, to bar immigrants over eighteen who could not read and write in their native languages from entering the United States. The provision made no mention of countries of origin, but everyone understood that it would effectively bar industrially unskilled immigrants from southern and eastern Europe, where, because of poor schools or none at all, a larger number of people from the countryside were unable to read.

In mid-December, when it was clear that the book would not be published until mid-January, Addams, in Washington, D.C., to lobby President Roosevelt about child labor issues, sent a desperate letter to her publisher at Macmillan, George Brett. "Affairs here are very critical in regard to the Immigration bill and I am very anxious to have some of the spiritual results of immigration put before certain people." She had given her page proofs to President Roosevelt the day before, she explained. Could Mr. Brett send page proofs to Senator Robert La Follette and to the Commissioner of Corporations in the Department of Commerce and Labor James R. Garfield, and send to Chicago four sets, which she would send out herself? Addams once wrote, "It is ideas which mold the lives of men," but her faith in the power of ideas was never more charmingly manifest than at this moment.[72]

Ethnic racism, always a strain in American politics, was heating up because of changing demographics. Between 1900 and 1906 the number of immigrants who arrived in the United States each year had more than doubled, with the biggest increases in the number of southern and eastern Europeans—Italians, Jews from Russia, Slavs, Greeks, Syrians, and Armenians—the "races" that, according to anthropologists, were objectively inferior to northern Europeans. One scientist wrote that the "new immigration" contained "a large number of the weak [and] the broken . . . drawn from the lowest stratum of the Mediterranean basin, the Balkans, [and] . . . the Polish ghettos." If the scientists were right, the trend looked most alarming for the country's future. The Immigrant Restriction League called immigration "the great American problem."[73]

Although Addams had no patience with xenophobia, the politics of the immigration bill were not simple for her. The American Federation of Labor wanted to keep cheap—i.e., nonskilled—labor out of the country; certain settlement house leaders, including Robert Woods of South End House in Boston, wanted an immigration policy to protect the so-called racial purity of "American stock"; and many women suffrage advocates favored a literacy test because they felt insulted that illiterate male European peasants could vote and they could not. On the other hand, immigrant organizations, including the 1.5 million-member German-American Alliance and a well-organized Jewish group, the National Liberal Immigration League, were stalwartly against restriction.

Addams stood with the immigrants. When the Speaker of the U.S. House of Representatives, Joseph Cannon, recruited her earlier in the year to write him a letter about the bill and to send a copy to the chairman of the Appropriations Committee, she sent him seven typed pages about the disruptions and suffering that the new restrictions would create in people's lives. "The regulation of immigration affects . . . the fate of hundreds of . . . persons desiring to join their families and friends in this country." She explained that she opposed the literacy test because it merely measured the level of education available in a person's community.[74]

In the end, President Roosevelt, who had supported the literacy restriction, agreed that it should be removed from the bill, not because he had discovered from reading Addams's book a new understanding of the "spiritual results of immigration" but in order to give himself and others the political leverage to add a provision, sought by some Californians, to ban not all Japanese but Japanese laborers, who had suddenly been flooding into the country, from entering the states. The bill passed Congress, and Roosevelt signed it. The new law was bad news for Japanese workers, now barred on racial and class grounds, but good news for European immigrants and their families. Clearly, President Roosevelt was neither the immigrants' friend nor their enemy. He was a consummate horse trader with his eye, in this case, on cultivating ties with Japan's leaders, who found the class-based restriction acceptable. Roosevelt used politics like a chess player, moving policies like pawns, always to strategic advantage and always with larger goals in mind.

Newer Ideals was published in January 1907 and met a mostly enthusiastic reception. William James read it immediately and wrote Addams with characteristic generosity and insight. He recognized the originality of her contribution to their shared interest in the idea of a "moral equivalent" of war. It is "hard to express the good [the book] has done me," he said, "in offering new view points and annihating old ones. Yours is a deeply original mind and all so quiet and harmless! Yet revolutionary in the extreme." On the other hand, some were uncomfortable with her subtle, circular style. Her friend George Herbert Mead, professor of sociology at the University of Chicago, reviewed the book for the *American Journal of Sociology*. He praised its ideas but added, "One does not feel, in reading Miss Addams, the advance of an argument with measured tread." The *New York Tribune* agreed, noting that the subject matter could have been "more logically organized." President Roosevelt, the passionate advocate for military preparedness, hated the book. In a letter to a friend he called Addams's ideas on militarism "preposterous" and Addams herself "foolish."[75]

With *Newer Ideals* Jane Addams, already a popular and admired figure, established herself as a major public intellectual. In 1907 she was one of the few women in the United States—possibly the only one—

to possess that stature. Believing in the power of large philosophical ideas to influence public attitudes and to improve the human condition, she remained an ethicist. But with her increasing skills as an advocate for state legislation and her greater interest in democratic institutions and the issues of international peace and patriotism, Jane Addams had become something very rare—an ethicist who was political too.

||||||||||||||||||||||||||||||||||||||||||||||||||||||||||||||||||||||||||||||||||||||||||||||||||||||||||||||||||||||||||||||||||||||||||||

CHAPTER FIVE

POLITICIAN

THE IMMIGRATION BILL was just the beginning of Addams's focus on federal legislative fights. By 1906 she and some of her friends on the National Child Labor Committee, including Florence Kelley and Lillian Wald, thought it essential to have a federal law banning child labor. "You can't protect children adequately if you pay too much attention to state lines," Addams told a *Chicago Tribune* reporter in late May. Protecting children and women state by state, she explained, was an uneven and frustrating process. If a strong law was passed in one state, the manufacturers often moved to another to keep children on their payrolls. She then posed a rhetorical question to the reporter: If the railroads could be regulated under interstate authority, ought not children's welfare be regulated, given that the country depended much more on its children than its railroads?[1]

It was a serious proposal. Addams and other anti–child labor advocates were seeking such legislation because it seemed the only way Congress would be able to ban child labor. The problem was the Tenth Amendment, part of the Bill of Rights. It stated that the powers that the Constitution did not delegate to the national government were retained by the states or the people. The idea of reserved state power was later referred to as states' rights, and it lay at the heart of the compromise that the thirteen original states, nervous about losing their independence, accepted in order to be willing to combine. They agreed that the new federal government had only the powers the Constitution authorized, leaving the states with the power to adopt legislation in all other areas.

But the Tenth Amendment also reserved whatever powers the national government or the states did not possess "to the people." The three words, heavy with unexplored implications, were as important to American democracy as another sentence in the Constitution, the first, "We, the people of the United States, . . . do ordain and establish this Constitution for the United States of America." The message of the Constitution was clear: The people held further, unspecified powers in their hands.

The rights of the states and the power of the people: These competing constitutional principles were the Founding Fathers' gifts to posterity; they set in motion conflicts that only politics could resolve.

||||||||||||

A few months after the *Tribune* reporter interviewed Addams, Senator Albert J. Beveridge of Indiana introduced a bill to ban states from shipping across state lines products partly or fully made by children. In a speech Addams gave at the National Child Labor Committee's annual conference soon after, she acknowledged with bite the need for the strategy: "If we have government in which human welfare is not to be considered as an [appropriate] object of direct governmental action and if we possess a well-rooted objection to humane legislation," then perhaps this is "the most American way to get at the matter."[2]

The committee's board hotly debated whether to endorse the Beveridge bill. The controversy was regional. Southerners thought it intruded on a state's right to regulate its own industries, but beneath this constitutional issue lurked a racial one—the white South was determined to protect its freedom to keep African Americans powerless. This was the historic burden of the constitutional argument, that it was a far more loaded question for the South than the North because for the South, whether the issue was a state's right to secede from the nation or to regulate child labor, it was always about race.

With some anguish, the board approved the Beveridge bill, and Roosevelt also endorsed it through a statement to the press. But the president, the son of a southerner, was really a states' rights man when it came to labor legislation, and he soon reverted to that position in his December 1906 annual message to Congress. Four months later the NCLC board did too, and for the same reason—in order, in Florence Kelley's words, "to please the south."[3] The Beveridge bill went nowhere in Congress in 1907, and the NCLC, and Addams too, dropped for the moment the idea of working for federal legislation. The committee would not try for a federal law again until 1913.

As both sides knew, the fight over the Beveridge bill was not just about child labor; it was about establishing the precedent of having Congress legislate a broad range of social reform proposals already accomplished in some of the states and now waiting in the wings for federal treatment. These included the eight-hour day, the six-day workweek, the right of labor to organize, a minimum wage for workers or, at least for women workers, and suffrage for women. The opponents to such a move included the Democratic Party, which had long been a states' rights party (it was the crucial reason it dominated in the South and vice versa). Furthermore, progressives in the South of *both* parties saw no reason to federalize such reforms.

But the biggest problem was the constitutional question, and the biggest obstacle was the U.S. Supreme Court, which also believed in states' rights. It was becoming clear that to achieve further progress in such reforms, Congress would either have to adopt legislation that the Supreme Court would judge constitutional or to pass an amendment to the Constitution that could then be ratified by three-fourths of the states. In the near future, reformers favoring the federal approach were to try both strategies repeatedly, though rarely with success. Nonetheless, their mere efforts were historic. It was not the New Dealers who started the revolution to make the federal government more powerful on behalf of the people; it was the progressives.

Wherever reforms were adopted, whether in city councils, state legislatures, or Congress, the push to undertake them came from millions of Americans. For more than two decades that political energy had been growing. The labor movement and farmers' cooperative movement of the 1870s became the farmers' and workers' populist movement of the 1880s and the People's Party of the 1890s. Both workers and farmers were frustrated. The workers thought that corporations kept wages too low and work hours too long. The farmers wanted the government to own the railroads and to loosen the money supply. They sought solutions from the state legislatures, but the legislators were generally too corrupted by corporate bribes to do much. Meanwhile, a third group began grumbling in the 1890s: the prosperous people in fast-growing cities who were frustrated with the poor public services of corrupt city governments.

The key to the progressive movement's rapid growth was its highly organized nature. The system's many rivulets were local groups, many of them not political in purpose, at least not at first. These were divided, as the cultural rules required, by class, sex, and race and included farm co-ops, trade unions, clubs (including ethnic ones), and civic federations, plus a few cross-class alliances. As frustrations grew, these groups began taking up political issues. Seeking greater influence, like groups flowed together into larger rivers of (still-segregated) state federations. By 1906 these had formed national bodies that had begun to coordinate state advocacy efforts. Those in the movement thought of the resulting river of civic energy as something akin to the great Mississippi, a river so wide and strong it could sweep away large obstacles in its path.

In fact the class, racial, and sexual divisions meant there was not one great Mississippi but something like six Ohio rivers and only partial agreement on reform goals. Only some in the upper middle class supported the demands of the working class for economic justice, few whites supported the demands of African Americans for racial justice, few men and not all women supported women's demands for political justice, and many Anglo-Saxon men and women wished to limit immigration and suffrage to those who could pass literacy tests. There were other divisions too: religious, urban-rural, and regional.

Who was a progressive? Populist farmers had begun using the word in the 1880s to signal their dissatisfaction with the status quo, and by the early twentieth century the label was widely popular. Generally it referred to anyone who was not a conservative. Conservatives distrusted the state. They believed that business should be unrestrained by government, that government's power should be strictly limited, and that progress happened naturally, over time, without organized effort and without government action. Progressives trusted government, believing that if it were reformed, it could improve life for Americans. They disagreed on what reforms to seek but agreed that businesses' corrupt influence on government should end and that governments—they were thinking at first only of local and state governments—should experiment with solutions and benefit from the expertise of the scientifically trained. So far, however, their impact on the United States had been spotty. Could the country's progressives sweep the states and become a national political movement? They would try. What reform movement would not want to be a single great Mississippi of American politics if it could?

||||||||||||

The social justice wing of the progressive movement tackled mainly problems resulting from the ongoing process, begun in the early nineteenth century, of massive industrialization, but two problems on its agenda had existed since the nation's founding: the unequal treatment of African Americans and the unequal treatment of women. By the time progressivism was organizing itself nationally in the early twentieth century, slavery was gone, but slavery's vicious, pervasive residue, racism, was not. Moreover, in most states, women still did not have the vote. Between 1906 and 1909 Addams began working on both issues through national organizations.

She joined the suffrage campaign first, recruited, it appears, by Florence Kelley. Kelley believed that working-class women could be a huge force for political change once they had the vote and that the National American Woman Suffrage Association was making a mistake in excluding them from its organized campaign. The National finally agreed, and Kelley joined its board in 1905. She recruited not only Addams but also labor organizer Mary Kenney O'Sullivan, her old friend from her Hull House days, who had worked for her as an assistant state factory inspector. Both attended the National American convention for the first time in 1906 and gave speeches.

The leaders of the convention were particularly honored to have Addams come. They put her up at the same Baltimore house where past president Susan B. Anthony and President Anna Howard Shaw were staying, and it was Addams who was the guest of honor at a dinner given by the hostess, the wealthy philanthropist Mary Garrett. Anthony, who celebrated her eighty-sixth birthday at the convention, was as determined as ever, telling the convention, "Failure is impossible."[4]

Anthony surely remembered having invited Addams to join the campaign eleven years before. We can easily imagine her greeting Addams in the Garrett parlor in her usual blunt fashion, "Well, it took you long enough." Addams's presence at the convention proved to be more than token. Although suffrage was not then her absorbing passion, it was to become so. She may not have realized it then, but her meeting with Anthony, who would die of heart failure a month later, amounted to the passing of the torch.

Beginning in 1906, Addams argued repeatedly for suffrage. She traveled thousands of miles, speaking from California to New York State and to every sort of audience: clubs, labor unions, colleges, reform conferences, teachers' meetings, churches, and large public gatherings, the Chicago Teachers' Federation, the New York City Women's Political Union, Smith College, and the Boston School Voters' League. In 1908 she even gave a suffrage speech at the International Women's Suffrage Alliance meeting in London. Mostly she was warmly welcomed but not always. The University of Michigan, for example, forbade her to speak on campus because the subject of women's suffrage was too controversial. Addams's speeches and essays circulated widely, in pamphlets, newspapers, magazines, and conference proceedings. For more than seven years, although she never stopped pushing for other reforms, she put her heart and soul into winning women the vote.

She tackled every argument the increasingly well-organized antisuffragists deployed. Their favorite was to insist that women's place was in the home and that the affairs of state were men's affairs. Women had been raised on this ideology, but now they were reminded of it everywhere, in churches and synagogues but also at the family kitchen, at the dining room table, and in bed, at the tea table and in the union hall, and in books and the pages of popular magazines, including those for which Addams wrote. They read about it in the pages of the *American Magazine*, in an article by a moderate progressive journalist and friend of Addams's, Ida Tarbell, who thought woman's role in the "inner circle" of society was to "breed and train the material for the outer circle," where men ruled.[5] They read about it in the pages of the *Ladies' Home Journal*, in an article by the archbishop of Baltimore, who argued that the home and motherhood were women's "Christian, . . . sacred obligations."[6]

The suffragists understood the devotion women felt to their homes and families; that devotion, they argued, was why women should seek the vote. Addams made that argument in *her* essay in *Good Housekeeping* (the magazine sought views on both sides of the question). How can a woman "preserve the home in its entirety," she asked, if she does not "extend her sense of responsibility . . . outside her own home?" If the city administration fails to remove the garbage, a child may die from disease. If the city does not inspect meat plants, a child may die from rotten meat.[7] Addams never directly criticized women for being housekeepers, leading some historians to assume she believed women ought to restrict themselves to the home. In fact Addams made the criticism obliquely when she noted the inhibiting force of tradition in making women think they did not want the vote. "Old-fashioned ways which no longer apply to changed conditions," Addams warned, "are a snare in which the feet of women have always become readily entangled." Someday, she boldly hinted, "social change . . . shall release her from that paramount obligation [to the home]," although she admitted it seemed impossible to imagine when that might be.[8]

Antisuffragists also liked to argue that women did not need the vote since their men were voting on their behalf. Illinois's leading anti-suffragist Caroline Corbin wrote approvingly that "men represent us in the cornfield, on the battlefield, and at the ballot-box." Addams cleverly took offense on behalf of the male. "A woman," she stated firmly, "has no right to persuade a man to vote against his own convictions."[9]

Though skilled at rebutting, Addams liked to make the positive case. She often argued the point that she and Kelley thought so important— that women should have the vote in order for society to reform govern-ment. She was not saying that women would vote in a bloc but that excluding half the adult population from voting was not good for a democracy. Only with "all points of view . . . represented" could a com-munity make "sane and balanced progress." She especially wanted her privileged audiences, so enmeshed in the pursuit of their own and their families' happiness, to think more about the dreams and challenges of people with fewer resources, to think about what would be good for the majority of Americans—i.e., working people and the poor. It would be best, she wrote about suffrage, if everyone could "view the whole situation as a matter of obligation."[10] To her the call of duty was not discouraging but arousing. It gave purpose to life.

It was the formation of the NAACP in 1909 that drew Addams into the national fight against racism. Two race riots had intensified her and the nation's concern, one in Atlanta in 1906 and a second in Springfield, Illinois, in 1908. Both were triggered by charges that black men had raped white women, and both led to white mobs rampaging through black districts, destroying huge amounts of property and killing black people. The underlying causes of the sudden eruption of crowd-based racist violence were demographic: African Americans had flocked to both cities in recent decades, unnerving white people with their more numerous presence. After the Atlanta riot in 1906, Addams wrote in 1907 in *Newer Ideals of Peace*: "The principle of racial and class equality is at the basis of American political life, and to wantonly destroy it is one of the gravest outrages against the Republic."[11]

In early 1909 three residents of New York City area settlement houses—William English Walling of the University Settlement, Mary Ovington of the Greenpoint Settlement, and Henry Moskowitz of the Henry Street Settlement—decided something had to be done. They put together a widely published invitation to citizens concerned about the persecution of African Americans to attend a conference in New York City. Addams signed the meeting call, along with more than sixty prominent white and black Americans, including W. E. B. DuBois and Ida Wells-Barnett. Those at the conference agreed a new organization was needed, but there were serious tensions about whether blacks would have an equal voice with whites in its governance. Still, a mission was adopted: to seek the legal enforcement of civil rights, equal education rights, and voting rights. It was a social justice agenda ambitious enough to occupy activists for the rest of the century and beyond.

Addams, who had to miss the conference, served on a committee that drew up plans. The organization's mission would be to work on behalf of all minorities, but especially African Americans, and within a year it had a name, the National Association for the Advancement of Colored People (NAACP). Addams agreed to join the board, which included friends Ida B. Wells-Barnett and Lillian Wald and former Hull House resident and friend Gertrude Barnum. What role the board played is hard to say since it did not meet often and its minutes are sparse. The organization may have been mostly staff-driven.

Of all the national groups to which Addams belonged, the NAACP was by far the most controversial—because of its interracial nature and

Annual meeting of the NAACP in Chicago, 1917. Jane Addams,
with the fur-collar coat, is just in front of the woman with the big hat in the
center of the back row; W. E. B. DuBois is somewhere in the group.

its use of lawsuits to achieve social justice. At one time Addams might
have thought lawsuits too confrontational a strategy, but by 1909 she
saw their uses, saw that just as workers might need the strike to compel
employers to respect their rights, so minorities might need the law to
compel society to respect their rights. Social harmony remained her
goal, but life, along with some solid nudging by Florence Kelley, had
taught her the realities of power—that it was not relinquished without
a fight.

Perhaps the least controversial organization Addams belonged to,
not that it did not have its own internal controversies, was the National
Conference of Charities and Correction. It was a membership organization for charity workers and for prison, asylum, orphanage, and
settlement workers (paid and volunteer). Now in its fourth decade the
conference's membership had burgeoned in the last fifteen years to more
than nine hundred, as more and more people chose these positions as
careers. Addams had been sporadically giving papers at the conference
since 1897 and had chaired two committees, one on neighborhoods and

the other on immigrants. In June 1909 she was elected president of the conference. It was her first national presidency or at least the first that she had accepted.[12]

There were other firsts achieved by her election that loomed larger for the members of the conference. Addams was the first president who came from a settlement house. It was a sign that the field of social work was increasingly willing to identify economic and social conditions, rather than individual character, as the main reason people struggled. The following year, because of Addams's leadership, the conference addressed industrial conditions and standards in a separate section of the program for the first time. As Addams said in her presidential address, "Charity and Social Justice," there is "a connection between industrial maladjustment and individual poverty."[13]

Addams was also the conference's first woman president. That was a sign of the times too. Mindful of the fears her election stirred among those who had opposed her election, she spoke with pointed humor on the subject. Calling it a "rather venturesome and unusual action," she added, "I can only say for your comfort that you have not been hasty, you have waited thirty-five years." Then, speaking of herself in the third person in her usual way, she playfully sought to allay male fears that their new president would prove to be an aggressive or impulsive female. "The woman whom you have elected will promise to walk as softly as possible, think twice before she speaks, and then speak only after counting to ten, that nothing untoward may happen."[14] Sometimes Addams managed to say wicked things without serious consequences; her earnestness, stellar reputation, and simplicity of spirit seem to have shielded her.

|||||||||||||

The rivers were joining. Between 1906 and 1909 the idea of forming a national organization for a particular branch of progressive reform, either to support local or state efforts or to push for federal laws or to file lawsuits (in the case of the NAACP), became so popular as to be irresistible. Addams was drawn into many of these new groups. She served as vice president of the Playground Association of America, which supported playgrounds and recreation programs for urban citizens; of the Committee of One Hundred, which urged the creation of a system of local clubs that would press Congress to create a federal department of health; and of the American Association for Labor Legislation, which circulated policy research findings and drafted and lobbied for state and federal legislation. Addams's fellow vice presidents on these boards included such male leaders as the former president of Harvard, the president of the University of Michigan, the president of the American Federation of Labor, and the steel magnate and philanthropist Andrew Carnegie.[15] Planning for a national federation of settlements began in 1908; Addams was to be elected its first president in 1911.

Jane Addams and other settlement house leaders at a meeting in 1908 to organize what, in 1911, became the National Federation of Settlements. Jane Addams is in the center, with her hand on a stooping friend's shoulder. The friend is Lillian Wald, head of Henry Street Settlement.

The peace movement was getting organized, or reorganized, nationally too. In 1907 Addams gave several speeches at the First National Peace Congress in New York City, convened by the nation's oldest peace organization, the American Peace Society (APS). It was gaining new branches and new members steadily. In these years the subject was viewed as educational and lawyerly rather than political. In 1909 the Chicago Peace Society, a longtime branch of the APS on whose board Addams sat, hosted the Second National Peace Congress. Peace was such a noncontroversial issue that Addams persuaded the businessmen of the Chicago Association of Commerce to sponsor the meeting. At the congress she spoke to a special session of clubwomen on "Woman's Special Training for Peacemaking." Again invoking women's experiences to justify a wider future for them, she urged those present to use their new "power of organization" to work for "the peace of the world."[16] Brick by brick, issue by issue, Addams was answering a central question of the age, "What should be the scope of women's concerns?" Her answer, in short, was "everything."

As her official titles piled up, it seemed as if every reform movement with which Addams was involved needed her to head it or serve on its board. This left the impression that she was leading the progressive charge, but she was actually more like a surfer riding the long, splendid wave of political energy that progressives across the country were creating. Just how she managed for a time to stay on top of the wave is unclear, beyond noting the obvious—that she was highly skilled at transforming splintering forces into forward motion and at traveling at a fast, precarious pace.

In the midst of all she was doing, but mostly in the summer, Jane Addams continued to write books. She loved to write, but she also had a purpose: to prepare the political ground for progressive reform. She published her third book in late 1909, this one on the temptations and longings of city youth. It was as different from her first two as they had been from each other. If she wielded the pen of a moral philosopher in *Democracy and Social Ethics* and of a political ethicist in *Newer Ideals of*

Peace, in the third, which she titled *The Spirit of Youth and the City Streets*, she wrote as a storyteller.

The book had many tragic stories about young people whose lives had been ruined by the temptations of the streets. Addams described one young woman who sought protection at the settlement house from her drunken and opium-addicted lover, Pierre. "I can see her now running . . . up the broad steps of the columned piazza then surrounding Hull House. Her slender figure was trembling with fright, her tear-covered face swollen and bloodstained from the blows he had dealt her."[17] Addams's voice here is that of the novelist she might have become.

The point of this story, like others she told, however, was not to elicit the reader's pity for the young woman, whom Addams did not name, but to inspire the reader's respect for the "tremendous force" that fed the woman's devotion to a man who was destroying her life. It was love, Addams wrote, that awoke in her the finest of virtues—courage, loyalty, and a willingness to sacrifice oneself for the sake of another. Its "manifestations . . . outside . . . moral channels . . . yet compel[s] our admiration."[18] This was Addams's gift: to see beyond the soul's mistakes to its fierce, marvelous strengths.

Each chapter treated how the spirit of youth—rebellious, passionate, searching—manifested itself in a different urban setting. In the chapter about youth and industry, Addams told how young people in their teens found it difficult to endure the monotonous, exhausting conditions of factory work and how some, unable to suppress their creative, independent, fun-loving spirits any longer, revolted by changing jobs often or running away. Addams called their response "an expression of the instinct of self-preservation."[19] The chapter was really the spiritual case for the urgent need to end child labor.

Though many of the stories were sad—some of them ended in disaster, with the child sent to reform school or the abandoned family sinking into poverty—the book in its essence was about the adventuresome, life-affirming spirit of children. Addams praised youth's fierce belief that all things were possible and urged the city, if it wished to thrive, to "feed the divine fire of youth," rather than "smother" it.[20]

Addams drew her own strength from that fire. It was the joyous voices of children and their laughter, echoing in the halls of Hull House every day, that restored her faith in life when it flagged. She assumed children affected everyone that way. "Nothing is more certain than that each generation longs for a reassurance as to the value and charm of life, and is secretly afraid lest it lose its sense of the youth of the earth."[21]

The book, partly serialized in the *Ladies' Home Journal*, struck many reviewers as her best yet. The ever-generous William James wrote her that he had been brought to tears by some of its passages. Full of admiration for her accomplishment, he added: "The fact is, Madam, that you are not like the rest of us, who *seek* the truth and *try* to express it. You inhabit reality; and when you open your mouth truth can't help being uttered."[22]

Meanwhile, she already had her fourth book, a memoir titled *Twenty Years at Hull-House with Autobiographical Notes*, under way. She wrote much of it at Bar Harbor, Maine, in the summer and early fall of 1909; several chapters were published in the *American Magazine* in the spring of 1910. She continued working on the rest of the book the following summer at Bar Harbor. In early September 1910 she wrote a friend, "I work on the book for four or six hours a day." Aiming for a November publication date, she was pushing herself to get it done. "I write so slowly," she added, "that it is hard to realize there are so many hours of work [left to do] on it."[23]

She made her deadline. The book was published on November 16, 1910 (publishers were remarkably speedy in those days). Her most widely read book, *Twenty Years at Hull-House* went through six printings in its first year and has remained ever after in print. The early chapters were autobiographical, but the rest dealt with topics, including immigrants, labor legislation, social clubs, and the arts. In each she placed the people of the Nineteenth Ward on center stage and told their stories.

She wrote of an old Italian whom she saw spinning a thread with a stick spindle, of a young Russian enrolled in law school whose real passion, pursued in the Hull House metalwork shop, was silversmithing, of an Irish mother who begged Addams from her deathbed to take care of her young son, of a Russian Jewish girl of thirteen years who committed suicide because she could not repay some money she had borrowed without impoverishing her family.[24]

The few deeds of her own that Addams described were tucked away in dependent clauses or hidden within the collective "we." She intended her presence first as a hook, a window, to draw the reader into her experiences and second as a witness stand-in, so that she could teach the lessons she had learned. "[T]his volume," she wrote, "endeavors to trace the experiences through which various conclusions were forced upon me."[25] Here, as with her earlier books, she wanted to awaken the social consciences of her upper-middle-class readers by bringing them into the urban industrial world of working people. She still thought personal ties were the best way to do that, but she knew that reading, through the power of the imagination, could also do the same thing.

The popularity of her books and her steady presence in the press, not to mention her positions on so many boards, signaled her emergence as a beloved national figure. In 1904 she became the first woman to receive an honorary degree from the University of Wisconsin, and in 1906 a poll chose her as the "best woman" in Chicago, a distinction for which only single women were considered, on the theory that married women were constrained by the wishes of their husbands. In 1908 the *Ladies' Home Journal* declared her the "Foremost American Woman."[26] In 1910 she received her second honorary degree, this time from Yale University, which, like Wisconsin, had never given such a degree to a woman before. Smith College gave her an honorary degree too, a symbolic version of the degree she had so long coveted but failed to earn. As a household name Addams was favorite copy for newspaper articles, and her writings boosted the circulation of the mass magazines. A British suffrage

Jane Addams in 1910

advocate lecturing in the United States discovered that if she mentioned Addams's name in passing in a speech, she had to endure a full minute of rapturous applause.[27]

Many conservatives found her views troubling, if not horrifying, but others respected and listened to her. Her friend in the Women's Trade Union League Margaret Dreier Robins noticed. She told her, "In all America I know of only one person who can reach the honorable conservatives of this country and rouse from them a rallying cry and that is you." In a 1910 editorial, on the occasion of Addams being named an honorary member of the Chicago Association of Commerce, the *Chicago Tribune* noted that while conservatives had once foolishly considered her "an anarchist" or "a dangerous meddler," most people now understood "the enlightened conservatism of her views . . . and [her] work[.]"[28]

Why had she become such a popular figure? Certainly her ideas had appeal. People were drawn to her vision of a generous-spirited, inclusive, more socially and politically democratic United States. And there was also the fame-generating nature of two of her main occupations of speaking and writing. Since 1889 she had been steadily and increasingly in the public eye—lecturing, recycling her speeches in a wide variety of publications, writing her own books. Finally there was the appeal of her personality.

People attending a lecture remembered her understated but compelling presence. They recollected her "earnestness," her "eager voice," and her "deep eyes."[29] Her niece, Alice's daughter Marcet, wrote, "She made no effort to be oratorical . . . yet . . . from the first word to the last she held the complete attention of her audience."[30] One resident thought she was the "finest impromptu speaker" he had ever heard.[31] Addams stood with her hands behind her and spoke in a natural tone of voice. Because of her elocution training at Rockford, everyone, even those in large audiences, could hear her (without a microphone, of course).

Then there was the way she made her arguments. She did not accuse, characterize, or judge. She interpreted. Although she supplied facts and endorsed principles, she often focused on matters of the heart—not on sentimentality, for which she had an aversion, but on "spiritual" matters, as she liked to refer to them: the human feelings of responsibility, compassion, and affection; the human longings for freedom, meaning, and connection. There was something magical about the way she could pry open closed minds and let light—in the form of empathy—flood in.

Her radical form of goodness needed labeling and containing. The popular stereotype of a "good woman"—a saint—came readily to mind. An Atlanta journalist struck the obvious note, writing in 1907, "In the hearts of thousands of Americans, high and low, Miss Addams justly ranks as Saint Jane."[32] Her friend John Burns, the British labor organizer, declared her "the first saint America had produced."[33] One newspaper reporter compared her with Joan of Arc. Another quoted a professor who had said: "She has attained the heavenly beauty of the Madonna[,] for she has borne the suffering of the people."[34] Kind, inclusive, interested in the "spiritual" side of human relations, she certainly fitted the female version of a saint better than did, say, the impatient Florence Kelley. It also helped that she was an upper-middle-class woman who worked among "the poor." She seemed to personify Christian self-sacrifice, not the least, it should be noted, to herself.

Yet the public knew Addams was more than that, since she advised presidents, pushed for legislation, and wrote about democracy. One reporter accepted head-on the challenge of working with contradictory stereotypes. He wrote in 1910: "Jane Addams is a blend of the saint and the statesman. She has the purity of life and character and immense capacity for self-sacrifice of the one, combined with the facility of looking at things in the large and the knack of securing results of the other."[35]

Being viewed as a saint had its complications. One admiring member of the public managed to corner Addams on a low windowsill at Hull House and was just bending over her and saying, "If you won't let me hold your hand, do let me hold your foot," when Addams's good friend Louise de Koven Bowen walked by. Bowen told the Hull House residents the story, and they often teased Addams about it. Bowen wrote, "For years afterwards, 'Let me hold your foot' became a byword and it always made Miss Addams very provoked."[36] Here at last was some anger! Apparently Addams felt she had failed in her quest for humility if she was treated worshipfully.

Humility is perhaps the most challenging virtue a person can aspire to since success leads right back to failure. Raised as a Christian *and* a Victorian woman, Addams had always sought humility. She was therefore willing to attend to her failures, which are one of the little-noticed themes of *Twenty Years* and part of its appeal. But humility required more than that. It took time for her to learn the difficult lesson that self-righteousness hid itself in a secret place of the psyche, where assumptions of superiority seemed justified. And then there was the new challenge of how to live with the complications created by her large fame, including the excessive admiration it inspired. Humility was helpful because it deflected some of the envy and meanness that might otherwise come her way.

Since she did not believe in taking pride in her accomplishments, she set herself the impossible goal of taking none. In 1901 she wrote: "To give up the consciousness of one's own identity and achievements is perhaps the hardest demand which life can make upon us, but certainly those who call themselves Christian . . . should be ready to meet this demand." She of course failed in this too, many times. A friend of her later years, Emily Greene Balch, once said that Addams "enjoyed even more than most people approbation and love."[37] What is interesting was not that she failed in her pursuit of humility but that she tried.

As for private affection, Addams received and dispensed it willingly. Her friends and family found her warm, sympathetic, and affectionate. She was joyous in greetings, generous with hugs and kisses, always ready to listen to both good news and to troubles and to help if she could. But ultimately she was a bit distant, reserved. One friend wrote, "It is her habit to be rather silent." Her good friend Alice Hamilton remembered, "She was . . . approachable" but "kept an impersonal atmosphere at Hull House." Another friend remembered there was "something impersonal" about her friendship; it was rather like "sharing in some blessing of nature that, like the sunlight, shone on the just and unjust."[38] Her nephew Weber Linn recalled how her nieces and nephews "sometimes felt her love as a radiation rather than as a direct and individual beam. They adored her but they felt her sometimes to be a little withdrawn." Her niece Marcet recalled the "impersonal sweep" of her aunt's emotions.[39] Ellen Gates Starr had described the same quality when she had complained that Addams's affection for her "included the 19th Ward."[40]

It would be good to know what Mary Rozet Smith felt, but that is a mystery. She kept no diary, and her few surviving letters disclose nothing. One letter Jane wrote her, however, captures a bit of Jane's rather spiritualized approach to love. "Do write to me, Dear One," she told Mary, "and know that if I am too rushed to write, I am never too rushed to be conscious of you and our affection."[41] In expressing her devotion, she managed to be warmly personal and ethereally impersonal at the same time.

Whatever Mary felt, it is clear that Jane tended not to share her deepest, most personal feelings with others. What was the source of this distance? Had she inherited her father's coolness of temperament? Or, given her greatness of soul, did she find profound attachments too narrow? Was she preoccupied with the world's burdens? Or was her impersonality part of the deeper sadness people saw in her eyes? Something she wrote in 1912 about friendship suggests the source was sadness. Her words evoke her struggle in her twenties to find an antidote to her depression. "It is strange we are so slow to learn," she said, "that no one can safely live without companionship and affection, that the individual who tries the hazardous experiment of going without at least one of them is prone to be swamped by a black mood from within. It is as if we had to build little islands of affection in a vast sea of impersonal forces lest we be overwhelmed by them."[42]

She had built just such an island for herself. In fact Jane Addams was famous among her friends for not liking to be alone. Louise de Koven Bowen, the wealthy Chicago woman who was an ally in many social justice causes and a great supporter of Hull House, recalled that when they traveled together, Addams would ask her to share her hotel room, saying, "I don't like to be alone very much." Alice Hamilton remembered Addams saying the same thing.[43] Mary Rozet Smith's companionship was another bulwark against loneliness, as was the busyness of Hull House.

The contradictions resolve themselves slowly. In Addams's world, where death had come too early as a devastating force and a loving mother's close tenderness had been absent, simple human affection and constant companionship were her lifelines. But her earliest loss also limited the kind of love she could bear to give. Deep intimacy was too great a risk; she did not dare suffer so much pain again. Although she spoke often of "interdependence" and although she and Mary Rozet

Smith were devoted life partners, it appears that the most revealing kind of intimate love remained beyond Addams's reach.

|||||||||||

By 1911 a new energy had come to the campaign for women's suffrage, an energy to which Addams both responded and contributed. After fourteen years of no progress at all, two more states had joined the suffrage column in the last two years. Now women could vote fully in six out of forty-six states, all of them west of the Mississippi River. Addams joined the board of the NAWSA in 1911 as a first vice president and began attending the monthly board meetings in New York City when she could. And the Women's Trade Union League, having added suffrage to its position platform, was now closely cooperating with the National, and its leadership regularly spoke at the annual conventions.[44] Moreover, the National had added equal pay for equal work and industrial safety to its platform.

Publicity was a big part of the National's work. One of Addams's speeches, "Why Women Should Vote," published in the *Ladies' Home Journal*, was widely circulated as an NAWSA pamphlet. She was game to try any medium to reach the public. In 1912 she appeared in a commercially made film melodrama, *Votes for Women*, which opened with a scene of Anna Howard Shaw and Addams speaking on suffrage at a labor meeting. It was shown in movie theaters across the country and used in state campaigns.[45]

Addams also worked hard on the Illinois campaign. Because of the obstacle created by that state's constitution, the goal was partial suffrage—i.e., the right to vote in federal and municipal elections (women could already vote in school board elections). In a move designed to generate political support and publicity, the Illinois Equal Suffrage Association rented a special train in 1911 to bring hundreds of women from forty women's organizations, including trade unions, from Chicago to the state capital. Addams and others gave speeches at whistle-stops to crowds consisting mostly of men, while college stu-

Jane Addams campaigning for the Illinois suffrage
bill on the train to Springfield, 1911

dents collected thousands of signatures on a suffrage petition.[46] The
effort was good, but not good enough. The suffrage bill passed the Senate but was defeated in the House.

As of 1911 Addams had been giving frequent speeches on suffrage
for five years. At the same time, she had been mulling over the question
raised by women's voteless condition: How had women come to be seen
as inferior to men? Drawing on ideas from the writings of Frederick
Engels and the more progressive social scientists, including ethnologists
Otis Tufton Mason and Lewis Henry Morgan and sociologist Lester
Frank Ward, she laid her synthesis out in a major speech, "The Woman
and the State." She gave it at least twice in 1911, both times to audiences

of women, first to the New York City Women's Political Union and second to the Boston School Voters' League. Though only a portion was ever published, it was the most complete analysis she ever wrote on how societal change shaped women's relationship to men, the family, and government.[47]

Woman, she said, founded the family (because she founded the home as a place to raise children), and the family, headed by the woman, was the first state, the place where government, law, and religion began. The matriarchy ended, however, when men began to fight over resources (land and women, the producers of future warriors) and war became a way of life. "[T]he warriors, [having] gained ascendancy, . . . pushed women quite outside state affairs." Since women's role in war was to protect the children, women also became objects of protection. In later centuries this led to the "sex idealization" of the woman as a lady, weak and leisured, despite the fact that "thousands of peasant women . . . worked in the fields through all the wind and weathers and carried the heavy burdens of beasts." Addams declared the ideal of the lady "totally unfitted to our own [age]" and urged the restoration of woman's central role in the state as a necessity whose time had come.[48]

She closed her speech with a playful but thought-provoking proposal. Consider, she suggested, the result "if the matriarchal period had held its own," if the state had developed along the lines of the family, women had retained control over society's "political machinery," and men, excluded from voting, were now asking women to grant them the responsibilities of citizenship. Women would say no, and they would have good reasons: Men had too long neglected family interests, men liked going to war too much, and men had failed to remember that the "object of the state is to nurture and protect life."[49] From beginning to end, the speech argued that centuries of men's dominance in governance had created a situation harmful to human life.

Addams had criticized the oppressive power of militarism before, but it was new for her to criticize the male gender. Apparently her years of fighting for suffrage had deepened her grasp of how pervasively patri-

archy was restricting women's freedom. Addams had recognized patriarchy's existence before—in 1894, when she had referred to a "military
code" that enchained women, and in 1895, when she had explored the
condescending benevolence that King Lear showered on Cordelia and,
by extension, that fathers showered on daughters. But this time instead
of hiding behind a metaphor or a simile, she was stating her point
plain. The implications of her greater understanding were important: It
meant that she now saw that her gender was a caste—i.e., that women
formed a group whose inherited characteristics were used to justify its
inferior status—and that she had another reason to doubt the justifica-
tions for war. "Feminism," a word just gaining currency in these years,
had entered Addams's vocabulary. She considered herself a feminist and
in this essay she called the women's movement, in which she was now
completely engaged, the "feminist movement."[50]

|||||||||||||

In 1912, across the country, men in political leadership remained over-
whelmingly uninterested in reforming the suffrage to admit women.
In the forty-two years since it had become an organized effort, not a
single presidential candidate from either the Republican or Democratic
Party had endorsed it, for either state or federal action, although a party,
the Republican Party, in 1872, had endorsed it once. In 1912, however,
an intriguing possibility presented itself. Former President Theodore
Roosevelt, out of office since 1909 and, like others, frustrated that President William Howard Taft had turned his back on reform, was considering running for president, either as the Republican nominee or as the
candidate of a new third party. The idea of a new party was circulating
because both the Republican Party and the Democratic Party had progressive and conservative wings. More than ever before in U.S. history,
social reform issues were positioned to drive party politics. Roosevelt
understood these emerging political forces as well as anyone. He had
not been an advocate for women's suffrage, but the question remained
whether he could be converted.

Theodore Roosevelt, 1904

Roosevelt considered himself a progressive, and in many ways he was a typical one, embracing widely popular reforms with a great deal of moral enthusiasm. Raised in an evangelical Christian family, he had the same impatience with selfishness, the same devotion to duty, and the same love of the language of social salvation that Addams and many others did. His language was also full of references to collective action and what would benefit "the people." In federal politics he favored regulating monopolies and expanding the role of experts in government, but unlike Addams and many of her settlement movement friends, he favored states' rights, was willing to restrict immigration, and was eager to expand the United States' dominance as a new world power. Ever since serving as assistant secretary of the navy in 1897–98, he had pushed relentlessly to expand the U.S. Navy, explaining that he wished to keep the peace by being prepared for war. Everyone in the country knew he was a passionate "militarist," though he demurely denied it.

As for women's suffrage, his stance had long been mysterious. As president he had not taken a position on the issue because, as he told a friend, "I do not regard it as a very important matter."[51] In early 1912, as it became likely he would seek the Republican nomination, Roosevelt published an editorial in the *Outlook*, the magazine where he was an editor, endorsing suffrage in a distinctly backhanded way. Noting that suffrage "should not be forced" upon women by men, he suggested that only women, not men, should vote on the question in their states and that "mothers" should have it in the states where they wanted it.[52]

His proposal was not only a rejection of a federal amendment (and of the argument of suffrage as a right) but a farce, since the men in a state were unlikely to give women the power to do what the men would not do for them. Many suffragists were furious with Roosevelt for making such a preposterous proposal, regarding it as an insult to a serious cause. But others saw in Roosevelt's fumbling foolishness a reason for hope. The man was a consummate politician, and he knew which way the wind was blowing. Perhaps he could be persuaded.

In the spring of 1912 progressivism was like a snowball rolling down a hill. Having made its presence felt in mayors' and governors' offices and in city councils and state legislatures for some two decades, it was primed to seize the stage of presidential politics. The only question was which of the two major parties would ride the progressive energy to the White House. Roosevelt wanted to be the Republican nominee, and the progressive part of the party was behind him. But those in control of the convention, held in Chicago in June, were for Taft, and by refusing to seat some of Roosevelt's delegates, they got their man nominated. Roosevelt and his delegates walked out, and formed the Progressive Party. Soon after, the Democratic Party, sensing the possibility of victory over a split Republican Party, resolved its differences enough to choose a progressive candidate at its convention, the nubile politician and two-year governor of New Jersey Woodrow Wilson, and adopted a platform that echoed many of the planks of the Progressive Party. Wilson himself was a more limited progressive. He was most interested in reining in corporate power and in the ideas of the progressive peace movement, such as treaties of arbitration and mediation and the creation of a world federation of states.

Suffrage fared no better at the Republican convention than Roosevelt did. Addams and the rest of the NAWSA delegation urged the Republican Platform Committee to adopt a suffrage plank without success. She was disappointed but fascinated by the experience. It was the first time she had ever addressed a party committee or set foot in a party convention. In her long road up from political outsider, she had never come so close to walking in her Republican father's shoes.

When the Progressive Party met in convention in Chicago in early August to nominate Roosevelt, she came even closer. Addams was not a member of the Illinois Progressive Committee; no woman was. But Roosevelt had figured out his suffrage strategy, and Addams was a key part of it. According to press reports, he converted to the cause just days before the Republican convention after Colorado progressive Judge Ben Lindsey told him that women voters in the West were voting to elect anticorruption officials. More likely, however, Roosevelt had made up his own mind to attract prosuffrage women to his campaign and staged the Lindsey conversation as a way to dramatize his shift in position.[53]

Roosevelt wanted Addams at the convention. At the last minute she was invited to be an at-large member of the Illinois delegation and accepted. Here she took an actual step in her father's shoes. He too had joined a new party with new ideas when he left the Whigs in 1854 to join the new Republican Party. But her father had been a state politician. His daughter was about to go further in her political career than her father ever did.

Addams was not just being nostalgic, however, when she joined the Illinois delegation. She did it, she later explained, because she thought the party offered the best way to get a federal amendment for women's suffrage. Given the Democratic and the Republican recalcitrance, it was clear that the amendment would pass Congress only when a new third party sent legislators already committed to women's suffrage. "What the situation demanded," she wrote, "was not more deference to Congressional opinion. . . . Woman suffrage needed to be pushed by men who had been elected to Congress pledged to that issue."[54]

With Addams now a delegate, Roosevelt and the Progressive Party chose her to be one of the two people to second his nomination. She was not the first woman to do so for a presidential candidate. That laurel had gone to a woman from a state where women could vote, Elizabeth Cohen of Utah, who had seconded the nomination of William Jennings Bryan for president at the 1900 National Democratic Convention. Cohen broke another historic barrier at the same convention since she was the party's first woman delegate.[55] But Addams was a national figure and therefore a more significant choice for the nomination honor. Beyond the fact that the suffrage advocates loved her, a broad swath of Americans held her in high esteem and affection. There had even been talk in suffrage circles of her running for senator or president as soon as she could legally do so.[56] Furthermore, Addams's most obvious constituency, progressive women voters, although still small, was beginning to look strategic. By 1912, 9 percent of the nation's women—some 1.2 million people—could vote for president, in six states, all in the West and Republican leaning. Jane Addams was something the world had never seen before, a woman in a democratic country with a large, diverse, loyal, and organizationally energized political base.

Meanwhile, the Republican Party and the Democratic Party had not yet sought to benefit from the political rising of women. During the 1912 campaign they continued to exclude women from membership in their formal party structures (women were segregated in their own "auxiliaries" for fund-raising and campaigning), and, as before, few women were delegates to their national conventions.[57]

Compared with them, the Progressive Party in 1912 was far more welcoming. There were twenty to forty women delegates at the convention (the exact number was never established) but whether delegates, alternates, or hangers-on, women were everywhere. There was even a woman delegate sitting on the party's all-powerful, otherwise all-male,

platform committee, the Committee on Resolutions: Alice Elinor Carpenter, from Massachusetts, another historic first.[58] The year 1912 was a
major milestone in the effort of American women to take possession of
their constitutional right to be part of "we, the people"; as a leader of
the freshly minted Progressive Party, Jane Addams symbolized the new
ground that women were seizing for their sex.

At the convention what mattered most to Addams was the content
of the party's platform. She was not on the platform committee, but
friends of hers from reform campaigns were. Following Roosevelt's
instructions, the party's Resolutions Committee adopted as the social
and industrial planks a set of recommendations just developed by a
committee of the National Conference of Charities and Correction,
on which Florence Kelley and Alice Hamilton served. Hamilton, a
medical doctor, had been living at Hull House since 1897 and was
developing an expertise in industrial health. The resolutions called for
legislation on unemployment, minimum safety and health standards,
child labor, the eight-hour day for women, the six-day week for workers, and the creation of a department of labor. Addams was speaking accurately when she told a reporter during the convention, "The
Progressive Platform contains all the things I have been fighting for
for more than a decade."[59]

Another thing that Addams loved about the platform was its morally
responsible and thoroughly democratic spirit. It opened with words she
herself might have written: "The conscience of the people, in a time
of grave national problems, has called into being a new party, born of
the nation's sense of justice." The platform also pushed for advances in
democracy by endorsing direct primaries for state and national offices,
including U.S. senators, and state referenda on state supreme court decisions dealing with state constitutional questions.

To her delight, the platform contained the strongest suffrage plank
any mainstream party had ever adopted. Rejecting the idea that "a true
democracy" would deny "political rights on account of sex," the party
did not simply endorse suffrage for women; it pledged to achieve it,

although it ducked choosing a side on the controversial question of federal amendment versus state law by not referring to how suffrage would be achieved.

But if the suffrage plank cheered Addams, the peace and national defense plank disappointed her. It started off well by declaring warfare "barbaric" and endorsing international agreements to limit naval forces, but it also pledged that in the meanwhile the government should build two battleships a year—something, she wrote, "I found . . . very difficult to swallow. . . ." Still, she cast her delegate vote for the platform because it promised to address so many issues that she thought needed action. Some of her friends in the peace movement thought she had "desert[ed] the cause [of peace]. . . ."[60] But a single action was never symbolic to her. She saw any one of her actions as part of a continuum of actions. How could one be interpreted in isolation? Furthermore, she believed she had the right to decide for herself the meaning of what she did.

Beyond the planks that were in the platform, there was the plank that was not. The NAACP had prepared a civil rights plank, drafted by W. E. B. DuBois and supported by Addams and other NAACP leaders. It insisted that the "10,000,000 people who have in a generation changed from a slave to a free labor system . . . must have justice . . . and a voice in their own government."[61] But the platform committee rejected the plank.

That was disappointing enough, but there was worse. The same racial politics that killed the NAACP plank kept the party from seating black or racially integrated delegations from the southern states. The white South had nearly completed its systematic political disenfranchisement and social segregation of the black South by 1912, and it would brook no northern interference from the new party. Roosevelt, knowing he had to build the party from scratch in the South, had devised a strategy to attract Democrats as well as Republicans to his ticket. African Americans could belong to the delegations from thirteen northern and border states, but not to the delegations from the South, where 90 percent of the nation's African Americans lived. There Roosevelt wanted what was called a "clean"—which was to say "white"—slate. The argument he used to explain this was the current white southern argument for white supremacy: Southern blacks were too easily bribed, too corruptible.

The white state party leaders in the South did their best to execute the plan. In the weeks before the convention, they used various tricks to create all-white delegations, but in Alabama, Mississippi, and Florida, African Americans refused to be shut out of the political process, organized their own state meetings, and elected their own delegations—some all black, some integrated. At the convention the Committee on Credentials refused to seat them.

Roosevelt arrived at the convention the next day to find the halls outside the meeting rooms filled with stunned and angry African Americans. Bitterly familiar with the racist stereotype of black debasement that Roosevelt was relying on, they emphasized to reporters and the Credentials Committee that they were lawyers and doctors, prosperous and respectable men. They tried to meet with Roosevelt to change his mind, but he angrily refused. Northern black delegates announced to reporters and to white party leaders that they would bolt the party if Roosevelt stuck with the current policy, but he ignored their threats. Several white male members of the NAACP met with him privately but failed to persuade him to seat the contested delegations.

Addams believed that the party's actions amounted to a colossal moral failure. That evening she and another white NAACP board member, Henry Moskowitz, appeared before a public session of the Committee on Resolutions, which oversaw the work of the Credentials Committee, to plead for justice. She said, "Some of us are much disturbed that this Progressive Party which stands for human rights should even appear not to stand for the rights of Negroes. It seems so inconsistent." She urged the committee to "Stop, look, and listen" before they disenfranchised the Negroes of the South. A few months later she asked in the pages of a white reform journal: "How far are we responsible that [the] civil rights [of African Americans] are often rendered futile, their political action curtailed. . . ?" She thought the nation too paid a heavy price.

When "great ranges of human life are hedged about with antagonism," she wrote, it meant "an enormous loss of capacity to the nation."[62]

The only other thing she could do was to threaten to resign from the party—that is, threaten to leave the convention and not be part of the election campaign. Most, if not all, of the African American delegates hoped she would do this, convinced she was so influential and the party's need for her endorsement so great that she could have reversed the decision if she had made the threat. But she did not make it. She did not believe in using coercion. One friend who was there remembered that "she could not do anything that was in the nature of compulsion or control . . . [because of] her respect for freedom of action and of choice." She did, however, seriously consider withdrawing from the party without announcing it ahead of time. In 1914, Roosevelt remembered what she or others told him later—that on the issue of seating the southern African American delegations she "came very near to leaving the Progressive Party."[63]

African Americans across the nation were split in judging her actions. Black women active in the club movement sent her telegrams praising her appeal to the Committee on Resolutions, but a black NAACP board member, William Trotter, who supported the Democratic ticket in the upcoming election, thought her failure to break with the Republican Party was a betrayal of his race. "Woman suffrage will be stained with Negro blood," he telegraphed, "unless women refuse alliance with Roosevelt."[64]

It was the old dilemma of how patient to be. Addams later explained that she did not resign from the party that day because she hoped more could be done in the future. Once the Progressive Party movement "crystallized" and "gained a national foothold," she wrote, "it is bound to lift this question of the races, as all other questions, out of the grip of the past and into a new era of solution."[65] In her willingness to wait, Addams was far removed from the radical impatience of her childhood heroes John Brown, Lucy Stone, and the other pioneers in the women's suffrage and abolitionist movements, Susan B. Anthony, Elizabeth Cady Stanton, Frederick Douglass, and Sojourner Truth. Her pragmatic view was that of an effective politician: that change often came incrementally, because of persistence and compromise, and only completely when the moment was right. And an effective politician, even if unelected, was what she had become. She was not temperamentally constructed to lead a revolution, but her times also gave her what their times had not given them, a chance to change society by direct political means. She seized the chance.

Still, one wonders, if the platform committee had rejected the suffrage plank, would she have stayed in the party? Or to say the same thing differently, was her commitment to the suffrage plank a major reason she did not resign? Probably. Black civil rights advocate and women's suffragist Frederick Douglass had faced a similar dilemma in 1866, when he decided to endorse the proposed Fourteenth Amendment because he believed it would protect the right of African American men in the South to vote, even though by speaking of "male inhabitants," it excluded women. He argued that while the Negroes' cause was "not more sacred" than the women's, it was "certainly more urgent."[66] Now, in 1912, although black men once more could not vote in the South, Addams thought that women's time had finally come. Her loyalties were as torn as Douglass's had been, but like him, she ultimately sided with her kind.

Meanwhile, the party convention churned merrily on. On the second day Roosevelt, breaking with the tradition that the nominee should not attend the convention, let alone address it, received a jubilant one-hour ovation before he delivered a two-hour speech on his ideas for the nation. On the third day he was nominated. Judge Ben Lindsey gave the first seconding speech, and Jane Addams's speech followed. When she arrived at the podium, the huge crowd's long roar of approval seemed to reporters and others to be at least equal to the one Roosevelt had received the day before; editor William Allen White described the response to Addams as "a volcano of emotion and applause." Then, as she began to speak, a *Chicago Tribune* reporter wrote, "all noise ceased. The usual walking about . . . stopped. Everyone listened."[67]

Her speech was an enthusiastic endorsement of the platform, which she spent four paragraphs discussing, and of Roosevelt, who received two sentences. She supported him, she said, because the program would require the kind of man he was, "a leader of invincible courage, . . . democratic sympathies, [and] one endowed with the power to . . . identify himself with the common lot." But she did not let the party's disenfranchisement of ten million African Americans go unremarked. Democracy would not be realized, she said, until a certain group of "10,000,000 people . . . [bore] the responsibilities of self-government."[68]

As she came down from the podium, a yellow banner urging VOTES FOR WOMEN was thrust into her hands, and a clapping, shouting, joyous line of women fell in behind her to parade around the convention floor as the band played. It may have been corny party politics at its best, but for the women there, so long excluded from the halls of party power, the moment was exhilarating. Addams, surrounded as she was by thousands of people whose faces were alight with happiness, could only have felt profoundly moved. She thrived on public affection, of course, but there was more to her feelings than that. The moment was one of solidarity, of feeling part of a larger whole. It was an experience she was to have again and again during the campaign. She wrote, "At moments we believed that we were witnessing a new pioneering of the human spirit."[69] For Addams, the delight of politics was the shared feeling of hope.

Presidential campaigns were short in those days. Roosevelt began his in late August. A powerful orator, he sounded the themes of progressivism on the campaign trail to rapturous audiences. "All of us taken collectively, the people as a whole," he said, "must feel our obligation to work by government action . . . to make the conditions better for those who are unfairly pressed down in the fierce competition of modern industrial life."[70]

A month later Addams launched her jam-packed speaking tour to twelve mostly midwestern states. She had already planned to campaign for suffrage in four of the six states where there was to be a referendum vote; now she added the Progressive platform to her speeches and more states to her tour. Determined to reach voters—i.e., men—with her message, she tried to speak only to mixed audiences.[71] Afterward she remembered that during the Progressive presidential campaign "I had the best chance to talk [*sic*] woman suffrage that I ever had in my life. I talked it [*sic*] to vast audiences of men. . . . [T]hey would not have come to a suffrage meeting or to a social reform meeting, but they would come to a political meeting, and there they had it driven into them night after night and day after day."[72] She loved it, writing to her sister Alice, "I am quite enjoying my campaigning." She also knew that her mere presence on the presidential campaign hustings made a better case for suffrage than any argument could. "What arouses attention is something that is done," she once wrote.[73]

Like many progressives, she did not think Roosevelt could win, but she thought the campaign valuable because it educated citizens about the issues. She made the point in the pages of the *Ladies' Home Journal* just before the election, using a Greek philosopher to bolster her case. She wrote, "Aristotle is reportedly to have said that politics is a school wherein questions are studied not for the sake of knowledge, but for the sake of action."[74] Perhaps only Jane Addams could have found a plausible way to quote Aristotle in the *Ladies' Home Journal*, and she may have been the first and last person to do so. Elsewhere she observed that a political campaign allowed reformers to present solutions as "a coherent political program" before the entire country.[75]

Addams's plunge into party politics shocked many. They thought she should have remained nonpartisan and above the fray, because she was a woman, a social worker, or the head of a settlement house. Letters and telegrams flooded her office at Hull House; people issued statements to the press. The president of the Red Cross told a *New York Times* reporter that Addams ought not enlist Hull House's influence

in a partisan cause; Addams replied, in a letter to the editor, that Hull
House had long worked for the cause of social justice embodied in the
Progressive Party platform and that an institution revealed its weakness
when it cared more "for its position and influence than for the cause
itself." As for destroying her own moral influence, she did not think it
was something she should worry about. That fall she wrote: "We all
forget that 'influence' . . . ceases to be of real value when it is consciously
cherished as a possession. . . ."[76]

Most suffragists thought it was fine that she had joined a party to
advance the cause, but a minority was horrified. The former chair of
the NAWSA's national press committee, Ida Husted Harper, published
a sharply critical letter to the editor in the *New York Times* in which she
dismissed the significance of the Progressive Party suffrage plank and
criticized Addams for "violat[ing] the unbroken tradition" that the
members of the National American Woman Suffrage Association "be
absolutely nonpartisan." She called for Addams to resign her position
as a vice president.[77] Addams issued a statement saying that while the
association was nonpartisan, its individual members were free to be as
partisan as they liked. Harper led a campaign, targeted at Addams, to
forbid NAWSA officers from affiliating with political parties at the
next NAWSA convention, but it was roundly defeated.

That Addams was a single woman was also controversial. Some were
offended that an unmarried woman should be promoted as an admi-
rable figure. The retired president of Harvard, Charles W. Eliot, told a
New York Times reporter that he thought Addams's nominating role at the
convention was in "very bad taste" and that he disliked seeing her held
up "in the limelight as an example for all other women to follow," given
that society needed women to bear children and take care of the home.
Roosevelt partly rebutted Eliot in a speech soon after by pointing out
that exceptions should be made and that "unmarried women" like Addams ought not to be "slurred" when they were serving all the people.[78]
In other words, Addams had proved herself to be selfless enough that
her unmarried status did not undermine her moral authority.

Eliot's criticism could only have evoked laughter at Hull House. Addams remained stalwartly confident that her decision to be partisan was the correct one, writing Lillian Wald that summer, "I never doubted for a moment that my place was inside, where there was a chance to help on such a program as this one."[79]

And she was definitely on the inside. Roosevelt instructed the party that women should have full and equal standing in the party structure.[80] During the campaign Addams was a member of the Illinois and Cook County Progressive committees and one of four women to be named to the National Progressive Committee. She joked to her sister Alice that in accepting the national position she had "become a full-fledged 'new woman.'" Soon after, she moved even further inside and was made a member of the nine-member Executive Committee, or governing board, of the national party, the first woman in American history to hold such a position. The unorthodox nature of her situation was highlighted several years later, when the Executive Committee, on which Addams still served, discovered at the last minute it could not meet in Chicago's University Club because of the club's rule that women were not allowed in its main clubhouse (women had a separate wing).[81]

It was through the meetings of the Executive Committee, often held in New York City, that Addams got to know Roosevelt a bit more. Sometimes he dropped by. She remembered that "'peace' was forever a bone of contention between us," although the discussion was never "acrimonious" and sometimes "hilarious." He loved to remind her playfully that he was more expert than she on the subject, since he had received the Nobel Peace Prize.[82] To this she was to have no sufficient rebuttal until 1931.

By election day, November 5, Addams was back in Chicago. Unable to cast a vote, she watched men troop to the polls as she awaited the returns at Louise de Koven Bowen's house, where she had collapsed in exhaustion. The results were, in a way, a win for progressivism, since the two progressive presidential candidates together got a majority of the vote. But with Taft and Roosevelt splitting the Republican vote, Woodrow Wilson swept into the presidency and Congress turned Democratic on his coattails. Roosevelt was trounced, winning only six states, all but one in the West or Midwest, and only 27 percent of the popular vote. He was "amused" to note afterward—"disappointed" would probably have been more accurate—that he had won in only two of the six suffrage states and in one prosuffrage territory.[83] His "suffrage strategy" had been a flop. But his biggest disappointment was undoubtedly losing the election. The many rivers of progressivism had not joined to carry him into the presidency after all.

Roosevelt had lost, but Progressive Party supporters were not shocked. The party was new. They expected that it would continue to build itself in preparation for the next national election, in 1916. But that proved impossible. While the party's local and state organizations put many Progressive legislators into office in the years before and after the 1912 campaign, it never again fielded a presidential candidate. After the party gave a poor performance in the 1914 congressional and local elections, Roosevelt decided it was "spurring a dead horse."[84] In 1916 he returned to the Republican Party.

Jane Addams's career in formal politics ended with the party's demise, but when the party was at its peak, she came closer to holding political office than she perhaps knew. In addition to the calls for her to run for senator or president, neither of which may have been politically feasible, her name was discussed during the 1912 campaign as a good choice for Roosevelt's cabinet. Roosevelt admitted afterward that this had been his likely plan.[85] Would she have accepted? Possibly. She would have found the opportunity to accomplish social change at the federal level difficult to resist.

||||||||||||

President Woodrow Wilson proved a disappointment to the progressives who wanted federal laws. There was progress on the economic front—he proposed legislation that created the Federal Trade Commission and the Federal Reserve during his first term—but it was Congress that took the lead in passing the laws, which Wilson simply signed, that created a department of labor, a minimum wage for women working in the District of Columbia, and prohibited child labor nationally—at last! Progressives barely had time to celebrate the latter two laws before they were challenged in court on the grounds of their unconstitutionality. Federal progressivism to insure social justice remained a dream for the moment. But two new constitutional amendments, endorsed by the Democratic and Progressive party platforms, made dents in the powers of the state legislatures. One established the direct election of U.S. senators (state legislators had elected them until then), and the other authorized Congress to create a graduated income tax (only the state legislatures had had that power before). Both proposals had been included in the People's Party platform of the mid-1890s.

As for progressivism's most ambitious and most democratic reform, women's suffrage, Wilson, a southerner, did nothing to advance it. He had artfully dodged the subject during the campaign, claiming it was an "arguable question" and he was still making up his mind.[86] In fact he was as lukewarm as Roosevelt was, which is to say he did not believe women had a right to vote but would accommodate states granting it. His party, the Democratic Party, whose leadership was dominated by the southern states, defended states' rights.

Meanwhile, the 1912 election had produced the biggest jump in suffrage states ever. Women in three more states, all of them western, could now vote. Suffragists correctly blamed the defeat in three other states on the liquor industry, which was fearful that women would vote for state prohibition laws. The fear was becoming the biggest obstacle to women getting the vote. At the same time, the federal amendment was going nowhere. Despite the annual ritual of hearings, the NAWSA still was not pushing hard for the Anthony Amendment, as it was also called, and the legislation remained politically unviable. The House had never voted on women's suffrage, and the Senate had not voted on it in decades.

When the National American Woman Suffrage Association held its 1912 convention shortly after the election, arguments about the state versus federal amendment strategy rose to fever pitch. Addams agreed with a group of younger women led by a former settlement house worker in her late twenties, Alice Paul, who wanted the National to start a forceful campaign to drive the amendment legislation through Congress. This group—college-educated, career-oriented, self-consciously feminist—also wanted to hold the party in power accountable if it failed to fight for suffrage. Addams, in disagreement with much of the leadership of the National, agreed with Paul's strategy. With Addams running interference on Paul's behalf, the leadership decided that Paul could chair the Congressional Committee and raise money from NAWSA members for its efforts, the first of which was to hold a massive suffrage parade the day before Wilson's inauguration in early March.

The parade was a big success but Jane Addams had to miss it. In February she and Mary Rozet Smith left the country for a five-month trip to Europe and the Middle East, paid for by Mary as her birthday gift to Jane. Ever the industrious students, they read up on Egyptian history as their cruise ship worked its way across the Atlantic and then the Mediterranean Sea. By the time they arrived in Cairo, Jane told a friend, she felt "quite learned" about the country. Exploring the tombs at Aswan, visiting various temples, traveling by steamer down the Nile, Jane had, as she put it, "fallen very much under the spell of this amazing country."[87] They went on to visit Jerusalem, in Palestine, and Italy; then Mary left for home, while Jane headed for Budapest, Hungary, to attend the International Women's Suffrage Alliance meeting as an NAWSA delegate. There she saw again some of the women she had met at the London IWSA meeting in 1909 and met new women as well. Her ties to European women were becoming stronger. She did not return to Chicago until early July.

The nearly five-month journey was Addams's first really sustained vacation in eighteen years, since a memorable trip she had taken with Mary to Europe in 1896, when they had actually managed to meet Leo Tolstoy. Now, as she traveled, she again found herself feeling wonderfully "stimulated and refreshed."[88] She was able not just to free her mind from reform politics and the responsibilities of Hull House but also to luxuriate in the stories of human experiences she always sought out in travel as well as at home. Egypt's vivid art, so prominent in its tombs and temples, of men and women preparing for and passing through the world of death touched her profoundly and drove her to write. On the ship coming home she finished an essay, "The Unexpected Reactions of a Traveler in Egypt," and mailed it to the *Atlantic Monthly* as soon as the boat landed in New York City. The editor's delighted acceptance letter was waiting for her when she reached Chicago. He predicted her essay "will stir many readers to new questionings."[89]

The piece was about how human beings encounter death and was at once the most personal and the most universalizing essay Addams ever wrote. She told how as she stood in the temples and tombs, looking at pictures that were some of the oldest records of man's ideas about "how to defeat death," she was often "submerged" by "primitive, overpowering emotions"—she meant fear, or rather, terror—she had experienced as a child. Memories came flooding back, including of her attempt to find the magic words in the Bible to save the souls of sinners at the town revival. And she recalled witnessing the burial of a classmate's mother that had also upset her. Her psyche could not retrieve the memory of her mother's death, the first devastating loss death had dealt her, but it bore the scar intact, the pain of which had long been buried. Egypt's art had restored the memories that had been linked to that pain.

The stories of her childhood Addams told in her essay were deeply personal, but she chose to see them as typical for any child. She called the "ghosts of reminiscences" that came to her in Egypt "manifestations of [a] new humanism."[90] She could not admit that death had put its black mark on her soul early. But perhaps she was not so wrong to insist on the universality of her Egyptian experience. The essay resonates with meaning for any reader who has ever known a loss from death or feared death. Jane Addams's spirituality was always there, informing her politics and her writing. When she freed her pen to write about the deeper questions of life, few could match her.

|||||||||||

When Addams returned to the United States, she returned to an energized and newly confident suffrage campaign. Just weeks before she
landed in New York City, the governor of Illinois signed the state's
suffrage law. It had passed the legislature thanks to a herculean effort
by suffrage advocates, who flooded legislators' offices with letters and
telegrams of support from every district and bombarded the Speaker's
home with coordinated phone calls every fifteen minutes the weekend
before the House vote. Addams could now, for the first time in her life,
vote for president and for the mayor of Chicago and other municipal offices, just not for state offices. More important for the nation,
Illinois was the first state east of the Mississippi to give women the
vote—granted, in modified form. What had been considered a western
phenomenon was now creeping eastward.

Meanwhile, Alice Paul was showing the suffrage movement what it
meant to really push for a federal amendment. As chair of the National's
Congressional Committee and of a separate but affiliated national organization she had founded, the Congressional Union for Woman Suffrage (CU) she used a national petition campaign to put U.S. senators
under pressure to pass an amendment. The strategy worked. By early
December 1913, when the National held its convention in Washington,
the Senate Suffrage Committee had reported out an amendment bill for
only the second time in history.

But Paul received no accolades at the convention for her work. Instead
President Carrie Chapman Catt charged her with trying to take over the
National and with financial irregularities. She told Paul that she and the
CU should stop organizing in the states. Clearly, the issue was one of
power. Jane Addams spoke in defense of Paul and her financial integrity, but the convention supported Catt, and over the next few months,
despite further effort on Addams's part, no solution could be found.
By early 1914 Paul and the Congressional Union had broken completely
with the National and were forging ahead with their own campaign.

Addams, to her credit, did not back away from supporting the controversial Paul, and the reasons why were clear: Like Paul, she believed in
using politics to achieve political goals and wanted a federal amendment. But the disunity in the movement could only have disheartened
her. Florence Kelley, too, had lost patience with the NAWSA. Calling
women's continued lack of the vote "ridiculous," she had resigned from
the board in 1913. The next year she joined the CU's advisory council.[91]

For years the nation's focus had been mostly on domestic politics,
but in the summer of 1914, foreign affairs abruptly seized the stage. In
late June, before Addams left Chicago for her vacation with Mary Rozet
Smith in Maine, she and the rest of the world learned that a Serbian
anarchist had assassinated the Austrian archduke in line to govern the
Austro-Hungarian Empire. The political implications of the deed were
huge, given the web of strategic alliances in place among European
nations. The spark required to light the bonfire of war-minded Europe
had been struck. A month later Addams and Smith were in the new
cottage they had bought together (with mostly Smith's money) in Hull's
Cove, near Bar Harbor, when the news came that war was declared
among the key European nations.[92]

The nations had gone to war like a row of dominoes. First the Hapsburg monarchy declared war on Serbia, Russia's ally; soon after, Germany, the Hapsburgs' ally, which had been arming itself aggressively
and was eager to reclaim territory it had lost in the Napoleonic Wars,
declared war on France and Russia. Troops mobilized. Germany invaded
Belgium on August 3, as the first step in its strategy to invade France
from the west. Two days later Great Britain, committed to stand by Belgium, declared war on Germany. The world's first war was between the
Allies, or the Entente, the main members of which were Great Britain,
France, Russia, and Japan, later joined by Italy, against the Central Powers of the German Empire, Austria-Hungary, the Ottoman Empire, and
Bulgaria. The neutrals were the United States, Spain, the Netherlands,
Norway, Sweden, Denmark, and Switzerland. Quickly the periodicals
were full of news of soldiers on both sides dying in battle by the thou-

sands, of Belgium women being raped by the invading German troops, of refugees fleeing.

The events sank Addams into despair. War to her was government-sponsored murder. Some hint of her bleak feelings appeared in a description she wrote later about how *other* people felt at learning the news. Thousands of men and women, she said, experienced a sense "of desolation, of suicide. . . ."[93] The second phrase was a reference to Tolstoy's claim, in *The Kingdom of God Is Within You*, the book Addams had read in 1894, that war was suicide for mankind. But what really drove home to her the news from Europe was the view from her window on August 4. She was startled to see a huge ocean liner anchored in Frenchman's Bay. Later she learned that it was German and that it was seeking refuge for its cargo of gold and silver bullion from the newly contested seas. The incongruously placed ship showed Addams vividly that, as she put it, "we were . . . required to adjust our minds to a changed world."[94]

|||||||||||||||||||||||||||||||||||||||||||||||||||||||||||||||||||||||||||||||||||||||||||||||||||||||||||||||||||||||||||||||||||||||||

DISSENTER

How DID ADDAMS adjust her mind to the changed world of war? She reached several fresh conclusions over the next four and a half years, but the most important was about her place in the political spectrum. Looking back on that period in 1922, she observed, "My temperament and habit had always kept me rather in the middle of the road; in politics as well as in social reform I had been for the 'best possible.' But now I was pushed far towards the left on the subject of the war."[1]

Her dilemma went to the heart of her political philosophy. If peace was about not just the absence of war but the health of democratic institutions that nurtured life, then war was about their sickness. To her a government at war was a government seeking to harm its citizens: it not only required them to kill other human beings and to risk being killed but redirected tax dollars from social programs into military expenses and restricted citizens' right to free speech. When it came to war, there was no "best possible" she could accept because democracy's essence—caring for its citizens—was at stake, and when it came to that, she was radical.

President Woodrow Wilson saw things differently. To him neutrality and war were strategies on the road to peace as well as tools to be used to advance the nation's and his own global standing. After announcing the country's neutrality in early August, he offered its diplomatic resources and himself as a mediator for peace negotiations and was uncharacteristically forthright about his motives: "America stands ready . . . to help the rest of the world. And we can . . . reap a great permanent glory out of doing it."[2] Wilson's belief that through him the United States could become the world's savior would drive the foreign policy of his presidency.

He did not expect his initial offer of mediation to be accepted. It was clear to him, as it was to others, that Japan and the strongest European nation-states and dynasties—Germany, Great Britain, Austria-Hungary, and Russia—wished to expand and, confident of their power, wanted war. Nor did Wilson think it an urgent matter that the war end quickly. His offer was designed to establish his role as the eventual peacemaker when the time was right, either when the warring nations were stalemated or after the war ended.

Wilson's offer was consistent with new international practice. The role of the neutral peacemaker nation was outlined in the much-admired Hague Conventions of 1907 that many nations, including the United States, Russia, China, Japan, and those in Europe, had signed. But there was something old-fashioned about the way Wilson was embracing the role. He assumed that the true force for change in the world was the morally responsible and courageous leader. Wilson would soon lead the nation to take a stance of heroic neutrality; later he would lead it into what he considered a heroic war; and still later, he would attempt to lead the world to a heroic peace. And he would try to do much of it by himself. He believed in solo accomplishments.

Addams had once been an acolyte of the heroic cult herself and still believed in the power of moral example, but it had become obvious to her that the pursuit of solo accomplishment was the road to practical failure and that self-righteousness and isolation were sure to follow. She thought a democratic society found the right path because people acted together through discussion, grassroots organizing, and compromise. Were not the collective successes of the progressive movement proof?

She thought, at least at first, that the peace movement in time of war offered the same possibilities. After World War I began and before the United States entered it, Addams would be part of a newly energized and politicized peace movement grounded in collective action. Once the nation declared war on Germany, however, all that would change. Support for the war would become every citizen's patriotic duty, and Addams would find herself standing against the majority view. Ironically, she would be forced into the role of heroic dissenter, a role that she had no desire to assume. Painfully isolated from popular support, she would become vulnerable to the devilish temptations—her old temptations—of self-righteousness and martyrdom, and would be tested in new ways.

|||||||||||||

Americans reacted to news of war variously. On the whole they thought a war in Europe was no business of theirs—unless they had relatives or friends there (30 percent of Americans were foreign-born or had at least one parent who was foreign-born). Many of the largest, mostly male, peace societies, believing the Allies' cause was righteous, averted their eyes from Europe and discussed the peace principles that should shape the postwar future.

A few peace advocates wanted action. Fanny Garrison Villard, a longtime member of the American Peace Society and daughter of the great abolitionist and pacifist William Lloyd Garrison, thought the peace societies were useless. "They are weak and ineffectual," she said. "The fear of being called peace-at-any-price men makes cowards of them all."[3] In late August in New York City, she led a parade to express women's sorrow over the war. With women refugees from the warring countries walking at the front of the column, some fifteen hundred women—mostly white but also black—marched down Fifth Avenue to the sound of muffled drums as thousands of people watched silently.

The parade, organized by a coalition of suffragists, pacifists, socialists, and settlement activists, marked the beginning of the separate women's peace movement in the United States.

Addams did not march. She wanted to discuss practical ways to influence the government's actions. At her suggestion, some twenty men and women—mostly colleagues from the settlement and progressive movements, including her good friends Lathrop, Kelley, and Wald—gathered in September at the Henry Street Settlement, with Addams traveling down from Maine. At first they talked about their fear that war would harm the social reform movements in Europe and the United States. As Addams told a newspaper reporter soon after, "When a million men are suffering in trenches wet and cold and wounded, what are a few children suffering under bad conditions in the factories? . . . It will take years before these things are taken up again."[4]

Then they debated whether to urge Wilson to go beyond the role of solo mediator and convene a conference of the neutral nations—the United States, the Netherlands, Spain, Switzerland, Denmark, Norway, and Sweden—that would call for a cease-fire and then mediate peace negotiations. This method was implied in The Hague 1907 Conventions, which stated that more than one neutral nation might mediate and that mediation might take place even after hostilities had begun. But the Henry Street group argued about whether it should urge the president to do this. A draft manifesto was circulated a few months later but not agreed to.[5]

Women suffragists had the next idea: to gather in Washington, D.C., in a big peace meeting. The proposal was promoted by moderate suffragist and ardent pacifist Rosika Schwimmer of Hungary and militant suffragist Emmeline Pethick-Lawrence of England, both of whom were lecturing in the states that fall. Pethick-Lawrence had been organizing suffragists into emergency peace committees in various cities. They wanted a meeting in the nation's capital to adopt a resolution urging Wilson to convene a conference of neutral countries that could end the war as soon as possible.

In November, Addams invited Schwimmer and Pethick-Lawrence, both of whom she had met at the international women's suffrage meeting in Budapest the year before, to come stay with her in Chicago to discuss the idea of a big peace meeting. Why just suffragists? Addams asked. She thought those pushing for peace should be all sorts of activists and also wanted the effort to be sex-integrated. Broadly, she wanted to shape public opinion; pragmatically, she wanted voters—most of whom were men—to support the effort; philosophically, she thought it only natural for men and women to work together.[6]

While Addams was still unsure about supporting a national women's peace meeting, she was ready to help organize an emergency peace committee in Chicago. With Pethick-Lawrence and Louis P. Lochner, the energetic twenty-seven-year-old secretary of the Chicago Peace Society, she convened a committee at Hull House to plan a peace rally. Their plan, not unusual in the early twentieth century, was to invite people not as individuals but as representatives of organizations. The final invitation list went to twenty-one groups with peace committees. The rally, to which the public was invited, took place in early December and included peace activists, socialists, trade unionists, women's club members, settlement workers, suffragists, businessmen, teachers, and clergy. One thousand people listened to speeches, adopted a platform, and elected Addams president of a new organization, the Chicago Emergency Federation (CEF).[7]

For critics of the war, creating peace platforms was the absorbing task. Addams would be involved in writing four in the war's first year. A peace platform was the collective answer a group of citizens supplied to the question, What new institutions and government policies would help prevent war? A platform risked being just words on the page, but as Addams and others knew from experience, policymakers sometimes raided platforms for ideas. Most of the answers the CEF's platform offered—a league of nations, international arbitration treaties, international courts, and arms control—came from the prewar peace movement's platforms. To this standard fare, however, the CEF added some unorthodox ideas. Pethick-Lawrence was promoting some—democratic control of foreign policies and an end to secret treaties—that were drawn from the platform of the Union of Democratic Control, a British peace organization her husband had just helped found. The suffrage resolution came, of course, from the suffrage movement.

Most unorthodox of all was the CEF resolution about a conference of neutral nations. It called on Wilson to convene one with diplomats sent by governments. If he would not, however, it called for an unofficial conference made up of private citizens with expertise in international law and peace terms to be convened. The resolution also set out a different role for each type. The official conference would urge the warring nations to declare an armistice. The unofficial one would simply offer its services of mediation to the warring nations.[8] For the next two years Addams and Schwimmer pushed for some kind of neutrals' conference repeatedly, refusing to give up on the one proposal they believed could shorten the war.

The idea of an unofficial conference had a second source of inspiration, also outlined in the 1907 Hague Conventions: Nations with disputes could create commissions of inquiry, made up of experts, *before* the dispute became a war. Early in his administration President Wilson had endorsed the idea, including the possibility that neutral nations might organize such commissions.[9] The CEF was just going one step farther and suggesting it be tried *during* a war. Addams favored the idea because she believed in drawing on experts for knowledge and thought, as she put it, that "the people themselves" should have a chance to discuss "the terms of peace" once the experts had outlined them. She also distrusted diplomats, who were famous for agreeing on terms behind closed doors.[10] Addams wanted there to be a lively public discussion before the choices were made. Still, she was willing to work for an official conference. As president of the CEF she tried and failed to meet with Wilson twice that spring to press him to convene one. But in wartime, as in times of peace, her priority remained educating public opinion so that democracy could work, and she would push for an unofficial conference when she could.

The CEF platform was historic in its scope. While it had many borrowed planks, taken as a whole, it was the most complete, bold, and democratic peace platform ever proposed. The product of a hugely diverse midwest American gathering, the CEF platform would prove to be a significant contribution to the international discussion about peace.

After the CEF peace rally Addams decided to support the idea of a big Washington women's peace meeting. She yielded on the point of gender—it would be a meeting for women only—but she won on including more than suffragists. The call, signed by Addams and suffrage leader Carrie Chapman Catt, was mailed, along with a copy of the CEF platform, in late December to the national women's organizations with peace committees. Each was asked to send a representative (most of whom turned out to live nearby) to meet in January in Washington, D.C.[11] The goal was "to enlist all American women in arousing the nations to respect the sacredness of human life and to abolish war."[12] Groups with a variety of purposes—social work, suffrage, antisuffrage, anticapitalist—were invited along with women's clubs, the Women's Trade Union League, and other labor unions, farm women's and mothers' congresses, the enormous and effective Woman's Christian Temperance Union with its wide-ranging reform agenda, the traditional-minded Daughters of the American Revolution, and the radical National Socialist Women's Committee.[13] Democracy had never seen such a gathering.

On January 10, several thousand women and a small number of men met at the Willard Hotel. About seventy women were official delegates; the rest were the interested public. They listened to speeches in the public sessions, while the Platform Committee, chaired by Carrie Chapman Catt and on which Addams sat, drafted the platform of a new organization, the Woman's Peace Party. It was virtually identical to the CEF platform, including its suffrage plank.

On the subject of a conference of neutrals the Woman's Peace Party platform, like the CEF platform, offered the choices of an official or unofficial one. If the first proved "impossible or impractical," then the party would work toward the "summoning of an unofficial conference of the pacifists of the world."[14] With even more boldness than the CEF, the Woman's Peace Party was urging that the world's citizens, not just international law experts, take the mediation of the war into their own hands. The idea was like the domestic progressive reforms of referendum, initiative, and recall in that it turned citizens into adjudicators of last resort. Going further back, it caught the spirit of the Declaration of Independence and the Constitution: If the government or governments were failing, the people would take responsibility.

Also striking was the new role in foreign policy the platform imagined for American women. Its preamble, after opening with the constitutionally inspired words "We, the women of the United States," applied the suffrage argument—that women were specially qualified for public policy debate—to the international realm. Since women had long been charged with the future of children, it argued, indeed been the custodians of life, and since women had built the foundations of the home and peaceful industry, they ought not to be shut out from debates about the life of nations and ought to be involved in the decisions too. "We demand that women be given a share in deciding between war and peace in all the courts of high debate. . . ."[15]

In discussing women, the preamble was artfully worded to mean different things to different people. Many women there, perhaps most, believed woman's biological nature made her more gentle and loving and therefore superior to men. They understood the preamble as endorsing that view, even though it never referred to women's nature as such. Addams, however, stayed focused on women's feelings about the value of human life. She told the gathering, "I do not assert that women are better than men . . . but we would admit that . . . women are more sensitive than men [when it comes to] . . . the treasuring of life."[16] While rejecting biological determinism, she was willing to grant that most women, having had the experience of giving birth and/or having raised children, felt the preciousness of human life more strongly than men did.

The delegates adopted the visionary platform and voted to create the first national women's peace organization in the United States, the Woman's Peace Party (WPP), and elected Addams its president. The time was right. The platform's unflinching preamble could not have been written in 1895 or even 1905; decades of effective organizing of women as a political force lay behind its self-confidence. By 1915 the demand that American women should have an equal voice in foreign affairs seemed merely obvious, at least to suffragists.

In calling itself a party, the new organization was imitating the Woman's Peace Party of New York, one of the new emergency peace committees formed that fall. "Party" was a good choice for the name of the new national group. It had a well-organized base, a platform of goals that required political action to achieve, and members ready to use political power to achieve their goals. If Jane Addams's role in the Progressive Party Convention of 1912 was the historical symbol of women's political coming of age, then the organizing of the Woman's Peace Party was the historical reality.

Meanwhile, Addams's itch to democratize the American peace movement was still not satisfied. In February she, Louis Lochner, and the other Chicago activists organized the National (or Emergency) Peace Federation (its title was to vary). Some three hundred men and women from the same broad swath of organizations that had gathered in Chicago before, now representing national bodies, adopted nearly the same platform as that of the CEF and WPP. The main difference was the plank on the neutrals conference: only the official one was endorsed. Clearly, the issue was controversial within the peace movement.[17]

Once again Addams was elected president. She had now accepted three presidencies in as many months. Before 1914 she had accepted only two, those of the National Conference of Charities and Correction and the National Federation of Settlements, although she likely received other offers. When the issue was peace in time of war, she said yes every time. It was an indication of her deep commitment.

Some European women, suffering much more from the war than Americans were, desired urgently to organize for peace. Dutch suffragist Aletta Jacobs convened a handful of suffragists from Belgium, Germany, Great Britain, and the Netherlands in Amsterdam to plan a meeting. They decided it would be held in late April in The Hague, the Dutch city that had hosted international peace conferences since 1899. Determined to ignore the battle lines of the war, they invited women from organizations in all the European nations and around the world. Had such a thing ever been done before in the history of the world? A *New York Times* editorial called it "a mad plan."[18] Addams was invited to lead the American delegation from the Woman's Peace Party and to chair the meeting. Hull House resident Dr. Alice Hamilton was to join her as a travel companion since Mary Rozet Smith was not going. She tended to stay home when Addams was going to a conference or lobbying in Washington.

Tragically, as Jane Addams was preparing to leave for Europe, her only surviving sister died. Alice Addams Haldeman had been seriously ill since October, when Jane had brought her from Kansas to stay at Hull House and, eventually, to be treated in a Chicago hospital. At sixty-one, Alice had suffered in recent years from obesity, rheumatism, and, finally, cancer, the cause of death. During the months she was dying, Jane was intensely busy with peace organizing and traveling to attend the WPP meeting and to give suffrage talks. The situation must have reminded her of the last time her social and family claims had been in difficult tension—when her oldest sister, Mary, had died during the Pullman Strike. At one point in the fall of 1914 Jane wrote guiltily to a family relation, "I am sorry to play the 'public woman' and it is very hard in the midst of distress and illness."[19] But she kept on going. She was not heartless; she believed her responsibilities to the nation and world placed a higher moral claim on her than those to her family. It was a choice that men had made since time immemorial, most notably in going to war, but for a woman to make it amounted to a stunning assertion of the equality of women and men as citizens, not to mention of the equality (at the very least) of peace and war as moral claims.

Fortunately, Jane was with Alice when she died in March, and she traveled with the coffin to Cedarville, where her sister was buried in the family plot. Since her stepbrother George Haldeman had died, still a recluse, in 1909, Jane's only living sibling now was her brother Weber. By 1915 he was living more or less permanently in a mental hospital. His schizophrenia had worsened over the years.[20] Alice's passing left a huge void.

Given that death always made Addams feel powerless and stirred her desire to act, the meeting at The Hague was a timely salve. But she had no illusions about what might be accomplished. The day before she boarded the ship for Europe, she tried to limit people's expectations in a speech in New York to Woman's Peace Party supporters: "We do not think we can settle the war. We do not think that by raising our hands we can make the armies cease slaughter. We do think it is valuable to state a new point of view. We do think it is fitting that women should meet and take counsel to see what may be done."[21] She was going to The Hague to be part of the debate about how to end the war. The Woman's Peace Party was putting the vision of its platform preamble into action.

||||||||||||

Broad fields of red and yellow tulips were in bloom as the women arrived in The Hague. An unusual gathering was taking shape. Present were some eleven hundred delegates from the United States (Canada sent none) and twelve European countries, including forty-three from the Central Powers of Germany, Austria, and Hungary (greetings were sent from as far away as India and South Africa). They represented 150 national organizations, mostly suffrage and peace societies but also cooperative guilds and labor unions. The United States had the largest delegation, with forty-seven women. And the public—another thousand women and a few men—came too, to observe.[22] The women from the belligerent nations were ignoring their governments' opposition and, in some cases, the disapproval of their husbands, brothers, and boyfriends. Addams found these women's moral courage profoundly moving. In a

The Woman's Peace Party delegation to the International
Congress of Women, The Hague, 1915. Addams is
in the front row, second from the left.

speech she said that their coming to the congress was "little short of
an act of heroism." She honored their moral courage. For a woman to
"even appear to differ from those she loves in the hour of their afflic-
tion or exaltation, has ever been the supreme test of [her] conscience."[23]

Addams presided over the three-day congress with a skill that others
called "masterly" and "magnificent."[24] There were public disagreements
among the delegates and attempts to maneuver behind the scenes, but
Addams managed it all deftly. One friend who watched her chair many
meetings remembered: "To see her handle difficult situations, difficult
personalities, conflicts, was as exhilarating as watching skillful rapier
play, only it was quiet and unspectacular and so humorous. . . ." As chair
she was exquisitely natural, yet "so quick and alert and alive all the
time."[25]

At the end the congress adopted a platform that was much the same as that of the Woman's Peace Party, including the suffrage plank. The distinctly American contribution was the plank calling for "continuous mediation" by a neutrals conference—whether official or unofficial was not stated.[26] The congress organized itself into the International Committee of Women for Permanent Peace (ICWPP).

Meanwhile, the war was raging in the nations to which many of the women, crossing battle lines, would be returning. Determined to do something immediate about the war, the delegates approved, by one vote, a daring proposal of Rosika Schwimmer's to send delegates to present the international committee's resolutions to government officials of the warring and neutral nations. The idea was bold and certainly dangerous. But these citizens who mostly could not vote or serve in government had few other options. Addams had her doubts but was willing to be one of the delegates. "I have not lost my head," she wrote to Mary Rozet Smith. "There is just one chance in ten thousand. . . . You can never understand unless you were here, how you would be willing to do anything."[27]

Once again Addams was elected president. It was agreed that the International Committee of Women for Permanent Peace would be governed by an executive committee made up of two women from each national branch—most branches did not yet exist—and its headquarters would be in Amsterdam. Within a few months, the Woman's Peace Party executive committee would vote to become the U.S. branch of the ICWPP. The International Committee decided it would meet again in the same time and place as the peace talks to be convened once the war ended.

Jane Addams gave the presidential address on the last evening. She wanted to strengthen the women's resolve as they prepared to reimmerse themselves in the overheated patriotism of their home fronts. Her ideas came from *Newer Ideals for Peace*, except that instead of crediting workers and immigrants with the new ideals, she now credited women. "By what profound and spiritual forces," she asked her audience, were they impelled to come? Why did they believe "the solidarity of women" would hold

fast when "internationalism is apparently broken down"? They understood, she explained, that a "spiritual internationalism . . . surrounds
and completes our family [and national] life" and that there are "universal emotions which have nothing to do with natural frontiers." Their
work, then, was to "dig new channels" through which this new internationalism might flow.

Lest the women doubt that they possessed the kind of power needed
to change the world, she assured them they did. "Our protest may be
feeble but the world progresses . . . only in proportion to the moral
energy exerted by the men and women living in it; social advance must
be pushed forward by the human will and understanding united for
conscious ends."[28] She was sharing with them the conviction that had
shaped her life, that progress came from putting organized spirit—
collective moral energy—into action. The women of the congress, by
putting their own convictions into action, gave that same moral energy
back to her.

The International Committee sent two delegations to meet with foreign and prime ministers in fourteen European countries. Crossing and
recrossing a continent at war, they spent almost two months completing
their journeys. Delegates Addams and Jacobs, who visited six warring
nations plus Switzerland and the Netherlands, found the response in
each warring country to be nearly the same. The officials said they could
not offer to negotiate but would consider it helpful if, as Addams put it
later, "neutral people" were to come together, study the situation, and
make proposals.[29] Her words suggest that she was discussing an unofficial conference and was taking advantage of the vague language to push
for her favored option. She, Jacobs, and Dr. Hamilton also met with
wounded soldiers in hospitals and with mothers who had lost sons in
the war and grieved to hear their stories.

By the end of their trip Addams and Hamilton were more convinced
than ever that an unofficial conference was the best way to move Europeans toward peace, and they thought their fellow citizens would agree.[30]
But they also knew that the Germans' recent sinking of the British ship

Lusitania, which killed more than 1,000 people, including 128 Americans, had stirred up anti-German feelings in the United States. When Addams and Hamilton arrived in New York City in early July 1915, they landed in a country that was still strongly isolationist but whose militarists were feeling newly confident they could bring the public to their side.

Soon after arriving, Addams shared what she had learned in Europe. Her first speech, given without notes, was to a friendly crowd of some three thousand people at a peace rally at Carnegie Hall. Perhaps their warm welcome loosened her tongue. She talked, toward the end, about her conversations with wounded soldiers in Europe. Intending to show her audience that spiritual internationalism was present even in the heat of battle, she told how soldiers were sometimes horrified at having to thrust their bayonets into other men's bellies and were given liquor by their officers to numb their feelings before the attacks. "They all have to give them the 'dope' before the bayonet charge is possible. Well, now, think of that."[31] She may not have known that this was tradition in Europe going back centuries. The practice was much less shocking to Europeans than to Americans.

The press covered her speech respectfully the next day. The *Chicago Tribune* reporter described accurately her assertion that many soldiers were fighting against their consciences. The *New York Times* quoted her at length about the views in Europe and noted it was a misconception to think that she and others at the congress had been trying to negotiate a peace agreement. But the *Times* paraphrased her as saying that "all nations make their soldiers practically drunk" in order to get them to bayonet each other.[32]

The *Times'* report created an opening for war advocates to attack her. The famous war correspondent and antisuffragist Richard Harding Davis fired off a letter to the editor in which he quoted the "drunk" claim, charged Addams with insulting the courage and honor of the dead, and called her a "complacent and self-satisfied woman."[33] Soon, with an efficiency that hinted at the influence of an experienced publicist's hand, Davis's letter was being editorialized upon favorably in newspapers across the country.

Many editors not only accepted Davis's charge against Addams but were even more hostile than he was toward the idea that a woman could speak with authority about matters of war. Ignoring her sixteen years of work in the peace movement, the *New York Topics* said, "Jane Addams is a silly, vain, impertinent old maid . . . who is now meddling with matters far beyond her capacity." The *Louisville Courier-Journal* called her a "foolish, garrulous woman." A *New York Times* editorial charged Addams was "unconvinced" that soldiers had the stomach to fight, and added that women did not understand war and soldiers.[34]

Theodore Roosevelt too was on the attack. He had already refused an invitation to greet Addams at the dock when she arrived in New York. Then, in an article in the *Metropolitan* magazine he demanded that the nation prepare for war right away, derided the women in The Hague— he did not mention Addams by name—for seeking "peace without justice and without redress of wrongs," and called them "amiable peace prattlers" who uttered "silly platitudes."[35]

Davis and Roosevelt each felt strongly that pacifists were dangerous, but they were also friends and capable of coordinating their attack. Davis was the journalist whose vivid reporting from Cuba in the Spanish-American War in 1898 made Roosevelt a war hero, and in these months the two men were seeing a good deal of each other. Davis often dined with Roosevelt in Manhattan, and both were writing regularly for the *Metropolitan* magazine, Roosevelt on the staff and Davis under contract.[36] It is easy to imagine that Roosevelt, the most aggressive of supporters for militarism in these months, urged his friend to write the letter.

Addams maintained her silence at first. When reporters tried to get her to respond to Roosevelt's comment, she replied, "I believe in free speech." She understood that certain claims in her Carnegie remarks had struck a raw nerve, the "long-cherished" idea of the heroic soldier. In fact she had been praising the soldiers' heroism—their moral honorableness—but it was a different kind of heroism than that for which soldiers were usually praised. A portion of the public was out-raged. Addams's mail was soon full of "bitter and abusive" letters.[37] As the weeks went on, friends urged her to answer the public criticisms, but, as she reminded them, it was not her practice. Finally she relented. She let a friend write a letter to the *Times*, gave an interview to an Asso-ciated Press reporter, and wrote an article, "Peace and the Press," for the *Independent*. She tried to clarify that she had not meant to imply the men at the front lacked courage, that she had never said the use of stimulants was widespread, and that she had never meant to describe all soldiers.[38]

The onslaught of negative publicity left her deeply shaken. She had never been criticized in such a sustained way and by newspapers across the country. Davis's letter, she wrote, started a "storm" that "broke sud-denly and with great violence."[39] But she was not the only one and in the months that followed, as she and other pacifists continued to receive hostile press, she came to see that there was nothing personal or random about it. For the first time in her experience, she wrote, newspapers "of all shades of opinion" were making a "concerted and deliberate attempt at misrepresentation. . . ." Their purpose was to "make pacifist activity or propaganda [she used the word in its neutral sense] so absurd that it would be . . . without influence. . . ."[40] Though she did not say so, she could not have failed to notice that the attacks on women pacifists were particularly nasty.

Nor could she have been entirely surprised. She had long known that women speaking the truth about war would not be believed. Thirty-four years before, at Rockford, she had written in her senior essay about Cas-sandra, and she was enduring the same scorn and disbelief Cassandra had endured when she had prophesied to soldiers their pending defeat in the Trojan War. It was as if Addams were the prophet, as if she had known that someday, during some future war, her femaleness would destroy her authority in the eyes of men.

Throughout the summer and fall of 1915 Addams kept trying to persuade President Wilson to convene an official neutrals conference.

In addition to her being committed to the idea personally, it was her job to urge it as president both of the Woman's Peace Party, which had endorsed both the official and the unofficial conferences, and of the ICWPP, which had endorsed the conference but not specified what kind. Addams, having been to Europe and met with European government officials, wanted the executive committees of both groups to embrace the unofficial version. They refused, still hopeful that Presi-

Woodrow Wilson, 1916

dent Wilson would convene an official one. They also instructed Addams not to be seen as a prominent supporter of the unofficial option, and she agreed to work behind the scenes.[41] Being president of these organizations was limiting her freedom, but she would not give up. A few months later, in January 1916, presumably after further negotiations with the two executive committees, she would go public with her support for the unofficial conference by publishing an editorial endorsing it in the *Survey*, where she served (from Chicago) as an associate editor.[42] Jane Addams was stubborn when it came to speaking her mind.

At the same time, she was not feeling well. Earlier, in August, a bad cold had become bronchitis. It was likely that cigarette smoke had irritated Jane's lungs. Mary, despite suffering from asthma, had taken up smoking—just how many years before is not clear. No one knew then the harm cigarettes could do (in fact Mary's doctor had instructed her to smoke menthol cigarettes because he thought they would be good for her asthma; also sometime before World War I, Mary had suffered from breast cancer and had had one breast removed).[43] Soon, Jane's bronchitis turned into pneumonia. Later, back in Chicago, she spent much of her time in bed at Louise de Koven Bowen's.

Meanwhile, events took an unusual turn. Henry Ford, the automobile industrialist-philanthropist, who was also a critic of militarism and one of the richest men in the country, agreed to finance an unofficial neutrals conference of experts. Addams, although still not recovered, joined him, Louis Lochner, and Rosika Schwimmer in New York to plan it. The first step, they agreed, was to hold a meeting with interested Europeans in Stockholm, Sweden. To transport all the Americans over there, Ford, without consulting his fellow activists, hired a ship, thinking it would generate fine publicity. Addams had serious doubts about the idea when she learned about it and said so. Newly stung by the press's dislike of pacifists, she sensed what fun it would have with a "peace ship." Still, she planned to go, out of loyalty to her friends and because she did not think "fear of sensationalism" should keep them from leaving "one stone unturned." She went home to Chicago to pack for the trip.[44] However, days before she was to return to New York, her lingering pneumonia worsened (antibiotics had not been discovered yet) and turned into pleuropneumonia. Her lungs' membranes had become badly inflamed, causing a persistent, racking, and painful cough, accompanied by fever. Seriously sick, she was hospitalized.[45] The ship left without her.

Ford's ongoing financing of the neutrals conference, which had strong support among pacifists in neutral countries in Europe, turned what had been a novel idea into a reality. Experts in international law, economics, and government founded the Neutral Conference for Continuous Mediation in Stockholm in early 1916 and later set up offices in The Hague, with Lochner as general secretary. In the coming months the conference proffered its mediation services, publicized the peace terms of warring nations, and issued its own proposal.[46]

Jane Addams must have been frustrated that she was sick when so much was happening. Unable to do much and having too much time to think in the hospital, she thought over and over about the attacks on her Carnegie speech. "I experienced," she remembered, "a bald sense of social opprobrium and wide-spread misunderstanding that brought me very near to self-pity." At other times her fighting spirit stirred, and she was quietly and privately outraged. She thought the swings in mood interesting. "Strangely enough," she noted, the pacifist in wartime "finds it possible to travel from the mire of self-pity straight to the barren hills of self-righteousness and to hate himself equally in both places."[47]

For the next three years, while she pushed herself to attend necessary meetings in New York and to testify at congressional hearings in D.C, she was ill much of the time. Generally when in Chicago she stayed at Louise de Koven Bowen's or Mary Rozet Smith's under doctor's orders and spent only a day or two a week at Hull House. She considered herself in these years, as she had considered herself in the 1880s, a semi-invalid.[48] As before, she did not shy away from the possibility that spiritual alienation was the real cause of her illness, although in print she chose to consider that explanation only regarding the illnesses of others. She wrote in 1922 of the "large number of deaths among the older pacifists in all the warring nations" and noted that this probably had something to do with the fact that "more than the normal amount of nervous energy must be consumed in holding one's own in a hostile world." To "suddenly ... find every public utterance willfully miscon-strued, every attempt at normal relationship repudiated," she concluded, must easily lead to a "health destroying ... suppression."[49]

As Addams lay in her hospital bed and as the Ford peace ship steamed toward Europe, the Wilson administration was preparing to rearm the United States. Earlier that fall Wilson had unveiled his plans to ask Congress to finance a number of new naval ships and aircraft carriers. At the same time, his administration's policies were not neutral toward the Allies. During 1915 the United States infuriated the Germans by shipping Great Britain crucial supplies and arms even as it techni-cally avoided breaking international laws governing neutrality. Wilson believed that helping Britain and the other Allies was key if he was to lead the peace process. This was also the view of his senior adviser, Colonel Edward House, who had put the case to him in early 1915: If the United States was to lose the Allies' goodwill, "we will not be able to figure at all in the peace negotiations."[50]

The battle between militarists and pacifists was now engaged. Wilson made a nine-day speaking tour in the Northeast and Midwest, beginning in late January 1916. "The world is on fire, and there is tinder everywhere," he warned. "America cannot shut itself out from the rest of the world."[51] But instead of calling for the United States to enter the war, he talked about the principles he thought should guide the peace process at the war's end—respect for a people's right to sovereignty, equal rights for large and small nations, and freedom from aggression—and about creating a new international institution to allow nations to act collectively, a league of nations.

Addams might have done more to oppose preparedness, but her illness prevented her. In February her doctor sent her, in the company of Mary Rozet Smith, to convalesce, first in Colorado and then in California. She watched from the sidelines as the Henry Street group finally published a manifesto against militarism, formed itself into an Anti-Militarism Committee (soon to be renamed the American Union Against Militarism), and launched a massive campaign of speeches, meetings, and editorials. Various branches of the Woman's Peace Party also organized educational efforts, including a traveling Hull House production of Euripides' *The Trojan Women*, the famous tragedy about women and war, for which Addams had raised the money.[52]

By April, still suffering from pleuropneumonia, Addams was back in Chicago but soon found herself in the hospital again. Doctors now discovered that she also had tuberculosis of the kidney, the result of her childhood bout with spinal tuberculosis. Following surgery to remove the damaged organ, she was not allowed to travel. She had planned to go to Stockholm later that month as an American delegate to the neutrals conference, but had to cancel.[53]

Part of what made the public debate about preparedness so lively was that the movement's most eloquent spokesperson, Theodore Roosevelt, was traveling the country, testing the waters as a possible presidential candidate for the Republican Party (he had declined to be considered for the Progressive Party nomination). Passing through Chicago, he visited Addams, who was recovering at Louise de Koven Bowen's house. He claimed he just wanted to visit an old friend; in fact he was there to do politics.[54] He wanted Addams to support the Republican presidential nominee that year, whether it was him or Charles Evans Hughes, the governor of New York State. Roosevelt may have vehemently condemned Addams and her fellow pacifists, but his party, eager to defeat Wilson, needed the small but useful progressive women's vote and therefore Addams's political endorsement. Addams let him come. Holding a grudge was not something she believed in; redemption was. Perhaps she hoped to help him see the dangers of preparedness.

Aside from whatever unrealistic hopes both may have had, Roosevelt's visit demonstrated that Addams's endorsement was a valuable commodity. Wilson knew it too. While she was recovering from surgery, he sent her a huge bouquet of sixty long-stemmed American Beauty roses.[55] The question was implicit: Would she vote for him now that the women of Illinois could vote in federal elections? He would have to wait to find out. Much later, in October, Addams was to make her announcement. After praising Wilson for domestic progressive policies, she informed the press she would cast the first presidential vote of her life for the president; grateful, he sent her another, equally massive bouquet.[56] Addams's enormous influence in presidential politics in 1912 and 1916 was a breakthrough accomplishment for a woman, not to be duplicated again until the twenty-first century.

Addams spent the summer before the presidential election in Maine, resting but also writing. Her new book, *The Long Road of Woman's Memory*, would be published late that year. It seems to have been inspired in part by the conversations she had had the previous summer with European women whose sons had died in the war. The rawness of their suffering and the horror of its cause had stayed with her. These women "sat shelterless in the devastating glare of Memory," she wrote in *Long Road*. Its "pitiless light" forced them "to look into the black depths of primitive human nature." More material for the book came from her essay about her Egyptian trip, which she edited and included in the book, and from her continuing conversations with female immigrants and workingwomen in Chicago about their memories of industrial work and troubled marriages. From all the stories Addams extracted the same lesson: A person could heal the pain of an experience by reinterpreting her memory of it. "Our chief concern with the past is not what we have done, nor the adventures we have met, but the moral reaction of bygone events within ourselves."[57]

Long Road was Addams's second book about women. In 1912 she had published *A New Conscience and an Ancient Evil* in support of a campaign women and men were leading in large cities against human trafficking in young girls, then called the white slave trade. That book was about girls in their teens, including many from the countryside who came to the city looking for work or had run away from home, being forced into prostitution by men using clever, emotional manipulation. This second book about women was different. *Long Road* was about older women using their inner resources to find meaning in their lives. Needing to interpret her own memories, Addams sought to understand how other women had done it. The connections she found comforted her.

|||||||||||||

Wilson was reelected in November. The result reassured voters that the nation would not go to war. But the president's subsequent actions revealed that he understood the situation differently. He thought his reelection gave him the freedom to enter the war if it would strengthen his position as postwar peacemaker. In December he again offered to mediate the war and was rebuffed by Germany, which replied that the belligerents should determine peace terms. Clearly, the United States' neutrality had become a handicap to Wilson's ambition.

Congress took up the president's proposal to expand naval armaments in January 1917, and Addams, still feeling unwell, went to Washington to testify and to chair the second meeting of the Woman's Peace Party. She told the House Committee on Military Affairs that the party opposed a large increase in military expenditures, but knowing that the

Jane Addams with Lillian Wald, head of Henry Street Settlement House,
speaking to reporters at the White House, 1916

all-male committee would be inclined to dismiss her views on the usual
ground that women were "too emotional" to speak about such serious
matters as war, she could not resist adding a bit of pointed feminist
commentary. "I do not want to say that men are more emotional than
women," she told the committee, but men are "much more likely to
catch this war spirit [and] . . . think they must prepare to defend the
country, even when there is no enemy to prepare against. . . . Women are
not quite so easily excited."[58] Perhaps she had her tongue in her cheek;
perhaps not.

On January 22, 1917, Wilson gave his "peace without victory" speech,
setting out his key peace principles again and promising that the United
States would add its "power" to that of other nations to "guarantee
peace" throughout the world. On January 31, Germany, tired of watching the United States supply Great Britain with weapons and essential

supplies, announced that its submarines would now conduct unrestricted warfare on all vessels approaching Britain. A few days later Wilson ended diplomatic relations with Germany.

The train was leaving the station, but peace advocates could not bear simply to stand by. In February a newly resurrected Emergency Peace Federation (EPF), gathering its troops in Washington, D.C., lobbied Congress to require a national referendum before the nation could enter a war. The idea had been endorsed earlier by the Chicago Emergency Federation as well as the American Socialist Party. Addams, back in Chicago and sidelined by illness, could only send supportive telegrams.[59] Although the resolution's chances of passing were slim, the EPF kept the public debate about the war going and the voice of those opposed to war in the press. A few weeks later Addams rallied herself to attend a board meeting of the Woman's Peace Party in New York City and agreed to let the EPF name her to a committee of five to meet with Wilson about alternatives to war.

The meeting on February 28 with the president left Addams feeling "bitterly disappointed." He told the group that he could not present the peace terms they desired at peace talks unless the United States participated in the war. Addams was dumbfounded. Suddenly she understood that Wilson's "heart's desire" was not to avoid war but to shape the peace. How could he rate himself so high as a "moral leader," she asked herself, when he was willing to thus sacrifice the lives of thousands of young American men?[60] That day Addams realized that the earnest peacemaker was leading the nation into war.

Addams spent March with Mary Rozet Smith resting in Oakland, Florida, where Mary's brother Charles and his family spent their winters on a large estate.[61] Meanwhile, German subs sank three American ships. This, combined with the news of Germany's secret negotiations for Mexico to become an ally if the United States entered the war, changed the public mood. Wilson and the militarists, aided by heated editorials in the press, further stoked the sense of threatening danger.

By April 1, feeling better, Addams was back in D.C. with the EPF as it rallied and lobbied against what everyone knew was coming—a presidential request to Congress for a war resolution against Germany. On the evening of April 2, Wilson, in a dramatic address to Congress, called for war, arguing that "the right is more precious than the peace" and that the United States needed to enter the war "to make the world safe for democracy." Addams was sitting on the stage at an EPF meeting that night when a newsboy came down the aisle waving his newspapers and shouting, "Extra! War declared!" Without saying a word she rose and left the hall.[62]

Congress adopted the war resolution on April 6 and, soon after, it passed two laws that Wilson also requested. The Conscription Act, despite the appeals of Addams and others, provided no exemptions from military service on ethical or broadly religious grounds for other than a few small, traditionally pacifist religious denominations. Conscientious objectors were required to do noncombatant service in military camps.

The Espionage Act eviscerated freedom of speech, despite Congress's stated intentions to protect it. It was the first law since the Sedition Act of 1798 to give the U.S. government the power to outlaw seditious speech. The federal government could now confiscate any mailed literature that might "embarrass or hamper the Government in conducting the war" and could arrest citizens who attempted through public speech to cause "disloyalty" or worse in the military or naval forces (the press escaped being formally censored, although Wilson had asked for that power). Since Wilson interpreted any expressions of dissent against the war as "stab[bing] our soldiers in the back," the new law gave him all the power he needed. He admitted in private he thought it "insanity" to protect free speech in wartime.[63] Addams, in testifying to a congressional committee against the Espionage Act before the legislation was passed, sought to clarify that she and others could still promote alternatives to war and oppose the draft without being in violation of the proposed law but got no real answers. It was a courageous effort.

A mood of unquestioning, prowar patriotism swept the country.

Wilson asked for all American citizens to give their "undivided and willing support" to the war's prosecution, and most Americans, including many newspaper editors and clergy who had earlier opposed U.S. entry, heeded his call. With war declared and Wilson calling the anti-militarists "tools" of Germany, people assumed that the war critics would now switch sides out of patriotic loyalty.[64]

Many did. The ranks of war critics thinned considerably. Some of Addams's oldest and dearest friends—Florence Kelley, Mary McDowell, Louise de Koven Bowen, Grace Abbott, and John Dewey—decided to support the war. So did her nephews Weber and John Linn. Two other friends, working for the federal government, did their best to duck the question. Hull House resident Alice Hamilton, who in recent years had become a leading industrial toxicologist, on occasion worked as a special investigator for the Department of Commerce and Labor. Julia Lathrop had left Hull House and moved to Washington, D.C., in 1912 to become the first chief of the new Children's Bureau in the same department. Both women remained pacifists but did not take a public stand because, in Hamilton's words, "we were deeply attached to our jobs and feared to lose them." Lillian Wald was a pacifist at heart but trusted Wilson as her president. Addams's passionate belief in free speech and her distaste for compelling someone else to agree with her helped her respect her friends' right to their own opinions. Still, when Addams received a supportive letter from an old settlement friend, Helena Dudley, who still opposed the war, she replied, "[Y]our letter was a great comfort to me. I feel as if a few of us were clinging together in a surging sea."[65]

In the months to come, when speaking to a skeptical, even hostile, audience about the war, Addams did not criticize the government or argue that only good could overcome evil. Instead she used practical arguments: She dismissed war as an ineffective way to solve international problems or advance democracy and proposed alternatives, like a league of nations. She also defended the patriotism of pacifists in order to make the point that one could love one's country and still criticize

its policies. She told audiences in Chicago and nearby that pacifists were
not traitors or cowards but patriots to urge the creation of an international organization to prevent further wars. Was it not courageous, she
asked, for a man to see "that which is invisible to the majority of this
countrymen" and to "assert his conviction" and be ready to "vindicate
its spiritual value over and against the world?"[66]

The reception she received was hostile. Silence greeted the speech she
gave to the Chicago Woman's Club. She had told those gathered, many
of them her friends, that she believed war was an invalid way to settle
disputes. As she was leaving with Mary Rozet Smith, she told her, "I do
not suppose I shall ever be applauded in Chicago again." The students
and faculty at the University of Chicago were also stonily silent. She left
there feeling "profoundly discouraged."[67]

The speech at an Evanston, Illinois, church, where the audience was
again silent, received a good deal of press coverage. An old colleague
from Addams's progressive reform days, Illinois Supreme Court Chief
Justice Orrin Carter, stood up and criticized her for not supporting
her government in time of war. A wire reporter filed the story, and
editors around the country ran it with headlines like FRIENDS TURN ON
JANE ADDAMS, and wrote editorials calling Addams pro-German and
un-American. Her Hull House mail was once again flooded with nasty
letters. (There were also some letters of praise.) Her pacifist friends
fumed at the unfairness of the attack. Alice Hamilton wrote her: "Well
it was detestable of Judge Carter, wasn't it, but men are going to be
that way . . . as long as the war lasts. . . . I do hope you are not letting
it hurt." These experiences, Addams wrote later, taught her a difficult
lesson: "[D]uring war, it is impossible for the pacifist to obtain an open
hearing."[68]

What Hamilton may not have known but Addams probably did was
that Carter was the vice-chairman of the Evanston's newly formed draft
board. Wilson had announced on June 1 that any eligible male failing to
register for the draft would be arrested and imprisoned for a year. On
June 5, just days before Addams's speech, the first national registration

day was held, and ten million men, ages twenty-one to thirty, registered. The first draft lottery was held soon after. The day Addams spoke, Carter and much of Evanston, as well as the nation, were in the grip of a fresh, sacrificial patriotism.

Hull House too was caught up in the mood. A settlement resident became head of the neighborhood draft board, and the other residents voted for the settlement to become a place for registration. Addams could have used her influence to discourage the decision, and she spent "a wretched night of internal debate" just before the board opened for business, wondering if she had done the right thing in allowing it.[69] But she rejected the idea that Hull House was an extension of herself; she could not justify forcing her beliefs on the residents' and neighborhood communities.

Hull House struggled to hold itself together during the war years. The government suspected that some of its immigrant neighbors from Central Power countries were spies. Officials often came to the settlement to observe, but to Addams's relief, no one was ever arrested. At the same time, the settlement's meeting rooms were open to all. Residents were split over the war—six of the men left to go fight—and there were passionate debates, but a resident remembered how they still managed to live together in "a spirit of ... good will." Many donors were less tolerant and stopped giving because they equated Addams with Hull House. In an unusual step, Addams published a fund-raising appeal in the *Chicago Tribune*, seeking gifts.[70] She had less income herself; her unpopularity reduced her lecture, magazine article, and book income substantially.

The Woman's Peace Party also struggled to hold itself together. Some of its suffragist members, led by Carrie Chapman Catt, withdrew from the party and supported Wilson and the war. Others stayed in the party but thought patriotism required them not to criticize the president. Addams, still president of the party and always a believer in the individual's freedom to think for herself, guided the depleted organization into a safe harbor of toleration for the time being. At the party's 1917 conference members adopted the resolution: "Let those of opposed opinions be loyal to the highest that they know, and let each understand that the other may be equally patriotic."[71] The party was waiting for a time when it would no longer be necessary to choose sides.

With the nation now at war, President Wilson and his administration launched the most ambitious propaganda campaign in American history. A new government propaganda office published millions of copies of pamphlets, speeches, and posters and wrote newspaper articles, all designed to establish "the absolute justice of America's position." Widespread war hysteria was the result, driven by hatred of the enemy. A committee film titled *The Kaiser, The Beast of Berlin* vividly portrayed German war atrocities.[72] Wilson encouraged citizens to report any acts of disloyalty they witnessed to the government, in an effort to turn everyone into a spy. The people became full of suspicion, especially of pacifists, another group Wilson considered pro-German.

Addams faced repeated persecution. Her nephew Weber Linn remembered: "She was stalked by charges of disloyalty. She was publicly booed, [and] her speeches were cancelled." A Justice Department agent shadowed her public appearances, and the Treasury Department's Secret Service, the agency that protected the president, ransacked the national headquarters of the Woman's Peace Party in Chicago seeking evidence of efforts to undermine national morale. A hostile portion of the public did its part, spitting on the mail that protruded from the office mail slot and, in Addams's words, "befoul[ing] the door in hideous ways."[73] Linn overheard a prominent Chicago woman remark at a dinner party that Addams should be hung from the nearest lamp post, while an old friend of Addams's told her bluntly he regarded her as dangerous and would not object if the government imprisoned her in a concentration camp.[74]

The war years were the loneliest of Addams's life. Now in her fifties, she had been drawing strength from common work and shared goals for more than two decades. As her nephew noted, she had spent her life "in seeking identification of her own spirit with the spirit of democracy." Losing that identification was painful. Characteristically, Addams thought of her pain as simply human. She recalled later how pacifists in wartime were "cast out" into an "unnatural desert . . . peopled with the "demons" of "solitude." They felt like "criminals," "fugitives from mankind." She described their state of mind—her state of mind—as a "consciousness of spiritual alienation." In *Democracy and Social Ethics*, she had written about thirsting "to drink at the great wells of human experience. . . ."[75] Now, for her, the wells had gone dry.

She had moments she thought she had made a terrible mistake. "In the hours of self-doubt and self-distrust," she wrote, "the question again and again arises, has the individual, or a very small group, the right to stand out against millions of his fellow countrymen?" She decided that such "dark periods of faint-heartedness" were the hardest to bear.[76] Those were the moments when she must have wondered whether she had been wrong to believe so strongly in democracy, in the wisdom of the people. The thought could only have been horrifying since it rendered her past efforts foolish and unmoored her life's work from its motive. But common sense rescued her. No one could say that the view of the people was really known since Congress had not allowed citizens to vote in a national referendum on the war, as she and others had urged. And, once war was declared, propaganda and the press's hysteria had made peace a treasonous subject and federal law had made dissent illegal. Debate had been silenced, and democracy could not work without debate.

She pulled herself out of her moods of black doubt by remembering that standing her ground was both morally and pragmatically necessary. Writing later of pacifists during that time, she said, "We could not . . . lose the conviction that . . . the moral changes in human affairs . . . [sometimes] begin . . . with the one who . . . is designated as a crank and a freak and in sterner moments is imprisoned as an atheist or traitor." Addams knew her history: Plato's suicide, Jesus Christ's crucifixion, the early Christians' martyrdom, Martin Luther's persecution, and Galileo's trial for heresy. She had grasped why the West admired the hero—not just because he stood alone but also because he stood for the truth as he saw it, regardless of the consequences. "[A] man's primary allegiance," she wrote, "is to his vision of the truth and . . . he is under obligation to affirm it."[77]

Her partnership with Mary Rozet Smith gave her comfort. After a vacation with Mary in Maine during the summer of 1917, Jane left her friend reluctantly to take a trip to Mackinac Island, but being a bit shy when it came to expressing intimate feelings, she did not manage to tell Mary of the gratitude that was in her heart. "I was more or less tongue-tied the day I left. It seemed absurd to tell you how heavenly good you have been to me month after month. I am filled with affection for you. . . . I don't know why I write it when I might have said it." A week later she wrote, "I am feeling so . . . battered that I am not of much use to anybody but I am always entirely yours."[78]

She sought the company of not just pacifists—opponents of war or certain wars—but also nonresistants, those who rejected the use of force. In 1915 she became a member of the Fellowship of Reconciliation (FOR), a Christian, mostly Quaker, group that believed in nonviolence. She soon joined its board and found at its meetings "a certain healing of spirit." She seriously considered becoming a Quaker, but Hull House residents persuaded her not to, arguing that people in the settlement's neighborhood saw her as nondenominational—they often asked her to officiate at weddings and funerals—and would not understand. But after the war she sometimes referred to herself as a Quaker.[79]

She also did what she could for the men who were serving time in either army camps or federal prisons as conscientious objectors. There were roughly a thousand men who registered but refused to do non-combat military duty overseas or, in some cases, any service at all. Both FOR and the American Union Against Militarism, whose board she was also now on, worked to expose the brutality of the camp and prison conditions—an unknown number were tortured, and seventeen died—and to protect their legal rights. In October 1917, after much painful debate, the two boards joined to create a freestanding organization, the National Civil Liberties Bureau, with Roger Baldwin, a Unitarian pacifist and social worker, as head. Addams agreed to serve on this new board. During the war the bureau, itself suspected of sedition, fought for the free speech and civil rights of conscientious objectors and "war resisters," who were convicted under the Espionage Act.

In these ways Addams clung to what was left of the peace movement. But as its scope narrowed, so did hers. That worried her. Some years before, in 1904, she had warned that the devil digs a "moral pit . . . for the righteous," when "[we] keep . . . on in one way because we have begun that way and do not have the presence of mind . . . to change. . . ." A person should be more flexible and adventurous, she believed. She took her own advice and looked around for a wartime cause she could sign up for without being "too conspicuous" or compromising either her pacifism or her belief in nonresistance and found it in the deeply humanitarian issue of food.[80]

As soon as the United States declared war on Germany, Wilson and Congress created a new Department of Food Administration to supply American troops with food overseas and to feed the starving civilian populations in Allied and neutral countries. Wilson asked Herbert Hoover, founder and head of the Commission for Relief in Belgium, a private, nonpartisan international organization, to run it. The commission was a wartime effort that, despite its name, was feeding hungry people across Europe. Now Hoover faced new challenges. To have enough food to ship, he needed farmers to increase production and citizens to eat less commercially produced food. Rejecting the idea of government rationing, he wanted the second effort to be voluntary. Soon Americans were practicing meatless Mondays and wheatless Wednesdays, and consumption had dropped by a remarkable 15 percent.

Hoover invited Addams, whom he had met in Belgium when she was there in 1915, to be a department spokesperson. From the fall of 1917 to the end of the war, as her health permitted, she made speeches across the country, sometimes to friendly audiences and sometimes to hostile ones, urging Americans to conserve food consumption. Later she remembered how she sought to arouse in her female audiences a "primitive . . . motive" as compelling as the "war spirit," that of feeding the helpless. She imagined, in her dreamy way, how women might thus "pour into the war torn world such compassion as would melt down its animosities." She believed that through feeding hungry people, "a new and powerful force might be unloosed in the world, . . . the positive incentive which arises from looking after economic and social needs."[81] It was the message of *Newer Ideals* and peacetime progressivism, reframed to address the new times.

Of course bread, the perennial symbol of food, was also a deeply personal subject for her. It was the product of her father's mill, that place of so many memories, and "breadgivers" had been her obscure metaphor in college for her philanthropic ambitions. Preparing to speak about food, she decided to read about the myths that gave bread a spiritual quality. She read "endlessly in Fraser's *Golden Bough*" of "the Spirits of the Corn [wheat]," who were "always feminine." Wishing to share with other women the stories that "brought . . . comfort to me," she wove the myths into her speeches.[82] Addams was traveling her own long road of woman's memory in order to interpret her wartime work in a way that relieved her heavy heart.

||||||||||||

Woodrow Wilson had spent much time beginning in August 1914 studying proposals and thinking about the peace principles that he wanted to recommend that the warring nations adopt when the war ended. The platform of the International Committee of Women for Permanent Peace particularly impressed him. Addams had presented it to him in August 1915, as soon as she had returned from Europe, and he had told her he thought it was "the best formulation" he had yet seen.[83] On January 8, 1918, although the Allies had not yet won the war, Wilson laid out his conclusions to Congress in his famous speech on the Fourteen Points. Six of these points were moderate versions of resolutions in the ICWPP's platform, which, as Wilson recognized, while having a good deal in common with many other peace platforms, was more complete.

By midsummer 1918 peace seemed imminent. The Allies were finally beginning to win the war. The American navy was protecting the flow of supplies and troops to Europe, and the American army, now numbering half a million overseas and soon to be much larger, were helping win crucial battles on the western front in France. At the same time, Germany and its allies were falling apart. Their soldiers were demoralized and deserting the battlefronts; their populations had long been suffering starvation. By early October, counting from the start of the war, some 4.4 million civilians, on all sides, had died of hunger. Germany was on the brink of civil war.

Under all these pressures the Central Powers collapsed. First the emperor of the Austro-Hungarian Empire and then the German kaiser asked for an armistice on the basis of Wilson's proposed Fourteen Points. Wilson's reply to Germany was especially forceful. Passionate about spreading democracy and willing to use his power as the head of a victorious nation to force the end of dynastic rule, he told the defeated nation it must become a constitutional republic.

And it did. On November 9, the kaiser abdicated and fled to exile in the Netherlands. The Austro-Hungarian dynasty collapsed soon after, falling into its disparate parts as its emperor withdrew from political power. The Russian dynasty had fallen earlier, with the outbreak in March 1917 of the Russian Revolution and the subsequent execution of the czar. Across Europe, ethnic groups that had been ruled by one conquering dynasty or another were in revolt and wanted self-government. If nothing else, the war, true to its destructive nature, had broken up the old Europe. The question became who would draw the lines of the new Europe and whether justice or revenge would dictate the terms.

||||||||||||||||||||||||||||||||||||||||||||||||||||||||||||||||||||||||||||||||||||||||||||||||||||||||||||||||||||||||||

AMBASSADOR

THE WAR'S END brought jubilation. In the United States the wire services sent out the news early on November 11. In Chicago it was 2:00 A.M. when the *Tribune's* giant sirens (newspapers owned sirens in those days), joined by the sirens from the city fireboats, roused people from their beds. Thousands headed downtown to celebrate. Musicians came together to play, leading impromptu parades of soldiers; citizens cheered and waved flags.[1]

With the war over, life had renewed urgency. People had been reminded that it was not a given but a gift. Jane Addams felt urgency for an additional reason. She was fifty-eight when the guns fell silent, and to people of her generation that was an age bordering on "old." Indeed, in 1914 she had published an editorial in the *Ladies' Home Journal* that, thanks to the editor, had the catchy title "Need a Woman over Fifty Feel Old?" The magazine's readers expected the answer to be no but did not think the question silly. In her piece Addams answered it by giving examples of older women "leading interesting and socially useful lives." She praised the contributions that "woman's matured capacity" could make to public affairs.[2] Her own life certainly illustrated the point.

The question for Addams was not whether she would remain useful and engaged—she did not know how, or want, to do anything else—but for how long. There was nothing to be done, of course, but the prospect of death was at the back of her mind, along with the coming inevitable loss of beloved friends and the chance that her health would decline.

Growing old also meant that the gap between Addams and the rising generation was widening. Those in their twenties were now some thirty years her junior. The decade of the 1920s was much more theirs to shape than hers. She had always believed in the need to respond to emerging issues, to connect with one's times. But at fifty-eight the task felt different. The possibility of obsolescence hung in the air. Her ideas about peace, however, ran no such risk. Twenty years after she had given her first speech on the subject, those ideas remained radical and, in the last years of her life, kept her a cutting-edge reformer.

|||||||||||||

The war's end left behind suffering. The loss of life for the United States, whose troops had fought for only a year or less, depending on when they arrived at the front, was tragic enough: 117,000 military personnel and 800 civilians. But the American death count was modest when set against the fact that France lost 1.3 million, Great Britain just under 1 million, and Germany, 1.8 million. Each loss was a separate tragedy. One of the American civilians who died was Jane Addams's nephew John Linn. The oldest of her sister Mary's children, Linn was an Episcopal minister and supporter of the war. When he was denied the chance to fight because of weak eyes, he became a Young Men's Christian Association chaplain with an artillery unit. He was killed in early October 1918, during the battle of the Argonne, and buried at the battle site.[3] Sorrowfully, Addams resolved to visit his grave.

With the guns finally silent, the mood of the victorious governments was stern. If another war was to be prevented, they argued, then Germany must be punished for violating the rights of sovereign nations. The major colonial powers of France, Great Britain, and Japan had already secretly agreed that, once they won, they would remove territory and colonies from Germany and divide up the colonies of the now-defunct Austro-Hungarian and Ottoman Empires. They also planned to replenish their badly depleted government coffers by forcing Germany to pay large fines to reimburse the victors for the costs of the war. In the United States the newspapers were filled with self-righteous hatred for the Germans. A *New York Times* editorial remarked that the best way to achieve permanent peace was to "realize that one side was mainly right in this war and the other side mainly wrong."[4]

Wilson had proposed his Fourteen Points as a means to prevent war. By 1918 war-bruised people around the world—for the war had been fought in far-flung colonies too—were hoping it was possible to do that. The idea was popular. One reason was that the Great War, with its new and powerful weapons of tanks, airplanes, massive guns, and submarines, was the most industrialized, and therefore destructive, war that had ever been fought. Another was the war's shockingly broad geographic scale, with Japan a major aggressor on its side of the world and European colonial battlefronts scattered as far as Africa, the Middle East, and Asia. Yet another reason was the efforts of the European and American peace movements before the war to spread pacifist ideas. With Wilson in the lead it now seemed unavoidable to many citizens that the peace conference, scheduled to begin in mid-January in Paris, would take the goal of preventing war seriously. Perhaps Wilson would be right, and this war would prove to be "the war to end all wars."[5]

Women pacifists were prepared to be part of the discussion. They wanted their International Committee of Women for Permanent Peace to meet in Paris too. But battered France would admit no Germans across its borders except the German government treaty representatives. The committee, believing strongly that women of all nations should be able to come to its meeting, decided to meet in Zurich, Switzerland, instead. Difficulties with visas and travel delayed their meeting until May.

Meanwhile, Addams was hoping the war's end would bring reasonableness to the American civic temperament and that pacifists in the United States would no longer be assumed to be the enemy. Others hoped so too. Her editor at Macmillan wrote her, "I believe the country is coming back to a saner attitude than it has shown of late." Another correspondent, Herbert Croly, editor of the *New Republic*, regretted the recent "intemperate condition of American opinion" but added, "I think the worst is over."[6] Both wanted to be able to publish Addams's writings again.

Addams soon had reason to doubt their upbeat predictions. In late January 1919 the Fortnightly Club of Chicago, a prominent women's club, nearly withdrew its invitation to her to lecture on the idea of a league of nations because some members objected to having a pacifist speak. The board stood its ground, and she spoke after all, but to a small audience.[7] The next day an employee of the War Department told a Senate committee that Addams was helping spread German propaganda. He presented an alphabetical list of sixty-two "radicals and subversives," and, as the *Chicago Tribune* reported, Addams's name was at the top. When a reporter asked Addams to respond, she went straight to the heart of the matter. "I cannot change my convictions," she said. "I have been against the war for many years."[8] A few months later she told the women delegates gathered in Zurich, "In America at the present day none is more detested than the pacifist."[9] Would she have to continue to bear the burden that she had borne during the war? It was a difficult future to contemplate.

Jane Addams left for Europe in early April with many of the same friends who had traveled with her four years before to The Hague. Florence Kelley, Alice Hamilton, and Emily Greene Balch all were delegates to the Second Congress of the International Committee of Women for Permanent Peace, as were several other newer friends, including Mary Church Terrell—the founder and president of the National Association of Colored Women, who was the only woman of color at the congress—and Jeannette Rankin. Rankin, a longtime suffragist from Montana, had been the first woman elected to the House of Representatives, in 1916, and was one of only fifty-six members of Congress to vote against the war resolution. Once the women arrived in Paris, their first destination, they were to meet up with Lillian Wald.

In gray, rainy weather, four of them—Addams, Hamilton, Wald, and Rankin—took a five-day trip to explore the devastated French country-side and to visit John Linn's grave. They saw, Hamilton reported to her family, "villages pounded to dust and great towns reduced to ruins and miles and miles of battlefields." The battlefield of the Argonne was still littered with the refuse of war—tin hats, canteens, and knitted socks. Finally they found Linn's grave in a small group of three rows of iron crosses. Afterward they walked a long way in the cold, slashing rain to reach their car. Addams, writing Mary Rozet Smith back home, said she was grateful to have seen it all.[10] Reality, good or bad, never failed to compel her attention.

Switzerland was a balm after that. But the war's cruelty was present at the congress at Zurich too, in the emaciated faces and bodies of the women who came from the defeated nations. Addams, walking in the city on the first day, met an Austrian woman delegate she had known at The Hague congress who was so thin and shrunken that Addams barely recognized her. Her condition filled Addams with sorrow for the woman's suffering, alarm at her poor health, and indignation that such things "were allowed to happen in a so-called civilized world."[11]

As for the 1915 congress, delegates to the Zurich congress were mostly professional or club women, and many were suffragists, but there were far fewer delegates, 150 instead of 1,100. This was presumably because of the toll the war had taken on the health and prosperity of European women generally, not to mention those who had died (the Austrian del-egate Addams met was to die three months later). The good news was that nineteen countries were represented, about 50 percent more than before. One likely reason was the spread of woman suffrage. Women in nine European nations and Canada had gained the vote between 1915 and 1919. The historic shift brought new energy to the meeting. More than ever women felt themselves to be players.

The Woman's Peace Party delegation to the International Congress of Women (which became the Women's International League for Peace and Freedom), Zurich, 1919. In the front row are Addams, third from the right; Emily Greene Balch, first from the right; and Jeanette Rankin, fourth from the left. In the back row are Alice Hamilton, third from the right; Florence Kelley, sixth from the right; and Mary Church Terrell, seventh from the right.

In some ways the work of this congress was the same as before. The 1919 platform endorsed the same principles of international law and international institutions, including a league of nations and women's suffrage. But with Europe now making peace, not war, the first part of the platform dealt with the treaty being worked on at the Paris Peace Conference. And because the women were to return home to nations at peace and therefore would be able to tackle reforms, the second part dealt with the work of the national sections. While the demand for women's equality permeated the platform, it dominated the second part. Delegates were charged to work for women's equal status in legislative bodies, for laws establishing legal and economic equality between husband and wife, for equal pay, and for equal education. This congress was a peace congress *and* a women's rights congress. Boldly the platform also called for racial equality and for civil and political rights for Jews.[12]

The Paris Peace Conference unveiled the peace treaty soon after the women's congress convened. The delegates in Zurich pored over its clauses with dismay. As expected, the treaty punished Germany by carving up portions of its territory, redistributing its colonies to the victorious powers (while ignoring ethnic groups and their right to self-determination), requiring it to pay massive reparations, drastically reducing its army and navy while leaving the victors fully armed, and forcing it to accept sole guilt for the war. The treaty thus violated most of Wilson's Fourteen Points. Despite Wilson's progressive internationalist vision and wartime maneuvering to be at the peace table, he had accomplished little. Frustrated that he had failed, the Zurich congress voted to "express its deep regret that [the peace terms] should so seriously violate the principles upon which alone a just and lasting peace can be secured." Such peace terms, it warned, would create "discords and animosities" throughout Europe, "which can only lead to future wars."[13]

Practically the only thing Wilson salvaged from his original vision was a proposed League of Nations, but there, too, much ground had been yielded. The Zurich congress found that the treaty provisions failed to allow all interested countries to join, failed to protect the right of self-determination for people living in territories that changed hands, failed to require that all member states reduce their armaments on the same terms, failed to give the League's Assembly any legislative powers needed to create a body of international law, embraced the use of military action to enforce League decisions, and excluded Germany from membership. Some delegates wanted to endorse the League and others thought such a flawed proposal should be categorically rejected. Finally they agreed to support the league idea in principle and recommend changes to the authorizing language.

The Zurich congress adopted a large number of resolutions spelling out its views and agreed to send five delegates, including Addams, to Paris to present the resolutions to representatives of Great Britain, France, and the United States. The purpose was more symbolic than practical. Even if the women could not persuade the victorious governments to revise the treaty, they were determined to be part of the discussion.

Not surprisingly, given the poor direction the peace conference had taken, there was plenty of determination at Zurich to convert their organization from a federation of national groups into a stronger international body. The group gave itself a new title, the Women's International League for Peace and Freedom (WILPF). It nicely summed up their program, as Lida Gustava Heymann, one of its international vice presidents, later explained: "Only when freedom is secured is permanent peace possible and only when women are free personalities will they be real workers for peace."[14] The group created a new international board, a portion of whose members were directly elected for the first time, and agreed that broad policy would be set by the congresses and be binding on the national sections. It would set up headquarters wherever the League of Nations was. Emily Greene Balch, who lost her Wellesley College professorship in 1919 because of her pacifist work, was named the head of the office, which turned out to be in Geneva. A brilliant and energetic organizer, she became the international league's driving force in its early years and, in a true sense, its founder. But one thing did not change: Jane Addams was again elected president, for a two-year term.

In her closing address, Addams tried, as she had at The Hague, to lift the morale of the delegates. Look at what you have accomplished, she urged. If the women from enemy nations could come together in "genuine friendship and understanding," then perhaps the same could be done "on a larger scale." In this moment "of sorrow and death and destruction, we shall have to believe in spiritual power.... We shall have to learn to use moral energy ... and believe that it is a vital thing ... [that] will heal the world."[15] It was the best advice she could give them or herself: Attend to the motive power of the human connection, and you will find strength.

Addams found strength at Zurich. Despite the problems with the treaty, she left the congress refreshed. She had felt like a "criminal" during the war, she later wrote, but her "sense of being apart" from her fellow human beings had been "broken into ... for a blessed fortnight." Alice Hamilton could see the change. In a letter to Mary Rozet

Smith, she reported that Addams was "happier ... than she had been in five years."[16] As much as Addams cared, and she cared deeply, about achieving actual social reforms, what kept her going in her long decades of sometimes Sisyphean effort was the joy of working with friends on shared goals.

Back in the United States, Addams watched as the U.S. Senate debated whether to ratify the treaty. Party politics were a factor (Wilson, a Democrat, was asking a Republican-controlled Senate to approve his treaty) but in addition, many senators were unhappy, not with the peace terms with Germany but with certain of the League provisions. The most troubling was the one requiring the United States, without prior Senate authorization, to act with member nations to aid another member nation if it was attacked. Also, it was impossible to approve the treaty without approving the League. Wilson had insisted the League language be embedded in the treaty to force the Senate to approve them together.

Opponents argued that the League threatened American sovereignty. They refused to ratify the treaty three times, in September and November 1919 and again in March 1920. (After Wilson left office, the United States signed a private treaty with Germany that omitted the League language.) Some Americans were embarrassed, and some—those with progressive hopes—were disappointed, but still others were relieved. Maintaining the traditional isolationism of the United States, upon which the war had intruded, seemed a lot simpler and safer than joining an untried, certainly entangling international body.

Addams was no enthusiast for the League as proposed, but she wanted the United States to be a member nation.[17] What mattered most to her was that for the first time in the history of the world forty-four national governments were creating a permanent institution as a forum for international policy debate. Addams believed that over time "an articulate world opinion" could reform it and make it a real force for peace.[18]

The world was shocked the United States was not going to be a member of the League. The United States was a world power, yet it had withdrawn itself from the new order of world politics. The exact opposite of what Wilson had promised had happened. Meanwhile, his life had taken a terrible turn. While campaigning in the West in September 1919 to stir up public support for the treaty, he had collapsed from exhaustion. Soon after, he suffered a stroke that partially paralyzed his left side and kept him bedridden for months. The man who had intended to save the world for democracy became an invalid at age sixty-two, still technically president until March 1921 (he refused to resign), but a shell of his former eloquent and vigorous self. Wilson's heroic self-righteousness had led to a tragic end. He was to die three years later.

Wilson left behind two legacies: a set of ideas—the principles embedded in the Fourteen Points, though none was original with him—and an institution, the League of Nations, an idea with a long history for which he had fought hard. To honor these accomplishments, the Nobel Committee of the Norwegian Parliament gave him the Nobel Peace Prize for 1919, which it awarded in 1920. The prize must have pleased him because it honored his ideals, about which he cared the most.

|||||||||||||

Addams continued her efforts to help those starving in Europe after the war, but now she was focused on the situation in Germany. After the Zurich congress, she and Alice Hamilton, along with some English Quakers, visited the country at the invitation of the American Friends Service Committee in order to bring food and money and inspect conditions. The two Americans returned to the United States with vivid memories of emaciated German children with sticklike legs and swollen bellies. That fall Addams and Hamilton traveled the country, giving talks to procure food and raise money for the Quaker effort in Germany, but their audiences were often hostile. Many Americans did not want to help feed the former enemy and charged the two women with being "pro-German," as of course, in a certain humanist sense, they were.

Addams understood the lingering appeal of the wartime vilification: "[N]othing save love stirs the imagination like hatred," she was to write in 1930. She wondered if people needed "some object upon which the hatred stirred up during the war could vent itself."[19] Pacifists, having been equated with the enemy, were an obvious target, as were socialists, with which they were also equated, since socialists had long been understood to be the enemy of capitalism. For the next decade Addams had to live with the fact that a group of Americans were determined to defame people who believed as she did.

Part of the nation may have been locked in a war mentality in 1919, but not all of people's fears—for fear always fuels hate—were ungrounded. While pacifists posed no real threat to the public order, anarchists who believed in violence did. In the early months of 1919 they began to terrorize the nation with bomb attacks. Between April and June thirty-four bombs were mailed to government officials in New York City; a bomb exploded at a U.S. senator's home, with two injured; another bomb blew up in the home of the new attorney general of the United States, A. Mitchell Palmer, with none injured; and one day bombs were exploded in eight cities simultaneously.[20] The violence was part of a familiar pattern. Before the war anarchists who believed in violence had assassinated six heads of state in Europe, had been rumored (incorrectly) to be behind Czolgosz's assassination of President William McKinley in 1901, and had also been given credit (wrongly) for the bomb at the Haymarket in 1886.

The nation wanted the government to act, and the task fell to the Justice Department. Under orders from President Wilson, Attorney General Palmer, his determination made all the fiercer by the attack on his family, launched a campaign in January 1920. Equating immigrant socialists with immigrant anarchists and immigrant anarchists with violent anarchists, the department instructed police in major cities to arrest immigrants with socialist or anarchist sympathies. Thousands of people were detained without trials; most of them were innocent of violent intentions, let alone actions; some were later deported. To identify which "dangerous radicals" should be arrested, Palmer turned to a young lawyer, J. Edgar Hoover, the new head of the department's General Intelligence Division. Hoover culled arrest records, subscription records of radical newspapers, and Socialist Party membership records for names.

For some Americans, the raids were something they read about in the newspapers; for others, like Addams, they took place next door and involved friends. In Chicago the Department of Justice arrested some Russian immigrants Addams knew, workingmen who were members of the Socialist Party. Thrilled by their nation's overthrow of the czar and hopeful that the Socialists would succeed in their struggle to control Russia, they had organized a school to train themselves in useful skills and planned to return to their homeland.

Upset at their being arrested without warrants and knowing some were headed for deportation, Addams helped raise bail for them and presided over a meeting protesting the violation of their constitutional rights. "An attempt is being made," she said at the meeting, "to deport a political party." All the men sought, she said, was "the right of free speech and free thought, nothing more than is guaranteed to them under the Constitution of the United States." And there was damage being done to the nation as well. "Free speech is the greatest safety valve of our United States. Let us give these people a chance to explain their beliefs and desires. Let us end this suppression and spirit of intolerance which is making of America another autocracy." She knew how much these Russian Americans had treasured their freedom in the United States to speak their minds without fear of persecution and how shocked and angry they were at being arrested. Though she kept her language mostly measured, she believed her country's oppression of free speech to be an outrage.[21]

Americans found the news of the Russian Revolution and Civil War gripping. Many working people were thrilled to see other working people rise up, and those who were socialists were thrilled to see their ideology come into power. Wealthier business people were horrified that Marxists, who were famous for their plan to take over the world, were gaining control of a nation for the first time in history. These

Americans feared not only the spread of revolution but also the end of property rights. The word "Bolshevik," the name of the workers' party in Russia, entered the American vocabulary as a nasty insult. As Addams put it, "To advance new ideas was to be . . . a bolshevik [sic]."[22] It was a drastic change. Just six years earlier reforms had been so popular that two presidential candidates had run on progressive platforms and one had been elected. Now such bold thinking was condemned by popular opinion as dangerous and un-American.

In such a political climate, Addams's unpopularity was bound to continue. Not only was she famous for advancing new ideas, but she also had, in the popular meaning of the phrase, "radical" sympathies. She was a pacifist, lived among immigrant and American socialists, had hosted famous Russian anarchists like Prince Peter Kropotkin, and was the head of a settlement house where socialists lived. Her sympathies for Russia were also obvious. In January 1919 she supported U.S. diplomatic recognition of the new government in Russia. In 1921 she served on a committee to raise funds for starving Russians.[23] Her membership on the board of the National Civil Liberties Bureau, and that of its direct descendant, the American Civil Liberties Union, organized in 1920, was seen by some as more evidence of the danger she posed to the nation. The ACLU was fighting the deportation cases in the courts. Clearly the war's end brought no reassessment of her patriotism. In fact the persecution to come was to prove far worse. J. Edgar Hoover would soon be compiling information on "radicals," including Jane Addams. She would have no respite from persecution for some years to come.

For Addams the happiest moment of 1920 was when the federal suffrage amendment was finally ratified. Support for the amendment had grown steadily during the war. Six more states gave women the vote in those years, and the NAWSA, its trade union and club allies, and Alice Paul's radical suffrage group, the National Woman's Party, all were pushing for it. (The party was her old group, the Congressional Union for Woman Suffrage, renamed.) Finally, in January 1918, President Wilson, prompted less by the NWP's picketing of the White House than by the politics of war, endorsed the amendment, and within months Congress approved it and sent it to the states. When, two years later, Tennessee, the final state needed to approve the amendment, passed it on August 18, Addams and other women suffragists celebrated, and they celebrated again on August 26, when the U.S. government officially declared the amendment law. The seventy-two-year campaign was finally over. It was a triumph to be savored.

Addams was no longer in the center of the fight by then. She had resigned from the National American Woman Suffrage Association board in 1914 because she objected to its endorsement of a states' rights suffrage amendment once she understood its racist implications.[24] She had given suffrage speeches and newspaper interviews for another year, but as the women's peace movement had absorbed the pacifist wing of the suffrage movement, she, like many others, merged the issues into one campaign.

The enfranchisement of women in 1920 was not complete, of course. Despite the words of the amendment, the majority of black women in the South, like the majority of black men in the South, still could not vote. Southern white men in power maintained racial domination through state and local voting laws and the extralegal tools of intimidation and violence. With women now legally voters, the moment was right for the women's rights movement to take up the issue of race. Seizing the opportunity, the National Association of Colored Women asked the National Woman's Party and the League of Women Voters (the organization into which the NAWSA had transformed itself) to support the proposal that Congress investigate these illegalities, but the two white organizations refused.[25] It was one more bitter betrayal of sisterhood to add to the others.

Organized white women, including Addams's good friends Florence Kelley and Julia Lathrop, took up many other causes with Congress, however. In 1920 ten progressive women's organizations whose leadership Addams knew well decided to improve on their informal collaboration of the prewar years. The League of Women Voters, the General

Federation of Women's Clubs, the National Women's Trade Union
League, and the National Consumers League formed a coalition, the
Women's Joint Congressional Committee, to coordinate their legislative campaigns. Between 1921 and 1924, they achieved notable successes,
including legislation to provide public services through the Children's
Bureau for maternity and infancy (the Sheppard-Towner Act, which
Lathrop ushered through Congress), an equal nationality rights act for
married women, and an amendment to the Constitution to ban child
labor.[26] These women picked up the banner of women's rights progressivism the war had forced them to put down. They were attending again
to the rights and needs of immigrant and working women and their
children.

Addams spoke on those issues from time to time, but her focus now
was on her international work as president of WILPF (she resigned
in late 1919 from the presidency of the Woman's Peace Party, just as it
reorganized itself into the U.S. Section of WILPF). The international
WILPF's program had been carefully conceived. The organization had
three goals, which Addams listed in her book about its early history,
Peace and Bread in Time of War. The first two were goodwill in international
relations and equality between men and women. It planned to achieve
these by influencing the work of the League of Nations in Geneva and
guiding the sections on which issues to advance in their national legislatures, WILPF did its reform work in its member countries (twenty-one
as of 1922) through pamphlets, meetings, lectures, legislative testimony,
newspaper interviews, petitions, exhibits, parades, and demonstrations.
Using facts, opinions, and dramatic deeds, it sought to stimulate discussion. WILPF was helping strengthen around the world the slow, messy,
vital process of democracy that Addams and her colleagues had worked
so hard to nurture in the United States.

The third WILPF goal was that future generations would also work
toward the first two goals. Much effort was put into education in the
schools. While these efforts, Addams admitted, could seem "ineffectual and vague," she had her answer ready: "[A]fter all[,] the activities

Jane Addams at sixty

of life can be changed in no other way than by changing the current ideas upon which it is conducted."[27] It was the kind of observation she specialized in—at once broadly philosophical yet somehow completely practical—and reflected her long-standing conviction that social change started from within.

Being president of a young and growing international organization at a time when the world could only communicate via expensive long-distance telephones and telegrams was not easy. Addams used postal mail to stay in touch with the presidents of the national sections and held face-to-face meetings whenever she could. After WILPF's international congress in Vienna in July 1921, she spent two months visiting the national sections in Europe and meeting with their executive committees.

Beyond Europe lay Asia, where women wanted to establish affiliated societies or national sections. To support them, the only real solution was to take a world trip. Addams, the lover of travel, hardly minded. It would be the adventure of a lifetime, a chance to learn about women in countries she had only read about, and to support the work of women's rights and peace advocates in faraway places. At age sixty-one, and with her uncertain health, the question must have occurred to her, If not now, when?

Addams left the United States in December 1922 with Mary Rozet Smith, who made the entire trip with her and possibly helped pay for it too. They went first to an emergency international congress at The Hague that WILPF had convened. The goal was to start a public campaign to push the signers of the peace treaty to correct its harsh terms—harsh to all except the victors, that is. Ethnic groups being governed by other countries under legal "mandates" wanted to govern themselves; colonies wanted independence; Germany's economy, crushed by the huge reparations it owed but could not pay, remained in shambles, and the German people were angry and humiliated. All this reinforced the worry that unless a new peace could be negotiated, another war was coming. Then there was the failure to design an equitable disarmament process. The delegates, from 111 national and international organizations from twenty countries, called for a new world congress to draw up better peace terms. Here was the unofficial neutrals conference in new garb, arising from the same faith in what citizens could accomplish if they acted together and with the same goal of pushing governments to do more for peace. Was it foolish for them to try something so difficult? But how could they do nothing when the stakes were so high? And what other choices did they have?

While in Europe, Addams went to two other international conferences, both organized by groups with which she had long-standing ties. The International Federation of Trade Unions met in The Hague right after the emergency peace congress. The labor movement, which had taught Addams so much about the meaning of democracy and to which she had been so loyal, remained her touchstone. Then she and Smith went on to Paris to attend an International Conference of Settlements.

The settlement movement's reach had grown massively since its start in the 1880s. A little more than three decades later there were five hundred settlements in the United States and many more sprinkled all over the world, from Egypt and India to Japan and Venezuela.[28] Addams, as head of Hull House, the most famous settlement house in the world, was the honored guest of the Paris meeting. Given the hostility she faced from many in the United States, the affection with which she was greeted at these European meetings must have been a comfort.

There was more to come. For almost nine months Addams and Smith traveled from Burma to India, the Philippines, Korea, Manchuria, China, and Japan. Addams was hosted by leaders of settlements, women's clubs, women's colleges, universities, women's labor unions, and peace and women's rights groups. She gave lectures, marched in parades, and dined with prominent people. Reporters covered her travels and, unlike reporters in the United States, wrote purple prose praising her as America's foremost woman. Addams's egalitarian humanism required her to disclaim the importance of it all, but no heart that had been as battered as hers had been by a nation's hatred could have minded being thus bombarded by love.

Mary had never stopped loving her, of course, and her company on the trip was another balm, not to mention a help. Mary was famous among Jane's friends as a solicitous caretaker of her partner. She was always there, Louise de Koven Bowen remembered, with a handkerchief, a shawl, or crackers, "ready to supply Miss Addams's needs, whatever they were." She was also bossy about Jane's failures to protect her health. "You go lie down," she would say. Sometimes Jane would. And sometimes, being an independent spirit, Jane would reply, "I shall do no such thing. I never felt better in my life."[29] And there were the reliable pleasures of Mary's quick wit and delightful conversation.

Best of all the gifts Mary gave Jane was her calm spirit, what Jane called "her inner serenity." Jane thought this grew out of Mary's receptiveness to people different from herself. But Mary was not always receptive. A few times on their trip they met with groups that Mary, in

Jane's words, found "utterly alien" and "difficult to understand." Perhaps she found it strange to be introduced to women with bound feet or men with shaved heads. Mary was always courteous, but afterwards, Jane remembered, she felt distressed that "her perceptions had failed her." After one such meeting she told Jane that if a person lost her consciousness of human solidarity while traveling around the world to acquire an awareness of human diversity, then "the game was scarcely worth a candle."[30] She intended to respect humanity in all its unfamiliarity, but when prejudice sneaked in, she acknowledged it and tried to keep it from affecting her conduct.

She applied the same high standards to those she loved the most. Although Mary had not been critical of Jane in the early years, that had changed over time. In 1933 Mary acknowledged to Jane that she had spent a good deal of their time together "scolding you roundly." Jane agreed. Mary, Jane later wrote, "was a very critical person . . . of herself and those friends she included in her inmost circle." Jane thought this was a good thing, that such criticism was part of the process of "self-discovery . . . essential to self-discipline."[31] Apparently Jane liked to have a partner who was critical. Ellen Gates Starr was the same way. Being criticized must have felt like home to Jane, revealing much about the way Anna had raised her, as well as her passion for self-improvement.

But Addams wanted personal affection too. In 1912 she had written, "No one can safely live without companionship and affection" if she wished to avoid being "swamped by a black mood from within." Even if she seemed to love impersonally, she readily sought love and did her best to give it. Believing what she had written in her first years in Chicago, that love "makes [men] human" by making them "interdependent," she embraced her vulnerability courageously, as part of her vision for a reformed world.[32] It was an unusual rationale for risking love, but entirely characteristic.

No doubt Addams's unending longing to improve herself was part of what compelled her to try to meet Mohandas Gandhi when she was in India. She had made the same sort of pilgrimage almost three decades before when she met Leo Tolstoy in Russia. Both men inspired her with their high characters and devotion to nonviolence. Gandhi, a lawyer with international experience who admired Tolstoy as much as Addams did, had drawn the world's attention in 1920, when he proposed that his countrymen use nonviolent noncooperation rather than armed revolt to gain independence from their colonial ruler, Great Britain. Named head of the political party that was leading the revolution for independence in 1921, he was sentenced to prison for sedition the following year. Thus he was in jail when Addams was in India in 1923.

Unable to meet him, she and Mary visited his ashram on the edge of the industrial city of Ahmadabad. In the Hindu tradition, an ashram is a place of spiritual learning. But Gandhi's ashram was hardly a retreat; it was a bit like Hull House, offering classes to farmers and laborers, hosting labor strike meetings, and generally supporting its neighbors in their struggles to pull themselves out of poverty. Gandhi's followers showed Addams the long-fibered cotton that they hoped Indians could grow to improve the quality of cotton cloth they produced and increase their income.[33]

Gandhi's moral leadership drew Addams the most. Gandhi, Tolstoy, and Addams held similar ideals: They believed in the moral power of all human beings, thought that spiritual values should permeate every action, and understood their lives as the best means they had to teach. Addams believed, as they did, that "[u]sing our life as an active moral principle, there is nothing we [can] not do with it." Apparently Gandhi admired Addams too. When *Life* magazine photographer and former Hull House resident Wallace Kirkland later visited Gandhi, the Indian leader's attitude changed from suspicious to friendly when Kirkland told him of his ties to Hull House and Jane Addams.[34]

The last leg of Addams's world trip was momentous in a less happy way. In Peking (Beijing), traveling in a rickshaw, she had an accident, hurt her arm, and suffered a pain in her side. The doctor treating her discovered she had a tumor in her breast. She decided to have a mastectomy in Tokyo, where she was headed next. Dr. Alice Hamilton, always attentive when Addams had a health crisis, hurried to Japan to be with her.[35] Once the surgery was completed and Addams had recovered, they left for home. A few days later a disastrous earthquake and a typhoon-driven fire leveled Tokyo, including the hospital where Addams had been staying. In comparison to dying in such a disaster, surviving with one breast must have seemed a relative blessing to her.

By late September she was back in Chicago and at Hull House. To the crowd gathered at the settlement to greet her, she told of her travels, including the progress that women's suffrage was making around the world and how she had narrowly missed the earthquake.[36] At a banquet the City Club gave for her, she spoke of the great desire she had found in every country in Asia to achieve "self-determination." But she knew how to mix humor with her politics. The Chinese, she said with mock solemnity, far from being uncivilized, learned banditry from watching American movies or sometimes by observing it firsthand. A famous Chinese admiral had told her, she explained, that once, when he traveled from California to Yale University, his stagecoach was attacked by Jesse James and his band.[37]

|||||||||||

While Addams was traveling in Asia, the U.S. War Department launched a direct attack on the U.S. Section of WILPF. The immediate cause was the organization's effort, along with that of other women's groups, to persuade Congress to cut the department's appropriations. Secretary of War John Weeks, a former prominent antisuffragist, launched a public relations campaign to ruin the reputations of the women's organizations and their leaders. Meanwhile, the international WILPF had decided to hold its fourth congress, the first to be held in the United States, in early May 1924 in Washington, D.C. The congress, by meeting in the War Department's hometown, was an easy target for the department to attack.

Although Weeks did not hide the department's role in the campaign, he wanted civic groups to lead it. He turned to local chapters of prowar veterans' groups like the American Legion, Daughters of the American Revolution, and Daughters of [the War of] 1812, all of them longtime critics of suffragists and pacifists. They used the now-familiar arguments that the women's groups were in sympathy with, and working as spies for, the Russian Soviet government and that the Russians, with WILPF's help, were planning to attack the United States and make it Soviet (Communist) too.

To help them make their case, Weeks had his department create and circulate among these groups a clever document, later versions of which were called the Spider Web. It showed, with connecting lines, that twenty-nine American women leaders were members of many of the same fifteen "socialist-pacifist" organizations, including the U.S. Section of WILPF. (Addams, because she was president of the international WILPF, was not in the original version but was added later, as were men; these versions were published privately.)[38]

Weeks also was in touch with Hoover, now the deputy director of the Justice Department's new Bureau of Investigation and soon to be its acting director. Perhaps at Weeks's request, Hoover assigned an agent from his office to spy on the congress. Afterward copies of the agent's report were placed in Addams's file at the bureau and sent to the Military Intelligence Division of the War Department.[39]

Addams likely headed to the D.C. congress with a sense of foreboding. In any case, by the time she and the other WILPF leaders arrived in Washington in late April, they knew what the *Washington Post* was also reporting: The War Department and the Justice Department were planning to send "observers" to the congress, and the Daughters of 1812 wanted a Senate committee to investigate if WILPF was financed by the Russian government. They had also heard through the grapevine (some WILPF members belonged to the patriotic women's societies) that a coalition led by the Daughters of 1812 was planning to shut down the WILPF congress. In response, the police chief of Washington, D.C., sent police to the congress to protect the league delegates' free speech. The result was a startling front page headline in the *Washington Post*,

ARMED GUARDS TO PROTECT WOMEN IN PEACE MEETING. The Daughters of
1812 later canceled their plan.[40]

In her opening address, Addams took up the sticky question of the
delegates' patriotism, the question that underlay the War Department's
attacks. "I am not one of those who believe that devotion to international aims interferes with love of country, any more than devotion to
family detracts from good citizenship. . . ."[41] She also disagreed with
those people who thought that to love one's country meant to love
the United States as it was. Addams thought it meant to love what a
country could become. A few years later she was to define patriotism as
possessing "courage and candid loyalty to the highest achievement of
which one's country is capable."[42] She apologized to the delegates for
the spirit of intolerance they had encountered and urged them to speak
freely and from their hearts.

WILPF was determined to be a truly international organization and
thus to break with a U.S.-European tradition of calling a body international if it consisted of countries on both sides of the Atlantic or even
on both sides of the English Channel. Women had traveled not only
from Europe but from Ceylon, China, India, Japan, Argentina, Brazil,
Chile, Bolivia, Ecuador, and Guatemala; the Iroquois Nation was also
represented. The congress drew a hundred delegates from more than
twenty-five countries. As Addams had hoped, the women debated freely
the current contested issues: whether nations should be allowed to send
their armies and navies to collect the debts or protect the properties
of their nations' corporations in foreign countries (a regular practice
of the United States), whether national governments should end the
draft and capital punishment, and whether there was a need for a world
economic conference to secure world peace.[43] At the end, the delegates,
having reelected Addams president, went home to continue their work.

The persecution of pacifists was to continue for several years.
Addams, as the most famous pacifist in the United States, was a frequent target. Sometimes she was called "the most dangerous woman
in America," though other women, including Typhoid Mary, Mother

Jones, and Emma Goldman, were called that too. (Nor is it clear who first called Jane Addams that epithet. Among those given the credit are Theodore Roosevelt, who had died in 1919, J. Edgar Hoover, the ROTC, and the DAR.[44]) In 1928 the DAR canceled her honorary membership, a title she had held since 1900. She quipped: "I had supposed at the time that [my membership] had been for life but it was apparently only for good behavior."[45] She reassured her colleagues that she was not upset. "I [do not take] these attacks very seriously," she told Carrie Chapman Catt, who was planning to write an essay defending Addams and several others, "having learned during the war how ephemeral such matters are."[46]

That, at least, was her public stance. But to say such attacks were ephemeral was a polite fiction. By the time she wrote the letter in 1927, she had been enduring continued attacks for twelve years, ever since her Carnegie Hall speech. Because the attacks stemmed from intolerance— from a refusal to acknowledge a citizen's right to hold dissenting views without being charged a traitor—they made her angry. She told her nephew Weber Linn that as he put it, she "resented the fact that tolerance seems to the fanatic either stupid or a crime."[47] She had reached the limits of her own tolerance and patience.

|||||||||||||

By 1929 Addams was mostly staying close to Chicago because her health, which had always been unreliable, was poor. She had bronchitis or the flu every winter, and in 1926, while in Dublin for a biennial WILPF congress, she had had a heart attack. Though only five feet four inches tall, she weighed about 170 pounds. Her girth had been growing steadily since her youth, and in her sixties, her weight had become a serious problem. Sometimes she fell. Alice Hamilton thought that her feet were too small to carry her large body.[48] Given her poor health, she knew it made no sense for her to continue as president of WILPF. At the August 1929 congress in Prague, she resigned over vociferous objections and was made honorary president for life. WILPF could think of no person to elect as president, so three cochairs, one of them Emily Greene Balch, were elected to carry on.[49]

Addams turned sixty-nine in 1929. It seemed time to consider the ever-widening generational divide. In a talk she gave to the Chicago chapter of the League of Women Voters, she took up the subject carefully, beginning with a bit of praise: "We older women . . . look to the younger ones with the utmost confidence and hope for the future." Knowing women in their twenties and thirties saw her as a remote senior stateswoman, she challenged the assumptions that she had any answers for them and that she and they could not work together. "The problems of their day," she said, "will be their own and must be met in their own way. We would not control them if we could[,] for we are ambitious to be remembered as comrades and not as mentors." Loving equality and fellowship, she felt uncomfortable and a bit sad to be put on a pedestal and to be asked, politely, for advice. The practice also seemed unwise. Elsewhere she wrote, "Perhaps there is nothing more dangerous in the world than the leadership of prestige based solely upon the authority of age."[50]

It was easy for Addams to believe that young people should design solutions to the social problems of their day; she had designed some herself when young. What puzzled her was that they were now ignoring those problems and pursuing a fascination with sex instead. She probed for answers in an essay, "Contrasts in a Post-War Generation," which she wrote as a chapter in the new book she was writing on her second twenty years at Hull House. Were young people fascinated by sex because they lived in a time when progressive democracy—political and social reform—"had been discredited"? Or did Freud's theory that repression was dangerous, which had been publicized widely in magazines, lead them to see danger in "self-control"? Or was it the war that made young people "decry sentimentalism and exalt sex"?[51]

Whatever the explanation, she thought they were traveling a morally dangerous road. Interestingly, it was not the pursuit of sex that troubled her. Rather it was the theory used to justify it. She summed that up as a belief in the "joy of self-expression" and the "power of the subconscious" and a denial of "the value[s] of self-criticism and of self-discipline." Since these values had been shaping forces in her life, she was worried what their rejection might mean. If this new generation refused to be "tied to conceptions of duty," she wrote, they might "become abject followers of blind forces . . . beyond their control." In that case, "the fear of missing some emotional stimulus may well become a tyranny worse than the austere guidance of reason." She saw unreflective seeking of personal pleasure as a tyranny, while young people saw it as freedom. She had put her finger on the nub of their disagreement.

But she also thought the rising generation's underlying motive was good and the same as her generation's: the desire for human potential to flourish. The new generation is "bent on the same quest" as "our[s]," to remove restrictions so that "each human being [could] develop to his utmost capacity."[52] She did not argue that one's sexuality should not be developed; she was not a prude. She strongly supported sex education at home and in the schools, rejecting the idea that it was a "dangerous subject."[53] But she did not think that sexual fulfillment was per se essential to human fulfillment. To her the question was which morality—one grounded in reason, self-discipline, and self-criticism or one grounded in the subconscious and the pursuit of the emotionally exciting—would lead a person to flourish more fully. She voted for the morality in which she had been raised and that she believed had allowed her to flourish.

Had she once again become a moral absolutist? Over the decades she had adjusted certain of her inherited beliefs. She had (mostly) rejected the ethic of benevolence, that faith in the superior wisdom of the prosperous, as out-of-date and embraced the wisdom of the demos, the public—except perhaps when it was manipulated in times of war. But when it came to the morality of self-development, she drew the line. Her profoundly psychological mind had extracted lessons from observing a wide swath of humanity. She could not agree that an ethic that nurtured character was passé. Had she herself become out-of-date? Or did her now old-fashioned ethic of self-mastery hold a wisdom to which society might someday return?

As usual, Addams gave her new book a cumbersome but descriptive title—in this case, *The Second Twenty Years at Hull-House, September 1909 to September 1929, with a Record of a Growing World Consciousness*. Some of the book was about Hull House—the settlement's work with children in the arts, its experience with a rumor about a devil baby, and the educational uses of current events—but mostly it was a set of essays about her wider engagements since 1909: the Progressive Party, the woman's movement, the peace campaign, the last ten years of "post-war inhibitions," the national experiment of prohibiting the sale of alcohol (a policy she was ambivalent about, in part because it appealed to racists and those who were anti-immigrant), the imposition of quotas on immigration, some recent famous court cases (including Sacco and Vanzetti), and the issue of racism against African Americans, which she said threatened democracy and was "the gravest situation in our American life."[54] It was not quite a history textbook, the writing was too interpretive for that, but it taught a lot of history, and she sprinkled the text with nuggets of philosophy. Her readers knew they could rely on her to be thought-provoking.

She wanted *Second Twenty Years* to be published in time for the fortieth anniversary of the settlement house's founding, in the fall of 1929, but it was not to be. She failed to finish it at Bar Harbor and, back at Hull House, was swept up into other things. Meanwhile, on October 24, 1929, the New York Stock Market started its traumatic collapse. As the months passed and unemployment worsened, no one was quite sure where the bottom was. President Hoover tried to be optimistic. In May 1930 he confidently announced: "We have now passed the worst."[55]

That same month Hull House celebrated its fortieth anniversary—a bit late, to be sure, since the event should have been held the previous September. Many people came back to reminisce, but some had never left. Fifteen of the seventy residents had been there for more than twenty

Florence Kelley, Jane Addams, and Julia Lathrop
at the 40th anniversary celebration of
Hull House, May 9, 1930

years, and nine for more than thirty years.[56] Sadly cofounder Ellen Gates
Starr was not among them. The year before, back surgery undertaken to
treat a spinal abscess had left her legs paralyzed. She had retired to live
economically in an academy attached to the Convent of the Holy Child
Jesus, in Suffern, New York, where nuns could care for her. (The place
delighted Starr; she had joined the Catholic Church in 1920.) Addams
visited her when she could, helped her with her monthly living expenses,
and set up a pension for her in her will.[57] Although they were no longer
close, the bond of a lifetime of friendship held fast.

Hull House had changed in forty years. Fewer young people were coming to live there now. Single women could live on their own, and educated women could sometimes pursue careers without relinquishing their chances of marriage. Nor were settlements the fascinating new idea that people were talking about; even idealism was out of fashion. The neighborhood around the settlement had also changed. When African Americans and Mexicans arrived on the Near West Side in larger numbers in the 1920s, they joined Hull House's existing clubs and classes and prompted new additions, including a "colored women's club" that worked on housing issues and Mexican pottery classes.[58]

The fortieth anniversary, however, was about looking back. In the rearview mirror, Hull House stood as a remarkable achievement. Over the years it had been a powerhouse in the best way an institution could be, by nurturing the human spirit. Thousands attended its clubs, classes, concerts, and plays, discovered talents, gained skills, made friends, and found lovers. Workers used its rooms to organize trade unions and strikes. People of prosperous backgrounds—whether as settlement residents, volunteers, or visitors—learned about the ambitions, talents, and frustrations of working people and immigrants, and, if they were men, about the leadership talents of women. Working people and immigrants learned about prosperous people: that not all were greedy, arrogant, and unkind. Hull House did not transform people—they brought too much to the table themselves—but it nurtured gifts and erased blind spots. It gave people a more balanced understanding of the world, and it taught them what living a democratic life meant.

The settlement residents gained some extra lessons for which Addams deserved the credit. Opinions freely circulated in the house because she loved a good debate. The residents were respectful of differences because Addams insisted on it. She once warned a young white southern woman who wanted to be a resident that Hull House welcomed all races and if that requirement made her uncomfortable, she should not come. Creativity was encouraged because Addams believed everyone had something unique to offer. One resident, Mary Collson, noted "her confidence in the ability of others. She gives everyone the feeling of calm assurance that one's best is better than one thought it was." Good friend Louise de Koven Bowen said, "She was . . . never condemning but always reassuring and encouraging. . . ." Resident Francis Hackett said, "She had the power to value human beings."[59] It was no accident that people flourished at Hull House; Addams meant it to be that kind of place. She had a light touch but paid attention. A frequent visitor in 1926 noted: "Miss Addams does not dominate affairs but she . . . know[s] what is going on. . . ."[60] Hull House was her theory of leadership in action. Sometimes, when advising new heads of other settlement houses, she made that theory explicit. She once told Mary White Ovington, cofounder of the Greenpoint Settlement in Brooklyn: "If you want to be surrounded by second-rate ability, you will dominate your settlement. If you want the best ability, you must allow great liberty of action among your residents."[61]

Living at Hull House was the first phase of its influence on residents. In the second phase they scattered across the country and took their memories of Halsted Street with them. Among those who had been residents were the first head of the Children's Bureau of the federal Department of Labor, the first head of the National Consumers League, a president of General Electric, a longtime prime minister of Canada, a president of AT&T, the first woman cabinet member in U.S. history, the first woman faculty member of the Harvard University Medical School, and a key author of the Social Security Act of 1935.[62]

And then there was Addams's influence in her later years on young people who had never been Hull House residents, but who knew her as an inspirational friend. Those fighting for social justice after she died remembered what she stood for and drew strength from it. The civil rights struggle was a case in point. Paul H. Douglas, a young professor of economics at the University of Chicago in the 1920s through the 1940s, knew and admired Addams for her independence of mind and her integrity. As a U.S. senator in the 1950s and 1960s, he kept her photograph on his office wall and looked at it daily as he fought in the Senate for the Civil Rights Act of 1964 and the Voting Rights Act of 1965.

Another young man, Myles Horton, frequently talked with Addams while he was studying in 1930 at the University of Chicago. When he left, he took with him her idea that democracy was about trusting that people, not government officials, had the best answers to their own problems. Horton went on to found the Highlander Folk School (now the Highlander Center) in Tennessee, which eventually, in the 1950s, trained African American organizers to teach African Americans how to vote and how to practice nonviolent civil disobedience, and also helped make "We Shall Overcome" the anthem of the civil rights movement. Many of the most important civil rights leaders of the era were involved with Highlander, including Rosa Parks, Septima Clark, and Martin Luther King, Jr. Thus, two of Addams's "students," working at either end of the problem, contributed hugely to the eventual political empowerment of African Americans and, in the fullness of time, to the election of the nation's first African American president.[63]

Addams's home was still Hull House in 1930, and when she was not traveling or seriously ill, she lived as she always had, in the middle of the stream of life that flowed through it. She sat in her office every afternoon from four to six, listening to what visitors had to say. It was the "swirl of the present" that always drew her.[64] She still knew the names of many of the children who came and went. She helped them find scholarship funds to go to college or encouraged them if they had other dreams. For those she was close to, she might give a wedding reception at Hull House. She also traveled to the suburbs and beyond to have dinner with those she had first known as children, some of whom had married each other, and took pleasure in the fine lives they had created for themselves.[65]

The fortieth anniversary party at Hull House was followed by a star-studded seventieth birthday party for Addams in Bar Harbor in August. The event had enough élan to attract the prominent people who summered nearby. The host was a former ambassador, Henry J. Morgenthau, and among the guests were Robert Hutchins, the president of the University of Chicago, and John D. Rockefeller, Jr., son of the Standard Oil industrialist. The United Press interviewed Addams about turning seventy, and the resulting story was printed widely across the country.[66]

The prominent guests' willingness to attend the party and the press's willingness to celebrate her birthday in honorific fashion were two signs that her popularity was returning. There were other signs. She was beginning to receive honorary degrees again from institutions of higher education, another good barometer of public opinion. Between 1920 and 1927 only one brave school, Tufts University, had given her a degree. Between 1928 and 1935 she received nine. In the first ten months of 1931 there were two awards, one from Bryn Mawr College and one from the popular magazine *Pictorial Review*. That same year mainstream *Good Housekeeping* magazine named her first among twelve living greatest American women, and several prominent men put her on their "greatest" lists.[67]

Peace remained Addams's first interest. Besides her WILPF presidency, she served on the boards of the National Council for Prevention of War, the League of Nations Non-Partisan Association, and the National World Court Committee.[68] Still, she did not forget her old causes: In the early 1930s, as in the 1920s, she sometimes lectured and wrote about child labor, immigration policy, minimum wage laws for women, old-age pensions, and unemployment insurance, and she continued to serve on the boards of the NAACP and ACLU.[69] She took up some new issues, opposing capital punishment and segregated housing and urging the public to give sympathy, not condemnation, to young out-of-wedlock mothers and their children.[70]

But the progressive moment had long since passed. Indeed, between 1918 and 1930 much of the progressive federal legislation had been dismantled. During the war the Supreme Court, as determined as ever to protect states' rights, had ruled the federal child labor law that Wilson had signed unconstitutional; in 1922 it knocked down a second federal child labor law on the same grounds. The next year it ruled that the D.C. minimum wage law for women, which Wilson had also signed, unconstitutional as well. Many in the country applauded these rulings, believing that such legislation was socialist. In 1924 Congress passed a constitutional amendment giving itself the authority to regulate child labor, a hopeful sign, but by 1930 only six states had ratified it. Meanwhile, the new immigration laws Congress put in place in the early 1920s severely limited the number of immigrants being admitted to the United States. In 1928, Congress condemned as socialist the maternity services program of the Children's Bureau, one of Julia Lathrop's proudest accomplishments, refused to fund it fully, and phased out the program. The times were fiercely conservative.

One issue Addams faced in the early 1930s was both old and new, the Depression. Between 1929, when the stock market crashed, and 1933, the worst year for finding a job, the unemployment rate rose steadily, finally reaching 24.9 percent.[71] As in the depression of 1893–97, Hull House was flooded with people looking for work. Distraught men, humiliated that they were failing in what they believed was their responsibility to be sole support for their families, told Addams their stories, and she repeated them on the radio.[72] Meanwhile, President Hoover continued his optimism. In May 1931 he announced that the Depression would soon be over.

As nations struggled with rising debt, many thought that international disarmament offered them the best chance to economize. In 1931, Hoover was preparing to participate in the Geneva Disarmament Conference, convened by the League of Nations, which was scheduled to start in early 1932. Addams put herself at the disposal of the U.S. Section of WILPF as it sought to arouse public support. In October 1931 she was part of its delegation that presented Hoover with a petition of 150,000 signatures, gathered during a cross-country automobile trip. The petition urged him to strongly support gradual but complete global disarmament. He favored only limiting armaments, but he was at least sympathetic. At the same time, WILPF's sections in thirty other countries presented petitions to their heads of state.[73]

Named a delegate to the conference, Addams was poised to fill an official diplomatic role for her government for the first time, but she was too ill to go. Seeking a cause for her illness, her doctors discovered she had a cyst on an ovary and decided she should have surgery to remove it in Baltimore in December. Surgeons there had a new anesthetic they thought was better for patients with weak hearts.[74]

The Nobel Peace Prize was probably not on her mind at the time. Nonetheless, history had its own ideas. The day after Thanksgiving she received a telegram from the Nobel Committee telling her that she, along with Nicholas Murray Butler, president of the Carnegie Endowment for International Peace, had received the award and asking her to keep the news "entirely personal" until the official announcement (she told Mary and her nephew Weber). She was not completely surprised; she had been nominated for the prize in 1916 and annually since 1928. But the reality must still have been a shock.

Addams was at the hospital in Baltimore on December 10 when the committee announced the award. Cables, letters, and flowers of congratulation flooded her hospital room. Mary Rozet Smith remembered that they kept Addams entertained as she and Smith waited the three days before the surgery, which was completed successfully (it is not known if the cyst was cancerous, but typically such cysts are benign). Addams had decided to give most of the sixteen thousand dollars that was her share of the prize money to international WILPF—twelve thousand to endow the costs of operating its headquarters in Geneva (she knew well the headaches of constantly funding building operation costs) and three thousand for the executive committee to use as it wished.[75] She was invited to give her Nobel lecture in Norway the following summer and looked forward to going.

It was lucky that she received the prize when she did. In December 1931 her two great friends Florence Kelley and Julia Lathrop were still alive to celebrate the news. But just barely. Kelley, who had been in the hospital for some time, died on February 17, 1932, at age seventy-one, from colon cancer. Two months later Lathrop died, aged seventy-four, after goiter surgery. Addams had thought the world of them both. When, in 1931, just for fun and because her family asked, she made a list of the women she admired most, she put Lathrop and Kelley at the top, just below Lucy Stone.[76] They were her friends from the trenches. We know more about her work with Kelley only because Kelley left extensive papers and a partial memoir; Lathrop did not. Addams once wrote that "the best kind of companionship" arises when people "have a mutual interest in a mutual cause." She had had the best companionship with them. She thought them both "brilliant" and admired their "zeal" and "their grace."[77]

In cooperative fashion, she planned to share with others the writing of the biographies of both. In *My Friend, Julia Lathrop*, she covered the first half of Lathrop's life (Grace Abbott was to write the second half but never did). It was published in 1935. She was also planning to contribute chapters to a life of Kelley.[78] Lathrop wrote about Kelley's and Addams's friendship in an obituary on Kelley for the *Survey*. Published just weeks before Lathrop's own death, it captured what was true of all three: "Miss Addams and [Florence Kelley] understood each other's powers and worked together in [a] wonderfully effective way...."[79] Kelley was the fearless, confrontational advocate, Addams, the gently persuasive interpreter, and Lathrop, the careful, wise government servant. They respected one another's strengths. No one thought the others should be like herself.

Addams usually pushed away two personal feelings, anger and sadness. Her solution to the first was to try harder to understand the other person's point of view. Her solution to the second was to celebrate what could be celebrated. When people died, Addams often celebrated their fine qualities in remarks at memorial services. In 1931 she decided to publish a collection of these, and the resulting book, *The Excellent Becomes the Permanent*, came out in March 1932, just after Kelley died.

She said in her introduction that she intended the book to answer a question she was often asked: Did she believe in a life after death? It was a question to which she had long wanted to know the answer. As a child she had asked it of her father, in trying to get him to explain what predestination meant. She never actually answered the question in the book, although she wrote in the introduction how, in rereading the speeches, she thought she saw hints that she just might believe in an afterlife. (She liked to treat herself as a mystery to be studied.) Perhaps, she guessed, this was part of the natural wish of those "who live in time and space" to reunite "with those who dwell in the timeless unseen."[80] It was a profoundly human longing. But it was also one that a person who lost her mother at two had had seared early into her soul.

Her book title gave her real answer: Achieving moral excellence was the path to living eternally. Moral excellence, for Addams, was finding the right balance among individual, family, and social morality and being sure that the social was not slighted and the individual and family not overemphasized.

Today we might call social morality a sense of civic responsibility, but the phrase hardly captures what she meant. Addams believed that all morality began with feelings of affection and that social morality began with having such feelings for people outside one's family and not just for those of a similar background. Morality is often thought to be about restraint and inhibition, but for Addams, it was about the widening of one's affections and the flowering of possibilities; it was about new feelings leading to new conduct.

Excellent was not a religious book in the traditional sense, but it fitted Addams's mature understanding of religion, an understanding that mirrored that of one of her favorite authors, William James. He argued in *Varieties of Religious Experience* for a "pragmatic way of taking religion." Whether God exists or not, he wrote, is an irrelevant question. Religion is tested by its results. The first of those is feelings, which in turn prompt experimental actions in pursuit of the good. The addresses in *Excellent* capture, for the most part, the way each person being memorialized had lived with just that kind of bold passion.[81]

Still, excellence, for Addams, was an ideal that not only individuals could act on. Nations could too. Hence, as noted earlier, she defined patriotism, which she thought was a form of social morality, as being, among other things, "loyalty to the highest achievement of which a nation is capable." And what about the world? "[W]hen patriotism becomes large enough," she wrote, "it will overcome arbitrary boundaries and . . . become a human term."[82] That was the path her own patriotism had taken; as she grew older, she became loyal to the world's possibilities. Yet she never lost touch with her family, her friends, and the people in her neighborhood and never stopped working on city, state, and national reforms. Not many people work effectively on so many levels of morality at once. Her moral scope was nearly without peer.

|||||||||||||

In summer 1932, Jane Addams was still not feeling completely well. Regretfully she canceled the trip to Norway to give her Nobel lecture. Being stateside, she again put herself at the disposal of national WILPF. It was a presidential election year, and that June both the Democratic and Republican parties were holding their national conventions, conveniently for Addams, in Chicago. The U.S. Section put together a peace platform to present to both parties. On the opening day of both conventions, Addams was in the lead car of a peace plank parade made up of members of peace societies from across the country riding in a hundred automobiles. In one of the parades there was an automobile full of youth from Hull House holding a banner that read, NO MORE WAR FOR OUR SAKES.[83]

The parade for the Democrats was particularly colorful. To rebut the military air show that the Democratic Party organized and that flew over the parade, the procession had a plane of its own that flew in the midst of the military ones. Piloted by Joan Thomas, a worker at Hull House, it trailed a banner reading PEACE. To top that off, the pacifists issued a statement to the press by the famous woman pilot (and former settlement house volunteer) Amelia Earhart. She said that she regretted she was unable to participate in the flyover and that she supported political efforts "to abolish war."[84] Addams made the presentations of the peace platform to both Resolutions Committees. It called for U.S. membership in the World Court, support for the Geneva Disarmament Conference, and cancellation or revision of war debts.[85] In the end, both parties endorsed joining the World Court and arms limitations but ignored or opposed changes in the war debts.

By 1932 Addams had advised seven presidents. She now added Franklin Delano Roosevelt to the list. Even before he was elected in November with the help of her vote, she had dinner with him at his home in New York. After he became president, she sent him telegrams to urge him to take certain positions (such as nominating the first woman to be a federal judge) or to thank him for doing as she had urged.[86] Roosevelt listened with great respect. Once, after meeting with Addams, he told Secretary of Labor Frances Perkins he thought Jane Addams "understands more about the real people of the United States than anybody else does."[87]

Meanwhile, her poor health was slowing her down more than ever. She regularly suffered from weeks of bronchitis or the flu. The other worry was her heart. Since the heart attack in 1926, it had become weaker, and at the same time, her weight had increased. By late 1932 she weighed two hundred pounds. In letters expressing her regret at being unable to accept an invitation she spoke of this "irritating" or "annoying" or "exasperating" bronchitis and her "poor heart."[88] She had no choice but to stay home a good deal.

Home, however, was no longer Hull House. Her doctor had forbidden her to live there because it placed too many exhausting demands on her and was too noisy to allow her good rest. He told her she could be there no more than four hours a day.[89] When she was not in Maine, she lived either at Mary Rozet Smith's or Louise de Koven Bowen's house in Chicago or at the hotels in Florida or Arizona where she and Mary regularly spent the winters.

Her great pleasure was Mary's abiding company. The partnership

Jane Addams and Mary Rozet Smith, 1930

that began in 1895, when Jane first retreated to Mary's house to recover from illness, had now lasted thirty-seven years. They had been closest in the last seventeen. Throughout their shared lives they were each other's family and were family to each other's blood relations. Jane's nephew Stanley, whom she had raised since he was eleven, called Mary, Aunt Mary. When Anna Haldeman Addams died while Jane was at the Zurich women's peace congress, Mary had stood in for Jane at the funeral. One summer when Mary was traveling in Europe, Jane spent a great deal of time keeping Mary's parents daughterly company.[90]

The times had changed around them, of course. Their same-sex partnership had raised no eyebrows in the 1890s, but by the 1920s male-female sexual relations had become a cultural obsession, as Jane was well aware. Freud and Havelock Ellis had also put the stamp of science on what was healthy or not in intimate relations, and homosexual relations were considered abnormal and presumed to be sexual. Whether Jane and Mary loved each other sexually is not known; such evidence rarely exists in any case. They sometimes, perhaps regularly, shared a bed (at Mary's house they had separate bedrooms, but each had a double bed), but for women of their generation, this fact in itself had no overtly sexual meaning.[91]

What is known is what they thought about love, or at least what Jane Addams thought. She had been a Platonist, a believer in the reality of the ideal since her teens, and seems to have remained one all her life. In *The Spirit of Youth and the City Streets*, she drew on Plato's thought to urge society to help young people deal with sexual urges by sublimating them into a love of beauty and broader ideals. If the aesthetic imagination is not awakened, she explained, then "the sex impulse [does not] over-flow into neighboring fields of consciousness." Mindful of the dreamy abstractness of her advice, she characteristically noted the need for self-discipline. "It is neither a short nor an easy undertaking to substitute the love of beauty for mere desire, to place the mind above the senses."[92] The sentence can be read as an endorsement of the need to resist temptation but also as an admission of having been tempted.

In the context of her Platonism, Jane Addams's puzzlement over the sexualized youth culture of the 1920s, something never seen before in American society, makes sense. Today we, the direct descendants of those 1920s pioneers, continue to see sex as the *essential* means to human fulfillment and therefore see Jane's partnership with Mary in this light. But Jane would have said that perhaps the important thing was not whether she and Mary loved sexually but that they loved.[93] As for who is right, that is more than a biographer cares to judge.

||||||||||||

By 1933 the two movements that Jane Addams cared most about—the peace movement and the women's movement—were struggling against a mood of despair, unable to overcome the historic forces aligned against them. With Hitler's rise to power in Germany, Germany's withdrawal from the League of Nations, and Japan's occupation of Chinese Man-churia, nations were rearming, determined to be better prepared for the coming war than they had been for the previous one. WILPF kept on with its work but with less hope than before.

By then, too, the prominent portion of the woman's movement in the United States was in disarray. For prosperous women, progress had realigned their lives. Those with college educations and ambition had more opportunities to pursue careers, at least until they married. And for all women, the now hugely popular mass women's magazines, intent on serving their advertisers, were skillfully repackaging the ideology of the family as women's duty into the family as women's career, making its appeal as hard to resist as ever. For workingwomen, the organizing continued, but more often now without the support of their cross-class allies. Earlier, in the 1920s, leaders like Florence Kelley had tried to keep the old alliance going via the National Consumers League, but she was gone now, as were so many of that generation.

Women activists of all classes were most painfully split over whether to support the Equal Rights Amendment. The amendment was not the creation of a cross-class alliance but of Alice Paul's National Woman's Party, and clearly most benefited its membership, professional women who wanted equal pay and equal job opportunities. Women trade unionists from the American Federation of Labor, the National Women's Trade Union League, and other women's unions opposed the amendment because it would have made protective legislation for women, like the eight-hour day or the minimum wage, illegal. Addams thought the amendment "legalistic," by which she meant "not pragmatic," although she took no public stand against it.[94]

At an international congress of women held in Chicago in the summer of 1933, convened by the National Council of Women to address the problems of the world, speakers, including Addams, struggled to find answers to where the two movements should be going. Emily Newell Blair, who had been vice president of the Democratic National Committee's executive committee in the 1920s, recalled the earlier "cohesion" of the suffrage movement and warned: "[W]e will have to evolve a way of working [together] fitted to the changing conditions of life." As always, Addams stressed the need to adapt ideas. Calling the present a transitional period, she said, "Never has there been a time when it seemed safer to hang on to concepts which are no longer as valuable as they were because the untried theories seem dangerous," and urged women to adjust "to the realities of human nature."[95] It was Addams at her elliptically philosophical best. She had been wishing since the 1890s that society would be more flexible in its thinking, and she never stopped urging people to open their minds.

The congress adopted a bold manifesto that announced nothing less than the beginning of a new international women's movement: "We believe that every person . . . is entitled to security of life [and] work, . . . to protection against war and crime, and to the opportunity for self-expression. Yet even in parts of the world where feminism has made its largest gains, these fundamentals . . . are sadly lacking. Hence it is against social systems, not men, that we launch our second woman movement." The congress's eyes were on the far horizon of history. But even as the women adopted the manifesto, they worried about the rising persecution of Jews in Germany. New laws had been adopted there in April banning Jews from working for the government and requiring citizens to boycott Jewish professional services and shops. The Chicago congress adopted a resolution that the National Council of Women cooperate with all efforts to "ameliorate the conditions of Jews and other groups in Germany."[96] World War II was coming; the second women's movement would have to wait.

|||||||||||

The death Jane Addams most feared was not her own but Mary's. It came in early 1934. Jane had had another heart attack and lay ill in Mary's house when Mary came down with a bad cold that became first bronchitis and then pneumonia. Everyone was worried about Jane, but Mary was the one who died, in a room across the hall from where Jane lay. Jane grieved every day after that. With Mary gone, she knew the temptation that any devoted partner feels. "I thought over everything,"

Jane Addams, January 10, 1934

she later told her nephew Weber Linn, "I suppose I could have willed my heart to stop beating, and I longed to relax into doing that, but the thought of what she had been to me for so long kept me from being cowardly."[97]

Slowly, Addams recovered some strength. She spent the summer at Alice Hamilton's home in Hadlyme, Connecticut, and the winter with Louise de Koven Bowen in Arizona, writing her biography of Lathrop, and reading. After a quick trip west to be awarded an honorary degree from the University of California—Berkeley, she returned to live with Bowen at her Chicago house in the spring of 1935.

In late April she traveled to Washington, D.C., for a big event, the twentieth anniversary celebration of the founding of WILPF, which had been made into a celebration of its first president. Twelve hundred people came to the banquet at the Willard Hotel, and the speakers included First Lady Eleanor Roosevelt. A former volunteer at a settlement house, she shared Addams's vision for a more socially just and peaceful world. She told those gathered, "It is quite evident to many of us that war rarely settles any question and that . . . it tends to bring more difficulties to solve, rather than less."[98] In a real sense, Addams passed the baton to Roosevelt that day. Roosevelt was to become the first delegate from the United States to the United Nations, the new international body that arose out of the ashes of the old League at the end of World War II, and the coauthor of the UN Universal Declaration of Human Rights.

There was also a reception at the White House, though Addams did not attend it, wishing to marshal her limited strength. She did join in an international radio broadcast, during which statesmen and leaders in London, Moscow, Paris, and Tokyo paid her tribute. Afterward Addams told her nephew how much she had enjoyed it all: "They made me feel as if I were still in the frontline trenches. Probably one never gets over that feeling, though[, of being in the trenches]. I have always wondered when I should understand that I am an old lady."[99]

Back in Chicago at Bowen's, she kept working on the Lathrop book, met with the Chicago Housing Committee, and visited friends in the hospital. Then, on May 15, she felt a sharp, persistent pain in her abdomen. A few days later she went into the hospital for exploratory surgery. The surgeons found that her lower cavity was riddled with cancer. They sewed her back up. As was customary then, her friends and family did not tell her what the surgeons had learned. Addams seemed a bit better at first and managed to write a letter or two but then weakened and sank into unconsciousness. A few days after her surgery, on May 21, 1935, at age seventy-four, she died.

Around the globe and the nation, but especially in Chicago, people mourned Addams's passing. At Hull House thousands passed by her coffin, and hundreds attended the memorial service in the courtyard. People filled the windows of the encircling settlement buildings and sat in the trees and on the rooftops, so many wanted to be there. Halsted Street was filled with many hundreds more. Around the country words of praise poured out of editorial pens, some of the same pens that had once sharply criticized her. She was called "a representative American," "the best kind of American womanhood," and even "an outstanding patriot." Some waxed sentimental. An ex-mayor of Chicago called her "the Mother of Men" and compared her with "Mary, Mother of God." The governor called her "an evening star." She was compared with St. Francis and Mary Magdalene (her nephew thought she would have taken a puzzled delight in that).[100] The excessive praise was well intentioned, yet it had the effect that such praise had had throughout Addams's popular years and that vilification had had in her unpopular ones: it rendered a powerful social critic harmless.

Some, though, came closer to grasping who she was. Emily Greene Balch praised her "love of life—of life as it is, not only as it might be," the "extraordinary penetration" of her judgment, and the "originality of her intellect" and her actions. John Dewey said that she was the most human person he had ever met. The editor of the *Nation*, Oswald Garrison Villard, who served with her on the board of the NAACP and was her ally in the peace movement, thought that her calmness and serenity perhaps concealed "deep fires within, as a doctor wears a mask in the face of suffering and death lest he be emotionally destroyed."[101]

Her casket went by train to Freeport, and a large crowd, some of them friends of her family, a few perhaps who had known her as a child, gathered to meet it at the station. A hearse took the casket to Cedarville and the village cemetery. Her family and close friends wept as her body was lowered into the grave, dug next to those of her parents and siblings. Her simple flat marker reads "Jane Addams for Hull House and the Women's International League for Peace and Freedom."

As Addams had grown older, her heart had looked back more often, where a sea of beloved faces kept her company, but she also had kept looking forward, unable to stop thinking about the future even though her own was short. Six years before her death she spoke of her work, which she succinctly described as trying "to change ... attitude[s]," and summed up how she lived. Although we may have "great doubt" about "what we might do," the essential thing as we move "to the end of the chapter" is that "we are continually filled with a holy discontent...."[102] Here was her self-doubt about knowing what action to take, the self-doubt that fed her willingness to listen and to experiment. Here was her feeling of being part of a larger whole. Her life was only a chapter in some longer book, she was saying, and there were many more chapters to be written. Here was her passion to make things better that she often kept hidden so well, the passion that had been there from the first, when she chose John Brown and Lucy Stone as her childhood heroes. Jane Addams had put that spirit into action. If she had done it imperfectly, still, it was excellent enough. And if the excellent becomes the permanent, as she believed, then her spirit is not gone.

POSTSCRIPT

ON THE WHOLE, history confirmed that the fears of conservatives were unfounded. The end of child labor, which Congress banned in 1938, did not force major industries out of business; women's ability to vote did not destroy the family; federal old-age pensions, the federal minimum wage, and state unemployment insurance did not destroy the American capitalist system. The United States's membership in the United Nations after World War II did not destroy the country's national sovereignty, although conservatives continue to claim that it has, or will soon.

On the other hand, seventy-five years after her death, many of the problems worked on by Addams and other reformers, of both genders and of every class and race, remain unfinished. At home, we still have poverty, obstacles to labor organizing, an inadequate minimum wage, discrimination against immigrants, unjust immigration policies, human trafficking, inadequate affordable housing, racism, and sexism. Around the world we still have war, although the work of the United Nations has prevented or shortened some conflicts. And the injustices that burden women around the world continue, although those injustices may soon receive more attention. At this writing the United Nations, under pressure from WILPF and other women's organizations around the world, plans to create a new high-level women's agency.

Meanwhile, the two institutions Addams did so much to help create live on. Hull House is the largest social service agency in Chicago. WILPF, the oldest women's international peace organization in the world, is still headquartered in Geneva and still works for peace and freedom.

ACKNOWLEDGMENTS

THERE ARE MANY people who have helped me along the way with this book. My sister Penny Knight and my friend Deborah Epstein have read every word of it in draft and made useful suggestions. Scholars from various fields have read selected chapters and shared thoughts, they include peace historians David S. Patterson and Harriet Hyman Alonso, historian and biographer Kristen Gwinn (whose biography of Addams's friend and colleague Emily Greene Balch will be published by the University of Illinois Press in 2010), progressive historian Robert D. Johnston, and philosopher Marilyn Fischer. Conversations with the members of the Midwest-based Jane Addams and Friends group have also been both fun and thought-provoking. Invitations to speak about Addams at the University of Michigan—Ann Arbor, University of Wisconsin—Madison, Harvard University, the Woodrow Wilson International Center for Scholars, and the Demos Project, among others, have helped me work through questions whose conclusions are reflected here. I thank my sister biographers and/or historians Kristen Gwinn, Blanche Wiesen Cook, Clare Coss, Sheila Tobias, Gloria Steinem, and Megan Marshall for their unflagging encouragement (and Megan for suggesting the title for this book) and my mother, Fran B. Knight, and my other sister, Elizabeth Knight, for their confidence in me.

Invaluable support has come from the Communication Studies Department of the School of Communication at Northwestern University, where I teach a rhetoric course every year as an adjunct professor; in addition, this book could not have been written without the wonderful resources and helpful staff of the university's outstanding research library. I am also in debt to Kristen Gwinn for her help in tracking down loose-end research questions in the final stages. My agent, Tracy Brown, president of the Tracy Brown Literary Agency, has been the best agent ever, right from the start. I am grateful to my editor, Amy Cherry, vice president/senior editor at W. W. Norton, who provided some fine editing and, believing in the book, helped me bring it into the world.

FOR FURTHER READING

JANE ADDAMS ALWAYS paid attention to the changing times and knew firsthand that historic events and trends influenced society's enthusiasms. These forces have certainly shaped her historical reputation. Within a few years of her death, the world was at war once more, which again cast her pacifism in a less than respectable light. In the years immediately after the war, the only biography of her, written by her nephew James Weber Linn in 1935, fell out of print.[1] Throughout the 1950s her memoir *Twenty Years at Hull-House* was taught in high school and college classrooms, as it had been in her lifetime, but the only new books published about Addams were those for children. These kept her name remembered in a hazy sort of way.

Two widely respected senior historians led a revival of interest in Addams in 1960, the hundredth anniversary of her birth. Henry Steele Commager wrote an essay about her for the popular magazine *Saturday Review*. Merle Curti gave a centennial lecture on Addams at Swarthmore College that was published in a scholarly journal. The Commager essay became the preface to a new mass paperback edition of *Twenty Years at Hull-House*, which led to the book's being taught more often in high school and college (years later, in college, I first encountered the book in that edition).[2]

Then the younger generation, with its interest in social activism, moved in. Christopher Lasch (Henry Steele Commager's son-in-law) published a collection of essays, *The Social Thought of Jane Addams* (Indianapolis: Bobbs-Merrill, 1965), graduate student John C. Farrell wrote a dissertation, later published—*Beloved Lady: A History of Jane Addams's Ideas on Reform and Peace* (Baltimore: Johns Hopkins University Press, 1967)— and Daniel Levine wrote a biographical study, *Jane Addams and the Liberal Tradition* (Madison: State Historical Society of Wisconsin, 1971). With the women's movement under way in the 1960s, two women historians, Anne F. Scott and Jill Kerr Conway, wrote briefly about Addams's life, Scott in an introduction to a reprint of an Addams book, *Democracy and Social Ethics* (Cambridge, MA: Harvard University Press, 1964) and Conway as part of her Ph.D. dissertation, "The First Generation of American Women Graduates," Harvard University, 1968. Finally, in 1973, Merle Curti's former graduate student Allen F. Davis published the first biography of Addams since Linn's and the first by a historian, *American Heroine: The Life and Legend of Jane Addams* (Oxford University Press, 1973; repr. Dee Books, 2000).[3]

Then there was a long lull. Between 1973 and 1998, for twenty-five years, no (adult) biography of Addams was published. Davis's biography was one reason. But historians and biographers were also more interested in uncovering remarkable but forgotten figures who deserved a place in history, particularly women and minorities of modest backgrounds. Addams, wealthy, white, and regularly mentioned in history books, did not fit this category. There were, however, two nonbiographical books about Addams published in these years. One was Mary Jo Deegan's study of Addams's influence on, and ties with, the sociologists at the University of Chicago, *Jane Addams and the Men of the Chicago School, 1892–1918* (New Brunswick, NJ: Transaction, 1988); the other was Ellen Condliffe Lagemann's edited collection of writings, *Jane Addams on Educa-*

tion (New York: Teachers College Press, 1985), which had a biographical introduction.

Then came the flood. Since 1999 there has been renaissance of interest in Addams, marked by a flurry of books. There have been three biographies about the first half of her life: Gioia Diliberto's *A Useful Woman: The Early Life of Jane Addams* (New York: Scribner's, 1999), Victoria Brown's *The Education of Jane Addams* (Philadelphia: University of Pennsylvania Press, 2004), and my book *Citizen: Jane Addams and the Struggle for Democracy* (Chicago: University of Chicago Press, 2005). There have also been two biographical studies, Jean Bethke Elshtain's *Jane Addams and the Dream of American Democracy: A Life* (New York: Basic Books, 2002), which examines the democratically inspired ideas in Addams's books, and Katherine Joslin's *Jane Addams: A Writer's Life* (Urbana: University of Illinois Press, 2004), which views Addams's life and books through a literary lens. In addition, there have been two edited collections of Addams's writings, *The Jane Addams Reader* (New York: Basic Books, 2002), half of the selections of which are chapters from the books, edited by Jean Bethke Elshtain, and *Addams' Essays and Speeches on Peace (1899–1935)* (New York: Continuum International, 2005), ed. Marilyn Fischer and Judy D. Whipps. Two interdisciplinary collections of essays have been published: *Jane Addams and the Theory and Practice of Democracy* (Urbana: University of Illinois Press, 2008), ed. Wendy Chmielewski, Marilyn Fischer, and Carol Nackenoff, and *Feminist Interpretations of Jane Addams* (University Park: Penn State University Press, forthcoming, 2010), ed. Maurice Hamington.

Philosophers have been especially busy. Marilyn Fischer published a succinct summary of Addams's ideas on five topics in *On Addams* (Toronto: Thomson Wadsworth, 2004), Maurice Hamington has his brand-new *The Social Philosophy of Jane Addams* (Urbana; University of Illinois Press, 2009). Two more books by philosophers are in the pipeline. Marilyn Fischer is working on a book on the sources and philosophical dimensions of Jane Addams's internationalism, and Charlene Haddock

Seigfried is working on a book about Jane Addams's philosophy of sympathetic understanding and cooperative inquiry.

Why the renaissance? It's hard to say, but I can think of at least three reasons. One is the influence of women's studies across the curriculum. For years now professors have been teaching about women's contributions to their fields, and Addams, whose wealth of writings and interests are relevant to many disciplines, has caught their attention. Teaching has led to research and publication. Philosophy has been out in front, at least as far as whole books on Addams are concerned, but it is only a matter of time until social work historians, peace historians, reform historians, rhetoric scholars, ethicists, philosophers of education, public administration scholars, women's history historians, progressive historians, cultural historians, urban sociologists, cultural anthropologists (Addams was a cultural anthropologist too), and others, many of whom are already teaching and writing articles about Addams, write books about her.

The other two reasons are a person and a press. The person is Mary Lynn McCree Bryan. Working steadily since the 1970s, she has single-handedly made it much easier to do research on Addams, first by publishing the microfilm of *The Jane Addams Papers* (Ann Arbor: University Microfilms International, 1985)[4] and, second, by editing, along with Barbara Bair and Maree de Angury, and publishing in book form *The Selected Papers of Jane Addams*, vol. 1, *Preparing to Lead, 1860–1881* (Urbana: University of Illinois Press, 2003), and vol. 2, *Venturing into Usefulness, 1881–1888* (Urbana: University of Illinois Press, forthcoming 2010, after *Jane Addams: Spirit in Action* went to press). Because of Bryan's skillful and determined efforts, anyone interested in doing research on Addams, be she student or scholar, need not travel to far-flung archives to read her correspondence or to dig through obscure publications to locate her published writings other than books; the researcher can consult the microfilm and get right to work. Bryan has also done many other things to nurture and support the field of Addams studies, including encouraging me to write about Addams when my first biography was only the faintest of impossible dreams. The debt anyone interested in Addams owes Mary Lynn McCree Bryan is enormous.

The press is the University of Illinois Press, which, under the guidance of editor in chief Joan Catapano, has not only published the first two volumes of Bryan's *Selected Papers* but also reprinted Linn's 1935 biography, as well as another edition of *Twenty Years at Hull-House*, seven of the other nine Addams books that have long been out of print, and several of the new books about Addams already mentioned. All this is a huge contribution to the field of Addams studies.

Where next for Addams studies? The work done by earlier scholars informs those who come after, but as the times change, so do the questions. What is remarkable about Addams is that her writings and her life are rich enough to have something interesting to say to new generations. In that sense, she is one who *can* keep up with the changing times.

JANE ADDAMS'S BOOKS

Democracy and Social Ethics.
New York: Macmillan, 1902

The Excellent Becomes the Permanent.
New York: Macmillan, 1932

The Long Road of Woman's Memory.
New York: Macmillan, 1916

My Friend, Julia Lathrop.
New York: Macmillan, 1935

A New Conscience and an Ancient Evil.
New York: Macmillan, 1912

Newer Ideals of Peace.
New York: Macmillan, 1907

Peace and Bread in Time of War.
New York: Macmillan, 1922

*The Second Twenty Years at Hull-House:
September 1909 to September 1929, with a Record of a
Growing World Consciousness.*
New York: Macmillan, 1930

The Spirit of Youth and the City Streets.
New York: Macmillan, 1909

Twenty Years at Hull-House with Autobiographical Notes.
New York: Macmillan, 1910

PHOTOGRAPH CREDITS

[Frontispiece]: Bettmann/Corbis

p. 4: Jane Addams Project, Fayetteville, North Carolina

p. 7: Jane Addams Project, Fayetteville, North Carolina

p. 14: Jane Addams Project, Fayetteville, North Carolina

p. 19: Jane Addams Project, Fayetteville, North Carolina

p. 33: Jane Addams Collection, Swarthmore College Peace Collection, Triptych: Tri-College Digital Library, Peace Photographs, scpc 00013

p. 48: Jane Addams Project, Fayetteville, North Carolina

p. 53: Jane Addams Project, Fayetteville, North Carolina

p. 60: Jane Addams Project, Fayetteville, North Carolina

p. 69: Jane Addams Project, Fayetteville, North Carolina

p. 72: Jane Addams Project, Fayetteville, North Carolina

p. 79: From *Scribner's Magazine*, vol. 24 (1898), p. 109

p. 83: Jane Addams Project, Fayetteville, North Carolina

p. 85: Courtesy of Jane Addams Project, Fayetteville, North Carolina

p. 99: Jane Addams Collection, Swarthmore College Peace Collection, Triptych: Tri-College Digital Library, Peace Photographs, scpc 00031

p. 114: H. R. Farr, Corbis Corporation

p. 121: From Jane Addams, *Twenty Years at Hull House* (1910), facing p. 310

p. 125: Courtesy of Jane Addams Project, Fayetteville, North Carolina

p. 128: Courtesy of Library of Congress

p. 134: Corbis Corporation

p. 153: *Crisis* magazine, 1917; General Research & Reference Division, Schomburg Center for Research in Black Culture, The New York Public Library, Astor, Lenox and Tilden Foundations

p. 155: Used by permission of Social Welfare History Archive, University of Minnesota Libraries (original contained in Box 191, National Federation of Settlements and Neighborhood Centers Records)

p. 160: Bettmann/Corbis

p. 166: Jane Addams Collection, Swarthmore College Peace Collection, Triptych: Tri-College Digital Library, Peace Photographs, scpc 00049

p. 169: Courtesy of Library of Congress

p. 200: Jane Addams Collection, Swarthmore College Peace Collection, Triptych: Tri-College Digital Library, Peace Photographs, scpc 00055

p. 206: Courtesy of Library of Congress

p. 212: Courtesy of Library of Congress

p. 229: Women's International League for Peace and Freedom, Swarthmore College Peace Collection

p. 239: From James Weber Linn, *Jane Addams* (New York: Appleton-Century, 1935), facing p. 360

p. 251: Corbis Corporation

p. 262: Jane Addams Collection, Swarthmore College Peace Collection, Triptych: Tri-College Digital Library, Peace Photographs, scpc 00109

p. 266: Jane Addams Collection, Swarthmore College Peace Collection, Triptych: Tri-College Digital Library, Peace Photographs, scpc 00188

NOTES

For chapters 1 through 3, the reader interested in sources used for material other than quotations is invited to consult my earlier book *Citizen: Jane Addams and the Struggle for Democracy* (Chicago: University of Chicago Press, 2005). For chapters 4 through 7, I have included references for certain obscure material, since those chapters cover years of Addams's life not covered in *Citizen*. Also all correspondence unless otherwise indicated is on the correspondence reels of *The Jane Addams Papers* microfilm, reels 1 through 26, on which the letters are organized chronologically.

People

EGS	Ellen Gates Starr
AHA	Anna Haldeman Addams (JA's stepmother)
FK	Florence Kelley
JA	Jane Addams
JHA	John Huy Addams (JA's father)
MHJ	Marcet Haldeman-Julius (JA's niece)
MRS	Mary Rozet Smith

Collections, Manuscripts, and Books

EGSP	Ellen Gates Starr Papers, Sophia Smith Collection, Smith College, Northampton, MA

HFP	Hamilton Family Papers, Schlesinger Library, Radcliffe Institute for Advanced Studies, Harvard University, Cambridge, MA
HHA	Hull House Association
JAC	Jane Addams Collection, SCPC
JAMC	Jane Addams Memorial Collection, UIC
SCPC	Swarthmore College Peace Collection
SSC	Sophia Smith Collection, Smith College, Northampton, MA
JAPCG	Mary Lynn McCree Bryan, ed., and Barbara Bair, assoc. ed., *The Jane Addams Papers: A Comprehensive Guide* (Bloomington: Indiana University Press, 1996)
JAPM	Mary Lynn McCree Bryan, ed., *The Jane Addams Papers* [microfilm] (Ann Arbor, MI: University Microfilms International, 1985)
Selected Papers	Mary Lynn McCree Bryan, Barbara Bair, and Maree de Angury, eds., *The Jane Addams Papers*, vol. 1, *Preparing to Lead, 1860–1881* (Urbana: University of Illinois, 2003)
Commonplace Book	Jane Addams, commonplace book [1877–83], series 6, JAC; *JAPM*, 27:0143

Preface

1 Jane Addams, "The Philosophy of a New Day" [July 1933], *Addams' Essays and Speeches on Peace*, ed. Marilyn Fischer and Judy Whipps (New York: Continuum International Publishing Group, 2005), 351–52.

Chapter 1: Dreamer

1 Jane Addams (JA hereafter) told her nephew what she remembered of that day. James Weber Linn, *Jane Addams: A Biography* (New York: Appleton-Century, 1935), 22. This story is also based on these sources: George Weber to Elizabeth Reiff, January 17, 1863, JAC; MHJ, Notes of Her Conversation with Alice Addams Haldeman, undated, File 39, Haldeman-Julius Papers, JAMC; MHJ, "The Two Mothers of Jane Addams," n.d. [1920s], 1, JAC;

See also Louise W. Knight, *Citizen: Jane Addams and the Struggle for Democracy* (Chicago: University of Chicago Press, 2005), 33, 425n70. MHJ was Alice Addams Haldeman's daughter. Alice married her stepbrother.

2 [Freeport] *Deutscher Anzeiger*, January 21, 1863, clipping, Addams-Reiff Family Paper and Genealogy, Box 1, series 8, JAC.

3 JA, *Twenty Years at Hull-House with Autobiographical Notes* (New York: Macmillan, 1910), 20–21.

4 JA, "Unexpected Reactions of a Traveler in Egypt," *Atlantic Monthly* (February 1914): 180. See also Knight, *Citizen*, 426n21.

5 JA, *Twenty*, 19–20.

6 Ibid., 9.

7 Ibid., 50.

8 Ibid., 18.

9 Ibid., 14.

10 JA, "Unexpected Relations," 181.

11 Re "was sure to be," see Isaac Carey to JA, August 21, 1881; re "the uncompromising enemy," see Allen F. Davis, *American Heroine: The Life and Legend of Jane Addams* (New York: Oxford University Press, 1973), 26. Davis's source is an undated document he cites as "Jane Addams Notebooks and Note Fragments," JAMC. The staff at Special Collections, University Library, University of Illinois at Chicago, which holds the JAMC, cannot locate this document.

12 Re "mental integrity," see JA, *Twenty*, 15; re her admiration for him, see ibid., 50.

13 Ibid., 2; See also JA to James Weber Linn, February 2, 1935.

14 JA, *Twenty*, 23, 21.

15 Ibid., 12–13.

16 Sarah C. T. Uhl to JA, November 15, 1896; MHJ, "Two Mothers," 16.

17 The Cedarville resident was Mary Fry. Mary Linn McCree Bryan, Barbara Bair, and Maree de Angury, eds., *The Selected Papers of Jane Addams*, Vol. 1: *Preparing to Lead, 1860–1881* (Urbana: University of Illinois Press, 2003), 454; Harry Haldeman to Anna Haldeman Addams, March 8, 1875, Sarah Alice [Addams] Haldeman Mss, Lilly Library, Indiana University.

18 See John Dewey's description of a discussion he had with JA about this. Knight, *Citizen*, 323.

19 John Huy Addams to Alice Addams Haldeman, January 6, 1874. JAC; John Linn to JA, December 21, 1910.

20 Re bread, see JA, *Twenty*, 276; re slippers, see Knight, *Citizen*, 420n10; re "babyhood," see JA, "The Subjective Necessity of a Social Settlement," *Philanthropy and Social Progress*, ed. Henry C. Adams (New York: Crowell, 1893), 14; the statement from the *Atlantic Monthly* was reprinted in the *Freeport Journal*, March 27, 1878, 2, col. 4.

21 John Huy Addams to Enos and Elizabeth Reiff, January 12, 1845, Sarah Alice [Addams] Haldeman Mss, Lilly Library, Indiana University.

22 Addams, *Twenty*, 32–33; Linn, *Addams*, 17.

23 Linn, *Addams*, 21.

24 JA, *My Friend, Julia Lathrop* (New York: Macmillan, 1935), 26.

25 "The Girl of Cedar Cliff," *Chicago Record*, June 17, 1897, news clipping, JAC, SCPC.

26 Ralph Waldo Emerson, *Ralph Waldo Emerson: Essays and Lectures* (New York: Library of America, 1983), 135, 143, 146.

27 JA, *Twenty*, 143; JA to MRS, August [4], 1904; Linn, *Addams*, 404.

28 JA to Vallie Beck, March 21, 1877.

29 Knight, *Citizen*, 76.

30 JA, *Twenty*, 43.

31 Quoted in Linn, *Addams*, 410–11.

32 JA, *Twenty*, 49.

33 Ibid., 49, 56.

34 JA to Vallie Beck, March 16, 1876; JA, Diary, June 2, 1875.

35 Charles Capper, *Margaret Fuller: An American Romantic Life*, vol. 2: *The Public Years* (New York: Oxford University Press, 2007), 111, 177–78.

36 Margaret Fuller, *Woman in the Nineteenth Century* (1845; repr., New York: Norton, 1971), 38, 36.

37 Caroline Potter, "Dear Friend," *Rockford Seminary Magazine* 12, no. 2 (February 1884): 54.

38 C. Potter, "The Madonna of the Future." Reprinted in "The Alumnae Meeting," *Rockford Seminary Magazine* 11, no. 7 (July 1883): 218–19.

39 AHA to JA, June 11, 1878; JHA to JA, June 17, 1878.

40 JA, "Resolved: That French women" (first version, November 13, 1878). *JAPM*, 45:1797. Also in Bryan, *Selected Papers*, 241–44.

41 JA, Ibid. The last quote is in a different version of the essay from that reprinted there. On this point, see *Selected Papers*, 353n4. The other version is available at *JAPM*, 45:1808–18.

42 JA to EGS, February 13, 1881; JA, "Follow Thou Thy Star," *Rockford Seminary Magazine* (July 1879): 183–85 (written February 1879).

43 JA, "Editorial," *Rockford Seminary Magazine* 7, no. 5 (June 1879): 166–67.

44 JA to EGS, August 11, 1879.

45 George Eliot, *Romola* (1863; repr., New York: Penguin, 1980), 145; Fuller, *Woman*, 51.

46 JA to EGS, August 11, 1879.

47 Alexander Bain, *English Composition and Rhetoric, a Manual*, 4th ed. (London: Longmans, Green, 1877), 171.

48 *Rockford Star*, March 30, 1933. Bryan, *Selected Papers* gives the date of 1932 (184n44). Her married name was Caroline Potter Brazee.

49 Bryan, *Selected Papers*, 350–51. Also at *JAPM*, 4:195–97. Emerson's "Man the Reformer" is full of metaphorical references to bread that carry the same meaning.

50 JA, Editorial, *Rockford Seminary Magazine* 9 (March 1881): 86.

51 JA, *Twenty*, 55–56.

52 JA to EGS, February 13, 1881.

53 JA, "The Magnificence of Character" (October 5, 1880), *JAPM*, 46:0219.

54 JA, Editorial, *Rockford Seminary Magazine* 8 (November 1880): 256; JA, Editorial, *Rockford Seminary Magazine* 9 (June 1881): 182.

55 George Eliot, *The Mill on the Floss* (1860; repr., New York: New American Library, 1965), 471; JA, Commonplace book. She replaced Eliot's word "natural" with the word "sacred."

56 S. Kendall to JA, August 24, 1881.

Chapter 2: Freedom Seeker

1 JA, "The College Woman and the Family Claim," *Commons* 3 (September 1898): 4, 7.

2 Ibid., 4.

3 Helen Harrington to JA, July 23, 1881.

4 *Freeport Journal,* July 6, 1881, 5, col. 2. The interview was not published until several days after the shooting.

5 John Weber Addams Documents, box 283, Stephenson County [IL] Court Records.

6 JA to EGS, September 3, 1881.

7 Ibid., October 23, 1885.

8 Charlotte Perkins Gilman, *The Charlotte Perkins Gilman Reader: The Yellow Wall-paper, and Other Fiction,* ed. Ann J. Lane (Charlottesville: University of Virginia Press, 1999), 10.

9 JA, Commonplace book, entries dated July 1882, Nantucket [MA]; JA, "Comments to Open Discussion, at Seventh Session, July 12, 1897," *Proceedings of the National Conference of Charities and Corrections, Twenty-fourth Conference, July 7–14, 1897,* 466.

10 JA, Commonplace book, entries dated April [n.d.] 1882, January 15, 1882, and July 15, 1882.

11 JA, "The Settlement as a Factor in the Labor Movement," in Residents of Hull-House, *Hull-House Maps and Papers: A Presentation of Nationalities and Wages in a Congested District of Chicago, Together with Comments and Essays on Problems Growing out of the Social Conditions,* intro. Rima Lunin Schultz (Urbana: University of Illinois Press, 2007), 147.

12 JA, Commonplace book, August 1882 entry.

13 JA to EGS, January 7, 1883.

14 Ibid., April 24, 1883.

15 JA to Alice Addams Haldeman, July 2, 1883.

16 JA, *Twenty,* 432 (see chap. 1, n. 3)

17 JA to EGS, August 12, 1883.

18 Ibid., July 11, 1883.

19 JA to Vallie Beck, May 3, 1877. See also Knight, *Citizen,* 433n46.

20 JA, *The Second Twenty Years at Hull-House: September 1909 to September 1929, with a Record of Growing World Consciousness* (New York: Macmillan, 1930), 196–97. Re the boyfriend, Rollin Salisbury, see Linn, *Addams,* 49–50, 53 (see chap. 1, n.1), and Knight, *Citizen,* 123–24 (see chap. 1, n. 1).

21 JA, *Twenty,* 66.

22 JA to EGS, November 3, 1883.

23 [Andrew Mearns] *The Bitter Cry of Outcast London: An Inquiry into the Condition of the Abject Poor*, ed. and intro. Anthony S. Wohl (1883; repr., New York: Humanities, 1970), 68–69, 73.

24 JA, *Twenty*, 68.

25 JA to Weber Addams, October 29, 1883; JA, *Twenty*, 66.

26 JA, *Twenty*, 68–69.

27 Ibid., 69.

28 Ibid., 84.

29 Ibid., 66.

30 JA to EGS, June 8, 1884; EGS to JA, April 28, 1885.

31 JA to EGS, February 7, 1886; JA, *Democracy and Social Ethics* (New York: Macmillan, 1902), 87.

32 JA, *Twenty*, 78–79.

33 Ibid., 261.

34 Leo Tolstoy, *My Religion*, in *The Novels and Other Works of Lyof N. Tolstoi*, vol. 17 (New York: Charles Scribner's Sons, 1902), 86, 87.

35 Giuseppe Mazzini, "Thoughts upon Democracy in Europe," in *Life and Writings of Mazzini* (London: Smith, Elder, 1847), 109.

36 JA, *Twenty*, 78–79.

37 JA to Alice Addams Haldeman, November 4, 1886.

38 JA, *Twenty*, 73.

39 JA, "A Book that Changed My Life," *Christian Century* 44 (October 13, 1927): 1196; Matthew 16: 24–26.

40 John Stuart Mill, *The Subjection of Women* (1869; repr., Cambridge, MA: MIT Press, 1970), 98. JA repeated this observation of Mill's, slightly edited, in her speech "Outgrowths of Toynbee Hall" (December 1890): 6, *JAPM*, 46:0480; and in a later speech she quoted this same sentence, with attribution. "The Subjective Necessity of a Social Settlement," 1–26 (see chap. 1, n. 20).

41 Mill, *Subjection*, 27, 22.

42 R. R. Bowker, "Toynbee Hall, London," *Century* 24 (May 1887): 158–59.

43 JA to Alice Addams Haldeman, January 6, 1888.

44 JA to Flora Guiteau, January 7, 1888; EGS to Anna Haldeman Addams, January 30, 1888, EGSP.

45 JA, *Twenty*, 86.

46 Marcus Aurelius, *Meditations*, Book 9, no. 3; JA to EGS, November 3, 1883.

47 Louise W. Knight, "Jane Addams's Theory of Cooperation," in *Jane Addams and the Practice of Democracy: Multidisciplinary Essays on Theory and Practice*, ed. Wendy Chmielewski, Marilyn Fischer, and Carol Nackenoff (Urbana: University of Illinois Press, 2009), 66–69.

48 JA to Anna Addams Haldeman, June 14, 1888.

49 Ibid., February 19, 1889. The poem is "Bishop Blougram's Apology," and the quotation is from lines 322–25.

Chapter 3: Activist

1 JA, "Alumnae Essay," in [Rockford Female Seminary Endowment speeches], *Memorials to Anna P. Sill, First Principal of Rockford Female Seminary* [June 1889], 74.

2 Matthew Arnold, "Democracy," in *Mixed Essays, Irish Essays and Others* (1879, repr., New York: Macmillan, 1924), 68–69.

3 JA to Mary Addams Linn, April 1, 1889.

4 JA, "Outgrowths of Toynbee Hall" [December 1890], 2. *JAPM*, 45:1756. This essay has been misdated by others. See Knight, *Citizen*, 472n66, for evidence of this 1890 date.

5 JA, *Twenty*, 94 (see chap. 1, n. 3).

6 JA to George Haldeman, December 21, 1890.

7 Robert Woods and Albert J. Kennedy, *The Handbook of Settlements* (New York: Charities Publication Committee, 1911), 2; JA to Mary Addams Linn, March 13 and April 1, 1889.

8 Mary Lynne Mapes, "Visions of a Christian City: The Politics of Religion and Gender in Chicago's City Missions and Protestant Settlement Houses 1886–1929," Ph.D. diss., Michigan State University, 1998, 78.

9 JA, "English and American Social Settlements," *Chautauqua Assembly Herald* 23, no. 24 (August 12, 1898): 7.

10 JA, *Twenty*, 109; JA to Katherine Coman, December 7, 1891.

11 JA, "Outgrowths," 16.

12 Re full-time work, see Richard Schneirov, *Labor and Urban Politics: Class Conflict and the Origins of Modern Liberalism in Chicago, 1864–97* (Urbana: University of Illinois Press, 1998), 188. Re the 1892 figure, see Mary Kenney, "Organization of Working Women," *The Women's Congress of Representative Women*, Mary Wright Sewall, ed. (Chicago: Rand McNally, 1894), 872.

13 Account Book #1, "JA's Ledger," *JAPM*, Addendum 3 (reel 74). Calculations are the author's. Re the farm and JA's income's being four thousand dollars, see Knight, *Citizen*, 117–18 (see chap. 1, n. 1).

14 Re JA's need to support herself, see, for example, Alice Hamilton to Agnes Hamilton, April 5, 1898, file 635, box 25, HFP. Re owning a small amount of property at the end of her life, see Linn, *Addams*, 352 (see chap. 1, n. 1).

15 The list of industries is drawn from Reuben Donnelley, comp., *Lakeside Directory of the City of Chicago* (Chicago: Chicago Directory Company, 1889).

16 Kathleen Banks Nutter, *The Necessity of Organization: Mary Kenney O'Sullivan and Trade Unionism for Women, 1892–1912* (New York: Garland, 1999), 7–9.

17 JA, "Settlement as a Factor," 140 (see chap. 2, n. 11).

18 Quoted in Kathryn Kish Sklar, *Florence Kelley and the Nation's Work: The Rise of Women's Political Culture*, vol. 1 (New Haven: Yale University Press, 1995), 132–33.

19 Maureen Flanagan, *Seeing with Their Hearts: Chicago Women and the Good City, 1871–1933* (Princeton: Princeton University Press, 2002), 41, 234n73.

20 JA, "How Would You Uplift the Masses?" [speech to the Sunset Club, February 4, 1892], reprinted as "With the Masses," *Advance* (February 18, 1892): 11–12. *JAPM* 46:0498.

21 JA, "The Objective Value of a Social Settlement," in *Philanthropy and Social Progress*, ed. Henry C. Adams (New York: Crowell, 1893), 49.

22 JA, *Twenty*, 202.

23 Linn, *Addams*, 135; Francis Hackett, "Hull-House—A Souvenir," *Survey* 54, no. 5 (June 1, 1925): 279.

24 Re "lioness," see Andrew Alexander Bruce, "Memorial Services for Julia Lathrop" (1927), vol. 17, *JAPM*, 38:0673. Re her laughter, see Edith Abbott, "Grace Abbott: A Sister's Memories," *Social Service Review* 13, no. 3 (September 1939): 377.

25 JA, *Twenty*, 201–22.

26 The Neighborhood Guild, founded in New York City in 1886, was not the first settlement house in the United States, according to its founder, Stan-

ton Coit, *Neighbourhood Guilds*, 2nd ed. (London: Swan Sonnenchein, 1892), 85–88. See also Knight, *Citizen*, 463n40. British-born Coit was really the first community organizer in the United States.

27 Louise W. Knight, "Jane Addams and Hull House: Historical Lessons on Nonprofit Leadership," *Nonprofit Management and Leadership* 2, no. 2 (Winter 1991): 128–31.

28 Patricia Lengermann and Gillian Niebrugge, "Thrice Told: Narratives of Sociology's Relation to Social Work," in *Sociology in America*, ed. Craig J. Calhoun (Chicago: University of Chicago Press, 2007), 97.

29 Residents of Hull-House, *Hull-House Maps and Papers* (see chap. 2, n. 11).

30 Josephine Starr, "Notes," 3, Box 1, folder 6, EGSP.

31 Ellen later recalled Jane's making the remark about Ellen. EGS to JA, April 12, 1935; the devil's tail quote is from Winifred E. Wise, *Jane Addams of Hull-House* (New York: Harcourt, Brace, 1935), 171.

32 EGS to Mary Allen, August 13, 1892, and October 14 [1892], EGSP. Starr says she is quoting FK.

33 EGS to Mary Allen, "Dearly Beloved," [September?] 1891, EGSP

34 Re MRS's activities at Hull House, see Linn, *Addams*, 115; Ann Mather-Smith Fishbeck (daughter of MRS's brother, Charles Mather Smith), interview by Louise W. Knight, April 13, 1995, Sarasota, Fla. For quotations, see Fishbeck, interview.

35 Fishbeck, interview.

36 Quoted in Eleanor Howard Woods, *Robert Woods: A Champion of Democracy* (1929; repr., Freeport, N.Y.: Books for Libraries, 1971), 82.

37 JA to MRS, August 26, 1893.

38 JA, *My Friend*, 67 (see chap. 1, n. 24); JA, *Twenty*, 260.

39 JA, *Twenty*, 259–60.

40 Ibid., 259.

41 Quoted in Flanagan, *Seeing*, 38.

42 Quoted in Edwin G. Burrows and Mike Wallace, *Gotham: A History of New York City to 1898* (New York: Oxford University Press, 1999), 1190, 1984.

43 JA, *Twenty*, 187.

44 See, for example, "Dictator Debs' Strike," *Chicago Tribune*, July 1, 1894, 11.

45 JA, "A Modern Lear" [1896/1912], in *The Jane Addams Reader*, ed. Jean Bethke Elshtain (New York: Basic Books, 2002), 163. For a more detailed discus-

sion of Addams's role in the strike, see "Biography's Window on Social Change: Benevolence and Justice in Jane Addams's 'A Modern Lear.'" *Journal of Women's History* 9, no. 1 (Spring 1997): 112–38, and Knight, *Citizen*, 352–59.

46 Alice Hamilton, "Jane Addams: Gentle Rebel," *Political Affairs* (March 1960): 34; and "Jane Addams of Hull-House," *Social Service*, vol. 27, no. 1 (June– August, 1953): 15.

47 JA, "Settlement as a Factor," 147, 148.

48 Ibid., 146, 148, 147.

49 John Dewey to Alice Chipman Dewey, October 10, 1894, John Dewey Collection, Southern Illinois University.

50 JA, "Modern Lear," 174, 175.

51 JA, "Claim on the College Woman," *Rockford Collegian* 23 (June 1895): 62.

52 The quotation is from a revised version of the "Modern Lear" speech. See JA, *Democracy*, 100 (see chap. 2, n. 31).

53 JA, *Twenty*, 282. For more on the garbage campaign, see Louise W. Knight, "Garbage and Democracy: The Chicago Community Organizing Campaign of the 1890s," *Journal of Community Practice* 14, no. 3 (2006): 7–27.

54 FK, "Hull House," *New England Magazine* 18, no. 5 (July 1898): 565.

55 *Chicago Tribune*, October 12, 1900, 12; JA, Editorial, *Rockford Seminary Magazine* 9 (May 1881): 155.

56 "Reception for Miss Addams," *Woman's Journal* (February 20, 1897): 60.

57 JA, "Growth of Corporate Consciousness," in *Illinois State Conference of Charities and Corrections Proceedings, 1897*, vol. 2 (Springfield, IL: n.p., 1897), 41.

58 JA, "The Social Obligations of Citizenship," *Chautauqua Assembly Herald* 23, no. 2 (August 10, 1898): 2.

59 JA, "Settlement as a Factor," 146; JA, "Modern Lear," 171, 175.

60 JA, "Modern Lear," 172, 171.

61 Ibid., 173.

62 JA, "Trade Unions and Public Duty," *American Journal of Sociology* 4 (January 1899): 450, 448.

63 Ibid., 459–60.

Chapter 4: Political Ethicist

1 JA to Henry Demarest Lloyd, December 1, 1894.

2 JA, *Democracy*, 178 (see chap. 2, n. 31); JA, "The Friendship of Settlement Work," *Charities* 10 (March 28, 1903): 316.

3 JA, *Democracy*, 10, 9.

4 Ibid., 9–10, 256.

5 Ibid., 158; see also JA, "College Woman and Christianity," *Independent* 53 (August 8, 1901): 1854.

6 JA, *Democracy*, 164–66, 170.

7 Oliver Wendell Holmes, quoted by Richard T. Ely, in a letter to JA, July 10, 1906; Edward Seligman to JA, April 26, 1902; Monroe quoted in Katherine Joslin, *Jane Addams: A Writer's Life* (Urbana: University of Illinois Press, 2004), 68; William James to JA, September 17, 1902.

8 JA to Anita McCormick Blaine, April 17, 1902; JA to MRS, May 3, 1902. Re taking the book off alone, see MHJ, *Jane Addams as I Knew Her, Reviewer's Library*, no. 7 (Girard, KS: Haldeman-Julius Publications, 1936), 12.

9 Anne F. Scott, "Jane Addams," in *Making the Invisible Woman Visible*, ed. Anne F. Scott (Urbana: University of Illinois Press, 1984), 131; Joslin, *Writer's Life*, 72.

10 William Jennings Bryan, "The Paralyzing Influence of Imperialism," Democratic National Convention, July 4–6, 1900, *Official Proceedings*, 205–06.

11 JA, Résumé, 1935. Women's International League for Peace and Freedom, U.S. Section Papers [microfilm], 19:0738, SCPC.

12 JA "Tolstoy and Gandhi," *Christian Century* 48 (November 25, 1931), 1485.

13 JA to MRS, October 24, 1898. Davis erroneously dates this letter October 6, 1898 (*American Heroine*, 141, 312n10, see chap. 1, n. 11)

14 *Chicago Tribune*, October 20, 1898, 11.

15 JA, "Democracy or Militarism," in *Addams' Essays and Speeches on Peace*, ed. Fischer and Whipps, 1 (see preface, n. 1).

16 Ibid., 2–3.

17 Ida Wells-Barnett, *Lynch Law in Georgia* (Chicago: privately printed 1899), n.p.

18 *Chicago Tribune*, September 12, 1895, 16.

19 Paula Giddings, *Ida: A Sword Among Lions: Ida B. Wells and the Campaign Against Lynching* (New York: HarperCollins, 2009), 417–18.

20 JA, "Respect for the Law," *Independent* 53 (January 3, 1901): 19. See also "Anti-Lynching Address," December 12, 1899, 2, *JAPM*, 46:0947.

21 JA, "Respect," 18, 20.

22 Ida Wells-Barnett, *Crusade for Justice: The Autobiography of Ida B. Wells* (Chicago: University of Chicago Press, 1970), 259.

23 Ida Wells-Barnett, "Lynching and the Excuse for It," *Independent* 53 (May 16, 1901): 1133–1136.

24 *Chicago Tribune*, September 8, 1901, 12.

25 JA, *Twenty*, 404–05 (see chap. 1, n. 3).

26 Raymond Robins quoted in Neil V. Salzman, *Reform and Revolution: The Life and Times of Raymond Robins* (Kent, OH: Kent State University Press, 1991), 122. Addams does not mention Robins's going with her in her version of the story.

27 JA, *Twenty*, 407; JA to Lillian Wald, September 17, 1901. In 1908 JA again sought justice for a Russian Jew, Lazar Averbuch, who was killed on the false suspicion he was a violent anarchist with the intent to commit murder.

28 JA, "Social Settlements in Illinois," in *Transactions of the Illinois State Historical Society*, pub. no 1 (1906): 163. For more on the residents and their departments, see *Hull House Bulletin*, 1905–06, 8, *JAPM*, 53:0850.

29 Louise de Koven Bowen, *Growing Up with a City* (New York: Macmillan, 1926), 88; re Lathrop, see, for example, JA to FK, June 30, 1901. Between 1905 and 1908 Addams served on the Chicago Board of Education, a demanding job that took up much of her time, and produced many frustrations. The complicated story is not told here only for lack of space.

30 *Critic* 64, no. 6 (June 1904): 489.

31 Walter Lippmann, *A Preface to Politics* (New York: Mitchell Kennerley, 1914), 152; Henry Demarest Lloyd to Anne Withington, September 13, 1903. Henry Demarest Lloyd Papers, Wisconsin Historical Society, Division of Archives and Manuscripts [Madison]; Ida M. Tarbell, "Jane Addams—Notes for Pen and Brush Talk" [1935], 10.

32 Anita McCormick Blaine, Diary entry, April 21, 1901. Anita McCormick Blaine Papers, McCormick Collection, Wisconsin State Historical Society.

33 JA, *Twenty*, 151.

34 Kathryn Kish Sklar and Beverly Wilson Palmer, eds., *The Selected Letters of Florence Kelley, 1869–1931* (Urbana: University of Illinois Press, 2009), 97, 122, 402.

35 JA, *Twenty*, 448.

36 Flora Guiteau, "Notes for a Talk on Jane Addams," April 7, 1936, 4, Memorials file, Jane Addams Collection, Rockford College Archives, Rockford College, Rockford, IL; Caroline Foulke Urie, "Jane Addams' Personality," 1, JAP, DGı, Series 4, Box 3, SCPC; Hannah Hull, "Jane Addams," *Pax International* 10, nos. 3–4 (May–June, 1935): 14.

37 JA, *The Excellent Becomes the Permanent* (New York: Macmillan, 1932), 65.

38 James Weber Linn, "Interpretation of Life," *Religious Education* 32 (July 1937): 221.

39 Alice Hamilton to Agnes Hamilton, May 10, 1897, HFP.

40 Harold Ickes, "Speech at the Jane Addams Memorial Dinner," May 11, 1949, p. 25. Alma Petersen Papers, JAMC, Special Collections, University Library, University of Illinois–Chicago.

41 JA to MRS, May 26, 1902, and August 4, 1904.

42 JA [untitled poem to MRS, December 23, 1900], *JAPM*, 46:0989. Smith's birthday was December 23. The poem refers to Addams's being forty.

43 JA to MRS, August 26, 1906, and May 3, 1902.

44 Ibid., April 8, 1902.

45 Bowen, *Growing Up*, 87; Ickes, "Speech," 25; JA, *Excellent*, 61.

46 JA, "Newer Ideals of Peace," July 10, 1902, in Fischer and Whipps, *Addams' Essays*, 23 (see preface, n. 1).

47 *New York Times*, November 27, 1904, SM8.

48 Robins quoted in Salzman, *Reform*, 90; JA, *Peace and Bread in Time of War* (1922; repr., Urbana: University of Illinois Press, 2002), 76.

49 Josephine Goldmark, *Impatient Crusader: Florence Kelley's Life Story* (Urbana: University of Illinois Press, 1953), 87–92; Allen F. Davis, *Spearheads for Reform: The Social Settlements and the Progressive Movement, 1890–1914* (New York: Oxford University Press, 1967), 129–31.

50 *New York Times*, April 24, 1904, 10; and January 19, 1905, 6.

51 May Wood, *History of the General Federation of Women's Clubs* (New York: General Federation of Women's Clubs, 1919), 166. Re JA's joining the NCLC board, see *New York Evening Post*, November 1, 1911, clipping, *JAPM*, 58:0570.

52 JA, "Ten Years' Experience in Illinois," in *Proceedings of the Seventh Annual Conference of the National Child Labor Committee, Supplement to the Annals of the American Academy of Political and Social Science,* no. 32 (July 1911): 148.

53 JA, *Newer Ideals of Peace* (New York: Macmillan, 1907), 164.

54 Quoted in *Chicago Tribune,* November 16, 1902, 35.

55 Philip S. Foner, *Women and the American Labor Movement: From Colonial Times to the Eve of World War I* (New York: Free Press, 1979), 301; re Chicago Federation of Labor, see James R. Barrett, introduction to Hutchins Hapgood, *The Spirit of Labor* (1907; Urbana: University of Illinois Press, 2004), xxi–xxii.

56 Samuel Gompers, "Should the Wife Help Support the Family?", *American Federationist* 13 (1906): 36; U.S. Bureau of Census, *Historical Statistics of the United States, Colonial Times to 1970* (Washington, DC: Government Printing Office, 1975), Part 1, Series D49-D62, p. 133.

57 Re the Chicago branch, see Meredith Tax, *The Rising of the Women: Feminist Solidarity and Class Conflict, 1880–1917* (New York: Monthly Review Press, 1980); re New York City branch, see Nancy Schrom Dye, *As Equals and as Sisters* (Columbia: University of Missouri Press, 1980).

58 Re founding board of WTUL, see Elizabeth Anne Payne, *Reform, Labor, and Feminism: Margaret Dreier Robins and the Women's Trade Union League* (Urbana: University of Illinois Press, 1988), 45–51; *Chicago Tribune,* January 5, 1904, 14. JA was not an officer of the Chicago branch.

59 JA, *Democracy,* 220.

60 Re JA on picket line, *New York Evening Post,* October 31, 1910, *JAPM* 53:0491. Re JA's working on relief fund, see Davis, *American Heroine,* 115 (see chap. 1, n. 12). Re Starr, see Gladys Boone, *The Women's Trade Union Leagues in Great Britain and the United States of America* (New York: Columbia University Press, 1942), 88. Re JA's mediating the strike, see *New York Evening Post,* November [?], 1910, *JAPM,* 53:0493.

61 JA [Extracts from an address on the WTUL to the Berkeley Lyceum], March 26, 1905], 2, *JAPM,* 42:0594.

62 *Chicago Tribune,* January 28, 1900, 5; re JA and Chicago Peace Society in 1902, see *Report of the Chicago Peace Society, 1912* (Chicago: privately printed, 1913), 28. JA, "Addresses of Miss Jane Addams," in Fischer and Whipps, *Addams' Essays,* 31–37.

63 JA to Richard T. Ely, November 20, 1905.

64 JA, *Newer,* 220, 28. See Herbert Spencer, *The Principles of Sociology* (Osnabrück: Otto Zeller, 1966). Spencer would have particularly disagreed with Addams's argument that the government's role should be expanded.

65 JA, *Newer*, 229.

66 Ibid., 29.

67 Ibid., 40, 15. JA's references in *Newer Ideals* and other writings to rural immigrants as "simple" and "primitive," "dull" or being "stupid" sound shockingly condescending to modern ears and seem to contradict her ethic of
respect. To understand what she meant requires a close study of her writings alongside those of some of her favorite authors, including John Stuart
Mill, Emerson, and Plato, as well as frequent recourse to an excellent dic-
tionary. One learns that her point, in all cases, was that rural immigrants
possessed untrained potential.

68 Ibid., 99, 91.

69 Ibid., 238, 141.

70 Ibid., 24.

71 William James, *Varieties of Religious Experience*, in *William James: Writings, 1902–
1910* (New York: Library of America, 1987), 333; Ralph Waldo Emerson,
"War," in *The Power of Nonviolence: Writings by Advocates of Peace* [no ed.] (Boston:
Beacon Press, 1992), 11. Seventeenth-century philosopher Baruch Spinoza
may have started this hare with his claim that peace was a virtue.

72 JA to George Brett, December 12, 1906; JA, "Recent Immigration: A Field
Neglected by the Scholar," *University Record* 9, no. 9 (January 1905): 282.

73 Madison Grant, *The Passing of the Great Race, or The Racial Basis of European History* (New York: Charles Scribner's Sons, 1916), 80; "The great American
problem," quoted in Daniel J. Tichenor, *Dividing Lines: The Politics of Immigration Control in America* (Princeton: Princeton University Press, 2002), 115.

74 JA to Joseph Cannon, June 11, 1906.

75 William James to JA, January 24, 1907; George Herbert Mead, "Review of
Jane Addams's *Newer Ideals of Peace*," *American Journal of Sociology* 13, no. 1 (July
1907): 128; *New York Tribune*, June 3, 1907, *JAPM*, 11-0218; Theodore Roosevelt
to Florence Lockwood LaFarge, February 13, 1908. *Letters of Theodore Roosevelt*,
vol. 6: *The Big Stick*, ed. Elting E. Morison (Cambridge, MA: Harvard University Press, 1952), 942–43. See also, Linn, *Addams*, 293–94.

Chapter 5: Politician

1 JA quoted in *Chicago Tribune*, May 27, 1906, D5.

2 JA, "The National Protection of Children," *Annals of the American Academy of
Political and Social Science*, vol. 29 (January 1907): 69–60.

3 *New York Times*, December 21, 1906; FK to Nicholas Kelley, April 6, 1908, in Sklar and Palmer, *Selected Letters*, 172–73 (see chap. 4, n. 34).

4 Ida Husted Harper, ed., *The History of Woman Suffrage*, vol. 1: *1900–1920* (New York: J. J. Little & Ives Co., 1922), 192.

5 Ida Tarbell, "The Irresponsible Woman and the Friendless Child," in *Antifeminism in America: A Reader*, ed. Angela Howard and Sasha Ranaé Adams Tarrant (New York: Garland Publishing, 2000), 114–15.

6 J. Cardinal Gibbons, "The Restless Woman" [1902], ibid., 108.

7 JA, "Why Women Should Vote," *Ladies' Home Journal* 27 (January 1910): 21–22.

8 JA, *Newer*, 186 (see chap. 4, n. 53); JA, "Why Women," 21.

9 Corbin, quoted in Rima Lunin Schultz and Adele Hast, eds., *Women Building Chicago* (Bloomington: Indiana University Press, 2001), s.v. "Corbin, Caroline"; JA, "Why Women," 22.

10 JA, "Why Women," 22; JA, *Newer*, 187.

11 JA, *Newer*, 141.

12 For the membership number, see Alexander Johnson, ed., *Proceedings of the National Conference on Charities and Correction* [Buffalo, NY, June 9–16, 1909] (New York: privately printed, 1909), 541. For complete details on JA's involvement with the NCCC, see *Jane Addams, September 6, 1860–May 21, 1935* [Memorial Meeting], *National Conference of Social Work, June 10, 1935* (Montreal, Canada: privately printed, 1935), 20–22.

13 JA, "Charity and Social Justice," *Survey* 24 (June 11, 1910): 449.

14 Johnson, *Proceedings, 1909*, 543.

15 Re her three vice presidencies and names of others on the boards, see *Charities and the Commons* 18, no. 10 (June 5, 1907): 339; "For a Federal Health Bureau," ibid., 293; JA to Phoebe Apperson Hearst, March 27, 1913.

16 JA, "Woman's Special Training for Peacemaking," *Proceedings of the Second National Peace Congress* (Chicago: American Peace Society, 1909), 253.

17 JA, *The Spirit of Youth and the City Streets* (New York: Macmillan, 1909), 40–41.

18 Ibid., 37.

19 Ibid., 116.

20 Ibid., 161.

21 Ibid., 3.

22 William James to JA, December 13, 1909. See also Charlene Haddock Seig-fried, *Pragmatism and Feminism: Reweaving the Social Fabric* (Chicago: University of Chicago Press, 1995), 135.

23 JA to Graham Taylor, September 4, 1910. See also JA to Ida Tarbell, August 23, 1909.

24 Re publication date, see JA to MRS, November 8, 1910; re stories, see JA, *Twenty*, 235, 376, 323, 200 (see chap. 1, n. 3).

25 JA, *Twenty*, ix.

26 Davis, *American Heroine*, 199–200 (see chap. 1, n. 11).

27 Margaret Tims, *Jane Addams of Hull House, 1860–1935: A Centenary Study* (London: George Allen & Unwin, 1960), 132.

28 Margaret Dreier Robins to JA, February 10, 1907; *Chicago Tribune*, April 22, 1910, 10.

29 For "earnestness," see unidentified Cincinnati newspaper clipping, May 15, 1894, *JAPM*, 55: 0022; for "eager voice," see Zona Gale, statement in *Unity*, 150, no. 10 (May 1935): 226; for "deep eyes," see unidentified newspaper clipping [June 28, 1894?], *JAPM*, 55:0025.

30 MHJ, *Jane Addams as I Knew Her*, 26 (see chap. 4, n. 8).

31 Victor Weybright, "Memories," *Saturday Review* 44 (August 12, 1961): 21.

32 Mrs. John K. Ottley, "America's Only Saint, Who Will Visit Atlanta," *Atlanta Constitution*, November 3, 1907, A5.

33 Burns quoted in William Hard, "Chicago's Five Maidens," *American Magazine* 62 (September 1906): 488.

34 Re Joan of Arc, see the *Caxton*, August [?], 1910, *JAPM*, 57:1207; for the quotation, see *Philadelphia Record*, March 4, 1912, *JAPM*, 58:0764.

35 *St. Louis Republic*, May 21, 1910, JAPM, 57:0978.

36 Louise de Koven Bowen, *Open Windows: Stories of People and Places* (Chicago: Ralph Fletcher Seymour, 1946), 226–27.

37 JA, "College Woman and Christianity," 1855 (chap. 4, n. 5); Emily Greene Balch, statement in *Unity* 115, no. 10 (May 1935): 199.

38 Elia M. Peattie, "Women of the Hour. Miss Jane Addams," *Harper's Bazaar* 38, no. 10 (October 1904): 1004; Alice Hamilton, "Jane Addams of Hull House and the Women's International League of Peace and Freedom," *Roundtable* [newsletter of the National Federation of Settlements and Neighborhood Centers] 19, no. 6 (June 1955): 2; Caroline F. Urie to EGS, May 25, 1935, Box 1, File 13, EGSP.

39 Linn, *Addams*, 433 (see chap. 1, n. 1); MHJ, *Jane Addams as I Knew Her*, 14.

40 EGS to Mary Allen, quoting FK, October 14 [1892], File 70, Box 7, EGSP.

41 JA to MRS, November 8, 1910.

42 JA, *A New Conscience and an Ancient Evil* (New York: Macmillan, 1912), 33.

43 Bowen, *Open Windows*, 206; Hamilton, "Jane Addams of Hull House and the Women's International League of Peace and Freedom," 1.

44 Steven M. Buechler, *The Transformation of the Woman Suffrage Movement: The Case of Illinois, 1850–1920* (New Brunswick, NJ: Rutgers University Press, 1986), 161–62.

45 JA, "Why Women," 21–22; Kay Sloan, *The Loud Silents: Origins of the Social Problem Film* (Urbana: University of Illinois Press, 1988), 111–13.

46 *New York Times*, March 8, 1911, 3.

47 JA, "Woman and the State," February 2, 1911, TM carbon, *JAPM*, 47:0096. The locations of the speeches are on the microfilm. Re the debate about the origins of the family, see Ann Taylor Allen, "Feminism, Social Science and the Meanings of Modernity: The Debate on the Origin of the Family in Europe and the United States, 1860–1914," *American Historical Review* (October 1999), http://www.historycooperative.org/journals/ahr/104.4/ah001085.html. For current knowledge of the history of matriarchy and patriarchy, see Cristina Biaggi, ed., *The Rule of Mars: Readings on the Origins, History, and Impact of Patriarchy* (Manchester, Conn.: Reading, Ideas, & Trends, 2006).

48 JA, "Woman and the State," 4–5. She wrote she had been reading Emily James Putnam's *The Lady: Studies of Certain Phases of Her History* (London: G. Putnam's Sons, 1910).

49. JA, "Woman and the State," 10. The part of the speech about men seeking the vote from women was later published as "If Men Were Seeking the Franchise" in the *Ladies' Home Journal* in 1913. See JA, "If Men Were Seeking the Franchise," in *The Jane Addams Reader*, ed. Jean Bethke Elshtain (New York: Basic Books, 2002), 229–34.

50. JA, "The Larger Aspects of the Woman's Movement," in *Women in Public Life*, ed. James Lichtenberger (Philadelphia: American Academy of Political and Social Science, 1914), 6. For a more complete discussion of the development of Addams's feminism, see Louise W. Knight, "The Feminist Consciousness of Jane Addams," unpublished (available from the author).

51 Quoted in John Milton Cooper, Jr., *Pivotal Decades: The United States, 1900–1920* (New York: Norton, 1990), 100; see also Theodore Roosevelt to JA, October 31, 1911.

52 Quoted in *Chicago Tribune*, February 2, 1912, 6.

53 *New York Times*, June 13, 1912, 1.

54 JA, "The Progressive Party and Woman's Suffrage," 5, *JAPM*, 47:0498.

55 Janet M. Martin, *The Presidency and Women: Promise, Performance, and Illusion* (College Station: Texas A&M University Press, 2003), 26.

56 Linn, *Addams*, 239, 260; *Los Angeles Times*, August 9, 1909, I1; *Chicago Daily Tribune*, August 9, 1909, 9.

57 Jo Freeman, *We Will Be Heard: Women's Struggle for Political Power in the United States* (New York: Rowman and Littlefield, 2008), 53–56, 58–65.

58 Ibid., 56; for twenty-two delegates, see JA, "Progressive Party and Woman's Suffrage," 5; re Carpenter, see *New York Times*, August 6, 1912, p. 2.

59 Quotation is from the *New York Evening Post*, August 8, 1912, *JAPM*, 58:1239. Ida Husted Harper wrongly claimed Addams was on the Resolutions Committee (*History of Woman Suffrage*, 706). This has misled historians. Addams added to the confusion by her typically loose use of the word "we" in writing about the party convention (*Second Twenty*, 29 [see chap. 2, n. 20]). For a list of the Resolutions Committee's members, see *New York Times*, August 6, 1912, 2. Re the NCCC committee, see JA, *Second Twenty*, 26.

60 JA, "My Experiences as a Progressive Delegate," *McClure's Magazine* 40 (November 1912): 14.

61 *New York Times*, August 7, 1912, 2.

62 JA quoted in *New York Times*, August 6, 1912, 2; JA, "Has the Emancipation Act Been Nullified by National Indifference?" *Survey* 29 (February 1, 1913): 566.

63 Sophonisba Breckinridge, statement in *Unity* 115, no. 10 (July 15, 1935): 191; Theodore Roosevelt to Raymond Robins, August 12, 1914, in Morison, *Letters of TR*: vol. 7, 801 (see chap. 4, n. 75).

64 William M. Trotter to JA, August 6–7, 1912.

65 JA, "The Progressive Party and the Negro," *Crisis*, 5 (November 1912): 31.

66 Frederick Douglass to Sophie White Griffing, September 27, 1868, in Philip S. Foner, ed., *Frederick Douglass on Women's Rights* (New York: Da Capo Press, 1992), 86.

67 William Allen White, *Autobiography of William Allen White* (New York: Macmillan, 1946), 531; *Chicago Tribune*, August 8, 1912, 2.

68 JA [Speech Seconding the Nomination of Theodore Roosevelt], Progressive Party Convention, Chicago, August 1912, *Congressional Record*, 62nd Cong., 2nd sess. (Appendix), vol. 48, pt. 12, 564–65.

69 JA, *Second Twenty*, 40.

70 Theodore Roosevelt, *Progressive Principles: Selections from Addresses Made During the Presidential Campaign of 1912*, ed. Elmer H. Youngman (New York: Progressive National Service, 1913), 206.

71 JA to Alde Blake, July 13, 1912.

72 *Woman's Journal* (December 14, 1912): 400.

73 JA to Alice Addams Haldeman, October 14, 1912; JA, "Newer Ideals of Peace," in Fischer and Whipps, *Addams' Essays*, 19 (see preface, n. 1).

74 JA, "My Experiences as a Progressive Delegate," 12.

75 JA, "The Steps by Which I Became a Progressive," 4, *JAPM*, 47:0505.

76 *New York Times*, August 15, 1912, 5; JA, "Pragmatism and Politics," *Survey* 29 (October 5, 1912): 12

77 *New York Times*, August 10, 1912, 6.

78 Ibid., August 21, 1912, 1; August 31, 1912, 2.

79 JA to Lillian Wald, August 15, 1912.

80 Theodore Roosevelt to Millicent Garrett Fawcett, November 19, 1912, in Morison, *Letters of TR*, vol. 7, 651.

81 JA to Alice Addams Haldeman, August 9, 1912; *Chicago Tribune*, December 1, 1914, 1.

82 JA, *Second Twenty*, 45.

83 Theodore Roosevelt to Millicent Garrett Fawcett, November 19, 1912, loc. cit.; Freeman, *We Will Be Heard*, 57–58.

84 Quoted in White, *Autobiography*, 513.

85 Theodore Roosevelt to Millicent Garrett Fawcett, November 19, 1912, loc. cit.

86 Quoted in Christine Lunardini, *From Equal Suffrage to Equal Rights: Alice Paul and the National Woman's Party, 1910–1928* (New York: New York University Press, 1986), 32.

87 JA to Clara Landsberg, March 1, 1913; JA to Katherine Coman, March 23, 1913.

88 JA to Helen Culver, April 11, 1913. Re JA's visit with Tolstoy, see Knight, *Citizen*, 371–74.

89 Ellery Sedgwick to JA, July 3, 1913.

90 JA, "Unexpected Reactions of a Traveler in Egypt," 178, 185 (see chap. 1, n. 5).

91 FK, "Women and Social Legislation in the United States," *Annals of the American Academy of Political and Social Science* 56 (November 1914): 70; Sklar and Palmer, *Selected Letters*, 203n2 (see chap. 4, n. 34).

92 JA to Lillian Wald, July 3, 1914. See also Linn, *Addams*, 353.

93 JA, *Second Twenty*, 119.

94 Ibid., 117–18; see also *New York Times*, August 5, 1914, 5.

Chapter 6: Dissenter

1 JA, *Peace and Bread*, 77 (see chap. 4, n. 48).

2 *New York Times*, August 4, 1914, 3.

3 *New York Times*, September 21, 1914; Charles Chatfield, *For Peace and Justice: Pacifism in America, 1914–1941* (Knoxville: University of Tennessee Press, 1971), 16.

4 *New York Evening Post*, September 30, 1914, 3.

5 FK to Paul Kellogg [February 12, 1915], in Sklar and Palmer, *Selected Letters*, 200–201 (see chap. 4, n. 34). See the 1907 Hague Convention for the Pacific Settlement of International Disputes, Articles 2 and 3.

6 JA to Lillian Wald, November 30, 1914.

7 *Chicago Tribune*, December 6, 1914, 1, F4; *Survey* 33, no. 15 (January 1915): 393–94; for platform, see *Survey* 33, no. 23 (March 1915): 597–98.

8 *Survey* 33, no. 15 (January 1915): 393–94.

9 *Encyclopedia of the New American Nation Online*, s.v. "Arbitration, Mediation, and Conciliation—The Hague Peace Conferences," http://www.americanforeignrelations.com/A-D/Arbitration-Mediation-and-Conciliation-The-hague-peace-conferences.html.

10 Quotation is from JA, "A Conference of Neutrals," in Fischer and Whipps, *Addams' Essays*, 136 (see preface, n. 1); re diplomats, see JA, *Peace and Bread*, 87.

11 JA to Lillian Wald, December 21, 1914.

12 Marie Louise Degen, *The History of the Woman's Peace Party* (New York: Garland Publishing Co., 1972), 40–41.

13 *Survey* 33, no. 15 (January 1915): 393–94.

14 Degen, *History*, 44. Julia Wales, an English instructor from the University of Wisconsin, wrote a proposal that a "commission of experts" do "con-

tinuous mediation" to bring about the war's end. Addams learned about it after the CEF meeting. She invited Wales to the WPP meeting, where the proposal was discussed. Since the WPP resolution refers to "pacifists," the party seems not to have embraced the "experts" concept, which, in any case, did not originate with Wales, although Addams later described it as such. JA, *Second Twenty*, 125 (see chap. 2, n. 20). See also David S. Patterson, *The Search for Negotiated Peace* (New York: Routledge, 2008), 48–49.

15 Degen, *History*, 40–41.

16 JA, "What Is War Destroying," in Fischer and Whipps, *Addams' Essays*, 62.

17 *Survey* 33, no. 23 (March 1915): 597–98. The "plank" was a petition. See also JA, *Second Twenty Years*, 123–24.

18 *New York Times*, April 28, 1915, 12.

19 JA to Sarah Hostetter, October 10, 1914.

20 Bryan, "Biographical Profiles," in *Selected Papers*, 480–81 (see chap. 1, n. 17).

21 Degen, *History*, 74, citing the April 13, 1915, *Chicago Record-Herald*.

22 JA, Emily G. Balch, and Alice Hamilton, *Women at The Hague: The International Congress of Women and Its Results*, intro. Harriet Hyman Alonso (1915; repr. Urbana: University of Illinois Press, 2003), 8; Degen, *History*, 78, 80.

23 JA [Address at The Hague], in Fischer and Whipps, *Addams' Essays*, 75.

24 Quoted in Patterson, *Search*, 75.

25 Caroline F. Urie to EGS, June 13, 1935, Box 1, File 13, EGSP.

26 Degen, *History*, 85; Addams described it later as a nondiplomatic, scientific conference. JA, *Second Twenty*, 125; see also Addams et al., *Women at the Hague*, 164. The phrase "continuous mediation" comes from the Wales Plan.

27 JA to MRS, May 9, 1915.

28 JA, "Women and War," in Fischer and Whipps, *Addams' Essays*, 76–77.

29 JA, "The Revolt Against War," in ibid., 85. Addams gave her address no title; this is the editors' title.

30 JA, *Second Twenty*, 131, 134. See also JA, "Settlement as a Way of Life," *Neighborhood*, vol. 2 (July 1929): 144.

31 JA, "Revolt Against," 83, 88–89, 94.

32 *New York Times*, July 10, 1915, 3.

33 *New York Times*, July 13, 1915, 10.

34 First two editorials quoted in Davis, *American Heroine*, 229 (see chap. 1, n. 12); *New York Times*, August 17, 1915, 8.

35 *New York Times*, April 16, 1915, 1; the magazine article is quoted in *Washington Post*, July 20, 1915, 5.

36 Kathleen Dalton, *Theodore Roosevelt: A Strenuous Life* (New York: Vintage, 2002), 449.

37 *Chicago Tribune*, July 22, 1915, 1; JA, *Peace and Bread*, 79–80 (see chap. 4, n. 48).

38 *New York Times*, August 18, 1915, 10; JA, *Peace and Bread*, 80; "Peace and the Press," *Independent* 84 (October 11, 1915): 55–56.

39 JA, *Second Twenty*, 131.

40 JA, *Peace and Bread*, 77.

41 Barbara J. Steinson, *American Women's Activism in World War I* (New York: Garland Publishing, 1982), 67–68, 73; Degen, *History*, 114–19; JA, *Second Twenty Years*, 134.

42 JA, "Conference of Neutrals," 136.

43 Fishbeck, interview (see chap. 3, n. 34).

44 Quotation is from JA, *Peace and Bread*, 29. Re discussion with Ford, see ibid., 21–22. Linn errs in thinking she was not there. Linn, *Addams*, 316 (see chap. 1, n. 1).

45 Linn, *Addams*, 317. Addams (*Peace and Bread*, 25) says this illness was the reappearance of a childhood illness—i.e., the tubercular kidney—but that came later, in April 1916.

46 Patterson, *Search*, 176; re conference's accomplishments, see JA, *Peace and Bread*, 25–27, 281, 291.

47 JA, *Peace and Bread*, 80.

48 Ibid.; re doctor's orders, see Lydia Rickman, "Personal Reminiscences of Jane Addams" [1959?], Series A3, Box 8, Women's International League for Peace and Freedom Collection, SCPC.

49 JA, *Peace and Bread*, 85.

50 Quoted in Patterson, *Search*, 117.

51 Cooper, *Warrior and Priest*, 298 (see chap. 5, n. 51).

52 Blanche Wiesen Cook, "Woodrow Wilson and the Anti-Militarists," Ph.D. diss., Johns Hopkins University, 1970, Chap. 5; re WPP activities in 1916, see

Steinson, *American Women's Activism*, 136–47; re *Trojan Women*, see Joslin, *Writer's Life*, 158–59 (see chap. 4, n. 7).

53 *Chicago Tribune*, April 7, 1916, 17; Linn, *Addams*, 317.

54 *Chicago Tribune*, April 30, 1916, 5.

55 Ibid., April 13, 1916.

56 Re Wilson's second bouquet, see Rickman, "Personal Reminiscences," 3. For her statement explaining her reasons for supporting Wilson, see Linn, *Addams*, 319–20.

57 JA, *The Long Road of Woman's Memory* (New York: Macmillan, 1916), 5, 50.

58 JA, Lucia Mead, and Anna Garlin Spencer to Woodrow Wilson, October 29, 1915, in Fischer and Whipps, *Addams' Essays*, 99. JA, "Statement of Miss Jane Addams" [January 13, 1916], ibid., 123–24.

59 *Chicago Tribune*, February 13, 1917, 3.

60 JA, *Peace and Bread*, 38–39.

61 Fishbeck, interview (see chap. 3, n. 34).

62 Alma S. Petersen, "The Social Conscience of Jane Addams as It Affected Fortnightly Members," 18. Fortnightly of Chicago Records, Midwest manuscript Collection, the Newberry Library, Chicago.

63 Cook, "Woodrow Wilson," 207.

64 Ibid., 215; *New York Times*, April 14, 1917, 6.

65 Alice Hamilton, *Exploring the Dangerous Trades* (Boston: Little, Brown, 1943), 192; JA to Helena Dudley, April 19, 1917.

66 JA, "Patriotism and Pacifists in War Time," in Fischer and Whipps, *Addams' Essays*, 162.

67 Quoted in Linn, *Addams*, 330; quoted in JA, *Peace and Bread*, 64.

68 JA, For nasty and praising letters, see JA's correspondence for June 1917; Alice Hamilton to JA, June 13, 1917; JA, *Peace and Bread*, 64.

69 JA, *Peace and Bread*, 67.

70 JA, *Second Twenty*, 141–43; Dorothy Detzer, "Memories of Jane Addams," *Fellowship* (September 1938): 5; *Chicago Tribune*, January 28, 1918, 19.

71 JA, *Second Twenty*, 136, 140.

72 George Creel, *How We Advertised America* (New York: Harper & Brothers Publishers, 1920), 99.

73 Linn, *Addams*, 347–48; JA, *Peace and Bread*, 73.

74 Linn, "Interpretation," 218 (see chap. 4, n. 38); Victor S. Yarros, "Jane Addams," *Character* I, no. 4 (September-October, 1935): 3, in Marian Young Papers, Box 1, folder 56, Special Collections, Chicago Public Library, Chicago, Ill.

75 Linn, *Addams*, 333; JA, *Peace and Bread*, 82; JA, *Democracy*, 11 (see chap. 2, n. 31).

76 JA, *Peace and Bread*, 81.

77 Ibid., 81, 86.

78 JA to MRS, August 25 and September 2, 1917.

79 Quotation is from JA, *Peace and Bread*, 74. Hannah Hull, "Jane Addams," n.p. (see chap. 4, n. 36); JA [Tribute to Allen B. Pond], in "Memorial Services for Allen B. Pond, City Club, Chicago, Illinois, April 21, 1929," 24, stenographic transcription carbon, *JAPM*, 48:1155.

80 JA, "Address to the Women's Meeting of the Universal Peace Congress" [October 5, 1904], in Fischer and Whipps, *Addams' Essays*, 32–33; JA, *Peace and Bread*, 44.

81 The word "primitive" is from JA, *Second Twenty*, 144–45; "pour into" is from JA, *Peace and Bread*, 48; "a new and powerful force" is from JA, *Second Twenty*, 144.

82 JA, *Peace and Bread*, 45. See also *Chicago Tribune*, January 24, 1918, 11.

83 JA, *Peace and Bread*, 35.

Chapter 7: Ambassador

1 *Chicago Tribune*, November 11, 1918, p. 1.

2 JA, "Need a Woman over Fifty Feel Old?" *Ladies' Home Journal* 31 (October 1914): 7.

3 Linn, *Addams*, 327, 339 (chap. 1, n. 1).

4 *New York Times*, November 18, 1918, 1; *New York Times*, May 18, 1919, 37.

5 Woodrow Wilson, Address to Congress, April 2, 1917.

6 Edward Marsh to JA, January 29, 1919; Herbert Croly to JA, July 26, 1918.

7 Muriel Beadle, *The Fortnightly of Chicago: The City and Its Women, 1873–1973* (Chicago: Regnery, 197), 149–51. See also Jean Bethke Elshtain, *Jane Addams and the Dream of American Democracy* (New York: Basic Books, 2002), 234–35.

8 *Chicago Tribune*, January 25, 1919, 3; JA quoted in Degen, *History*, 223 (see chap. 6, n. 12).

9 Quoted in *New York Times*, May 20, 1919, 5.

10 Alice Hamilton to Hamilton Family, May 12 and 19, 1919, *JAPM*, 12:0350 and 0390; JA to MRS, May 1, 1919.

11 JA, *Peace and Bread*, 91 (see chap. 4, n. 48).

12 *Report of the International Congress of Women: Zurich, May 12–17, 1919* (Switzerland: Women's International League for Peace and Freedom, 1919), 260–61 (hereafter *Zurich Report*).

13 Ibid., 242.

14 *Report of the Fourth Congress of the Women's International League for Peace and Freedom, Washington, May 1–7, 1924* (Switzerland: Women's International League for Peace and Freedom, 1924), 42 (hereafter *Fourth Congress Report*).

15 JA, Closing Address [May 17, 1919], in Fischer and Whipps, *Addams' Essays*, 202 (see preface, n. 1).

16 JA, *Second Twenty*, 149 (see chap. 2, n. 20); Alice Hamilton to MRS, May 12, 1919, *JAPM*, 12:365.

17 JA to Emily Greene Balch, October 16, 1919.

18 JA, *Peace and Bread*, 123.

19 JA, *Second Twenty*, 151.

20 Geoffrey R. Stone, *Perilous Times: Free Speech in Wartime from the Sedition Act of 1798 to the War on Terrorism* (New York: Norton, 2004), 221.

21 JA quoted in Davis, *American Heroine*, 261 (see chap. 1, n. 11); re the Russian Americans' reactions, see JA, "Immigrants and Social Unrest," in National Conference on Social Welfare, *Official Proceedings of the Annual Meeting: 1920* (Ann Arbor: University of Michigan Library, 2005), 61.

22 JA, *Second Twenty*, 153–54.

23 Re diplomatic recognition, see Davis, *American Heroine*, 254. Re committee, see JA, *Peace and Bread*, 142.

24 Harper, *History*, 422–24 (see chap. 5, n. 4).

25 Lynn Dumenil, *Modern Temper: American Culture and Society in the 1920s* (New York: Hill and Wang, 1995), 102.

26 Freeman, *We Will Be Heard*, 161, 167n5 (see chap. 5, n. 57).

27 Degen, *History*, 239–40; JA, *Peace and Bread*, 145, 138.

28 Robert A. Woods and Albert J. Kennedy, *The Settlement Horizon: A National Estimate* (New York: Russell Sage Foundation, 1922), iii.

29 Bowen, *Open Windows*, 227 (see chap. 5, n. 36); Linn, *Addams*, 354.

30 JA, "Dedication of the Mary Rozet Smith Cottage, Bowen Country Club" [1935] [Waukegan, Ill.], 2–3, *JAPM*, 49:0516.

31 MRS to JA, September 3, 1933; JA, "Dedication," 3.

32 JA, *New Conscience*, 33 (see chap. 5, n. 42); JA, "Subjective Necessity," 19–20 (see chap. 1, n. 21).

33 JA, "Tolstoy and Gandhi," 1487 (see chap. 4, n. 12).

34 JA, "Count Tolstoy," *Chautauqua Assembly Herald* 27 (July 11, 1902): 5; Wallace Kirkland, *Recollections of a Life Photographer* (Boston: Houghton Mifflin, 1954), 14.

35 Barbara Sicherman, *Alice Hamilton: A Life in Letters* (Cambridge, MA: Harvard University Press, 1984), 294. Davis says the breast tumor was benign (*American Heroine*, 271) but gives no source for his claim. Linn says it was kidney trouble, but he seems confused. Linn, *Addams*, 355. MRS lost a second breast to cancer around this time. Fishbeck, interview (see chap. 3, n. 34).

36 *Chicago Tribune*, September 24, 1923, 16.

37 Ibid., October 13, 1923, 4.

38 Kim E. Nielson, *Un-American Womanhood: Antiradicalism, Antifeminism and the First Red Scare* (Columbus: Ohio State University Press, 2001), 74–78, 83–84; Nancy Cott, *The Grounding of Modern Feminism* (New Haven, CT: Yale University Press, 1987), 249–50; chart is on 242; for later chart, see Davis, *American Heroine*, 265.

39 A. P. Davidson, *Report of Fourth International Congress* [1924], File 287, May 7, 1924. Federal Bureau of Investigation, "Jane Addams," Part 1a, http://foia.fbi.gov/foiaindex/addams.htm.

40 Carrie A. Foster, *The Women and the Warriors: The U.S. Section of the Women's International League for Peace and Freedom, 1915–1946* (Syracuse: Syracuse University Press, 1995), 47–48; *Washington Post*, April 4, 1924, 5; April 24, 1924, 2; April 25, 1924, 10; April 26, 1924, 1; April 27, 1924, ES8; April 28, 1924, 5; April 28, 1924, 1; April 30, 1924, 8. The headline was in *Washington Post*, April 2, 1924, 1.

41 JA, "Presidential Address [1924]," in Fischer and Whipps, *Addams' Essays*, 259 (see preface, n. 1).

42 JA, *Second Twenty*, 184.

43 *Fourth International Congress Report.*

44 Davis (*American Heroine*, 266–67, 325n29) credits "most dangerous" to ROTC in 1928. See biographies of the other persons for information on them.

45 JA, *Second Twenty*, 180. See also JA to Alice Addams Haldeman, December 10, 1901.

46 JA to Carrie Chapman Catt, January 3, 1925.

47 Linn, *Addams*, 432.

48 JA, Weight diary, *JAPM*, 28-0745; Alice Hamilton to James B. Herrick [JA's doctor], November 19, 1929, James B. Herrick Papers, box 4, file 9 ("Hamilton"), Special Collections, University of Chicago Library.

49 Gertrude Bussey and Margaret Tims, *The Women's International League of Peace and Freedom, 1915–1965: A Record of Fifty Years' Work* (London: George Allen & Unwin, 1965), 82.

50 JA, "The Leadership of Women," April 10, 1929, 15, *JAPM*, 48:1137; JA, *Second Twenty*, 5.

51 JA, *Second Twenty*, 192, 193.

52 Ibid., 194, 199.

53 JA, "As I See Women," *Ladies' Home Journal* 32 (August 1915): 11, *JAPM*, 47:1256.

54 JA, *Second Twenty*, 401.

55 Quoted in Robert Heilbroner and Aaron Singer, *The Economic Transformation of America Since 1865* (New York: Harcourt, Brace, 1994), 144.

56 Tims, *Jane Addams*, 138 (see chap. 5, n. 27).

57 Suellen Hoy, "The Unknown Life of Ellen Gates Starr," *Chicago History* 36, no. 2 (Spring 2009): 15–18.

58 JA, *Second Twenty*, 97; Cheryl R. Ganz and Margaret Strobel, eds., *Pots of Promise: Mexicans and Pottery at Hull House, 1920–1940* (Urbana: University of Illinois Press, 2004).

59 Re the southern woman, see Delores Waldorf, "Thirty Organizations Will Honor Pioneer," *Oakland* (Calif.) *Tribune*, May 1, 1960, S1. The resident was Sara Southall. Mary Collson, "My Search for an All Right World," 27, manuscript 85, file 5, Box 5, Edward J. Meenan Papers, Mississippi Valley Collection, University of Memphis, Memphis, TN; Bowen, *Growing Up*, 88 (see chap. 4, n. 29); Francis Hackett, *American Rainbow: Early Reminiscences* (New York: Liveright, 1971), 199.

60	Margaret Carol Dunn, "Jane Addams as a Political Leader," master's thesis, University of Chicago, 1926, 151. For other facts, see "Notes on Hull House," September 1935, Madeline Wallin Sikes Collection [one file], Special Collections, University Library, University of Illinois at Chicago.

61	For JA's advice to Ovington, see Mary White Ovington, *Black and White Sat Down Together: The Reminisces of an NAACP Founder*, ed. Ralph Luker (New York: Feminist Press at CUNY, 1996), 8.

62	These are, in order, Julia Lathrop, Florence Kelley, Gerard Swope, Mackenzie King, Walter Gifford, Frances Perkins, Alice Hamilton, and Grace Abbott.

63	See Paul H. Douglas, *In the Fullness of Time* (New York: Harcourt, Brace, Jovanovich, 1971), 149; Myles Horton, *The Long Haul: An Autobiography* (New York: Teachers College Press, 1998), 48–50, 158.

64	Frances Perkins Interview, Arthur Hepner, ed., *The Invitation to Learning Reader* 4, no. 14 (May 1954): 139.

65	Hilda Satt Polacheck, *I Came A Stranger: The Story of a Hull-House Girl*, ed. Dena J. Polacheck Epstein (Urbana: University of Illinois Press, 1989), 126; JA, "Settlement as a Way of Life," 140–42 (see chap. 6, n. 30).

66	Linn, *Addams*, 377–79.

67	Ibid., 380–381.

68	JA to Frederick J. Libby, November 3, 1934; re other two boards, see JA to Kathleen Courtney, August 15, 1932.

69	Linn, *Addams*, 406, 403, 382; re JA's appointments, offices, and memberships, see *JAPCG*, 284–87.

70	Re capital punishment, see JA, Letter to the Editor, *Chicago Tribune*, December 6, 1920, 8. Re segregated housing, see JA, *Second Twenty*, 396–98. Re her talk on unwed mothers, see *San Francisco Daily News*, March 29, 1927, *JAPM*, 67:0415.

71	Heilbroner and Singer, *Economic Transformation*, 143.

72	JA, "Social Consequences of Depression," in *Aspects of the Depression*, ed. Felix Morley (Freeport, NY: Books for Libraries Press, 1968), 12–21.

73	*Washington Post*, October 10, 1931, 6; October 11, 1931, 8.

74	Linn, *Addams*, 389–90, 392.

75	Quotation in Harriet Hyman Alonso, "Nobel Peace Laureates, Jane Addams and Emily Greene Balch: Two Women of the Women's International League for Peace and Freedom," *Journal of Women's History* 7, no. 2 (Summer 1995): 16; Linn, *Addams*, 389–92.

76 Linn, *Addams*, 404. Stone famously kept her maiden name after marriage, but Linn gave her last name as being that of her husband.

77 JA, "Count Tolstoy," 5; JA, *My Friend*, 127–28 (see chap. 1, n. 24).

78 See JA correspondence for the winter of 1934–35.

79 Quoted in JA, *My Friend*, 129.

80 JA, *Excellent*, 4 (see chap. 4, n. 37).

81 James, *Varieties of Religious Experience*, 462–63, 453, 22 (see chap. 4, n. 71).

82 JA, *Second Twenty*, 184; JA, "Newer Ideals of Peace," in Fischer and Whipps, *Addams' Essays*, 20.

83 *Chicago Tribune*, June 15, 1932, 10; *Chicago Tribune*, June 28, 1932, 3.

84 Ibid., June 28, 1932, 3.

85 Ibid., June 16, 1932, 6.

86 *New York Times*, July 24, 1932, 6; JA to Franklin Delano Roosevelt, September 4, 1933, JA to Franklin Delano Roosevelt, December 26, 1933; Secretary to the President to JA, January 9, 1934.

87 Frances Perkins, Remarks, *Jane Addams Memorial Meeting, June 10, 1935* (New York: National Council of Social Work, 1935), 19.

88 JA, Weight Diary, *JAPM*, 28-0745; re her frustrations, see JA's correspondence for the winters of 1932–33 and 1933–34.

89 Edmund Wilson, *American Earthquake* (New York: Farrar, Straus and Giroux, 1958), 454.

90 Stanley Linn to JA, August 30, 1933; re Anna Addams's funeral, see Bryan, "Biographical Profiles," in *Selected Papers*, 465–66; JA to MRS, August 14, 24, and 30, 1899.

91 Re JA and MRS's sharing bed: MRS to Esther Loeb Kohn, May 22, [n.y.], *JAPM*, 1:0088; see also Knight, *Citizen*, 216–18, 470n57 (see chap. 1, n. 2); MHJ, *Jane Addams as I Knew Her*, 10 (see chap. 4, n. 8); Joslin, *Writer's Life*, 193 (see chap. 4, n. 7).

92 JA, *Spirit*, 16, 30 (see chap. 5, n. 17).

93 See also Knight, *Citizen*, 217–18, 470n57, and Knight, "Love on Halsted Street," in *Feminist Interpretations of Jane Addams*, ed. Maurice Hamington (University Park: Penn State University Press, forthcoming).

94 Re trade unions, see *New York Times*, December 13, 1923; for JA quotation, see Nancy Cott, *The Grounding of Modern Feminism* (New Haven: Yale University Press, 1987), 139–40.

95 Re conference, see *Chicago Tribune*, July 17, 1933, 13. For quotations, see *Chicago Tribune*, July 22, 1933, 9; July 18, 1933, 4.

96 Ibid., July 22, 1933, 9.

97 Quoted in Linn, *Addams*, 407–08. MRS left Addams a living trust in her will. A copy of the will, which is dated November 29, 1933, is in the author's possession, provided to her by Richard S. Bull, Jr., MRS's great-nephew.

98 Address of Mrs. Franklin Delano Roosevelt, May 2, 1935, Women's International League for Peace and Freedom, U.S. Section Papers (microfilm), 19:1065, SCPC.

99 Quoted in Linn, *Addams*, 418. Re the participants in the broadcast, see Paul Kellogg, Remarks, *National Council of Social Work, Jane Addams Memorial Meeting, June 10, 1935* (New York: privately printed, 1935), 15.

100 Davis, *American Heroine*, 290–92; Linn, *Addams*, 426–27.

101 Balch and Villard are quoted in Tims, *Jane Addams*, 149–51. Dewey's remark is summed up by Katherine F. Lenroot, Remarks, *National Council of Social Work, Jane Addams Memorial Meeting, June 10, 1935* (New York: privately printed, 1935), 5–6.

102 JA, "Settlement as a Way of Life," 146.

For Further Reading

1 James Weber Linn, *Jane Addams: A Biography* (New York: Appleton-Century, 1935).

2 Henry Steele Commager, "Jane Addams: 1860–1960," *Saturday Review* (December 24, 1960). Reprinted as the foreword to *Twenty Years at Hull-House* (New York: New American Library Signet Classic, 1961); Merle Curti, "Jane Addams on Human Nature," *Journal of the History of Ideas* 22, no. 2 (April–June 1961): 240–53. In 1961 a British writer and fellow peace activist of Addams's, Margaret Tims, also published a brief study of selected aspects of Addams's philosophy that reads like a bit like a biography, *Jane Addams of Hull-House, 1860–1935* (London: George Allen & Unwin, 1961).

3 See Louise W. Knight, "Afterword: Scholarship and Jane Addams," in *Citizen: Jane Addams and the Struggle for Democracy* (Chicago: University of Chicago

Press, 2005), 405–12, for a more complete discussion of the history of this scholarship.

4 There is also the invaluable, though out-of-print guide to the microfilm that was published as a book, separately from the microfilm. Mary Lynn McCree Bryan, ed., and Nancy Slote, assoc. ed., *The Jane Addams Papers: A Comprehensive Guide* (Bloomington: Indiana University Press, 1996). Addams scholars will want to request the *Guide* through inter-library loan.

INDEX

References to illustrations are italicized.

National Association for the Advancement
of Colored People (NAACP), xiv,
115-16, 151-54, *153*, 174-76, 255,
268
National Association of Colored Women,
227, 237
National Child Labor Committee
(NCLC), 129, 133, 144-46
National Civil Liberties Bureau, 221,
236
see also American Civil Liberties Union
National Conference of Charities and
Correction (NCCC), 153, 173,
197
National Consumers' League, 123, 128,
238, 264
National Council for Prevention of War,
255
National Council of Women, 264-65
National Federation of Settlements, 197
National Peace Federation, *see* Emergency
Peace Federation
National Socialist Women's Committee,
195
National Woman Suffrage Association
(NWSA), 98
National Woman's Party (NWP), 236,
237-38, 264
National World Court Committee, 255
NAWSA, *see* National American Woman
Suffrage Association
neurasthenia, 40-41
neutrals conference, 192, 194-97, 201-2,
205-9
New Conscience and an Ancient Evil, A, 211
Newer Ideals of Peace, 95, 135-40, 139, 140,
142, 152, 156-57, 201, 222
New York Child Labor Committee,
128-29
nineteenth ward, *see* Chicago, nineteenth
ward of
Nobel Peace Prize, xiii-xiv, 181, 233, 257

nonresistance, 119
see also Addams, Jane, on nonresistance
Noyes, John, 10

O'Sullivan, Mary Kenney, 75, 80, 130-32,
149
Ovington, Mary White, 152, 253
Owen, Robert, 18

pacifists, 245-46
see also Addams, Jane, on pacifists
Palmer, A. Mitchell, 234
Paris Peace Conference, 229-30
patriarchy, 16, 95-96, 167, 303*n*47
see also Addams, Jane, on patriarchy
patriotism, 218
see also Addams, Jane, on patriotism
Paul, Alice, 184, 186-87, 264
peace movement, 135, 156, 191, 263
in Europe, 197-202; *see also* International Committee of Women for
Permanent Peace
platforms of, 192-98, 200, 222-23,
229-30, 260-61
role of women's suffrage advocates in,
192-95, 197-202
women's, 191-93, 195-202, 211
peace platforms, *see* peace movement,
platforms of
People's Party, 147
Perkins, Frances, 261
Pethick-Lawrence, Emmeline, 192-93
Plato, 263
Plutarch, 12
politics:
women and, 76-78, 80-81
see also Addams, Jane, political career of;
Addams, John Huy, political career of
Potter, Caroline, 22-25, 27, 29-30, 34,
42, 50
poverty, 62, 67, 88
see also Addams, Jane, on poverty